Digital Education and Learning

Series Editor
Michael Thomas, Liverpool John Moores University, Merseyside, UK

Much has been written during the first decade of the new millennium about the potential of digital technologies to produce a transformation of education. Digital technologies are portrayed as tools that will enhance learner collaboration and motivation and develop new multimodal literacy skills. Accompanying this has been the move from understanding literacy on the cognitive level to an appreciation of the sociocultural forces shaping learner development. Responding to these claims, the Digital Education and Learning Series explores the pedagogical potential and realities of digital technologies in a wide range of disciplinary contexts across the educational spectrum both in and outside of class. Focusing on local and global perspectives, the series responds to the shifting landscape of education, the way digital technologies are being used in different educational and cultural contexts, and examines the differences that lie behind the generalizations of the digital age. Incorporating cutting edge volumes with theoretical perspectives and case studies (single authored and edited collections), the series provides an accessible and valuable resource for academic researchers, teacher trainers, administrators and students interested in interdisciplinary studies of education and new and emerging technologies.

Alexander van Deursen · Jan van Dijk

Digital Skills

Key to the Smart Society

Second Edition

palgrave
macmillan

Alexander van Deursen
University of Twente
Enschede, The Netherlands

Jan van Dijk
University of Twente
Enschede, The Netherlands

ISSN 2753-0744 ISSN 2753-0752 (electronic)
Digital Education and Learning
ISBN 978-1-349-96161-0 ISBN 978-1-349-96162-7 (eBook)
https://doi.org/10.1057/978-1-349-96162-7

Cover credit: stellalevi/GettyImages

This Palgrave Macmillan imprint is published by the registered company Springer Nature America, Inc.
The registered company address is: 1 New York Plaza, New York, NY 10004, U.S.A.

About This Book

We are experiencing a transformative moment in human history. The world around us is becoming not just digital but intelligent, powered by artificial intelligence, interconnected through the Internet of Things, and guided by algorithms that shape what we see, think, and do. From the phones in our hands to the sensors in our devices, digital media now weave through every aspect of our daily lives. They influence how we learn, work, communicate, and even understand ourselves and others. In this complex media landscape, digital skills are central to participation, opportunity, and empowerment. And yet, while digital media advance at breathtaking speed, the human capacity to use them effectively often struggles to keep pace. This book begins with the question of what it means to be digitally skilled in a smart society. From this question unfolds a journey through seven essential digital skills. Three of these skills relate to mastering the medium itself, how we choose, operate, and navigate digital media. Four focus on mastering content, how we locate and evaluate, communicate, create, and strategically apply online content.

Chapter 1 introduces the comprehensive digital skill framework and traces the evolution through history, from oral societies to the early days of computing and the Web to today's algorithmic, data-driven society. It shows how digital skills have accumulated and expanded, and why they are now indispensable for everyone, regardless of background or profession.

Building on this, Chapter 2 explores how the seven skills apply to internet and intelligent media that define our era: online platforms, social media, AI-driven platforms, and smart connected devices. This is where digital skills meet the world of automation, data analytics, and personalization. It is the heart of the book, bridging scholarly insight and practical relevance.

Chapter 3 turns theory into evidence. Drawing on empirical data from survey research and task-based performance tests, it examines the actual levels of digital skills across populational groups. Who has the skills needed to benefit from internet and connected intelligent media, and who is being left behind? The findings expose gaps across age, education levels, income groups, traditional literacy, and social capital, offering a sobering picture of digital inequality that persists beneath the surface of connectivity.

Chapter 4 widens the lens. Digital skills do not exist in isolation; they are embedded in a broader social context. This chapter investigates how digital inequalities intersect with traditional forms of inequality and shape economic, educational, political, social, cultural, spatial, and institutional participation. It asks: Are disparities in digital skills simply a reflection of existing divides, or do they represent a new and growing layer of social inequality? How do AI, automation, and algorithmic bias further complicate these patterns?

The second half of the book turns toward solutions. Chapters 5 and 6 explore two complementary strategies for addressing and improving digital skills. The first considers the design of digital media and platform interfaces to be more inclusive, transparent, and user-friendly. The second focuses on people: education, training, and lifelong learning as pathways to digital empowerment. From classrooms to workplaces and from self-directed learning to peer collaboration, these chapters show how digital skills can be cultivated across life stages and contexts. They also highlight the importance of reaching those most often excluded from digital progress: older adults, people with disabilities, migrants, and individuals with limited literacy.

Finally, Chapter 7 looks ahead and brings together insights and implications for policy, outlining how governments, institutions, and industries can foster digitally skilled societies. It identifies strategies and partnerships that can ensure that digital transformation becomes a force for inclusion rather than division.

This book can be considered as both a roadmap and a call to action. It invites readers—scholars, students, practitioners, educators, developers, and policymakers—to rethink what it means to be skilled in a world shaped by internet and intelligent media. It argues that digital skills are not a fixed checklist of technical skills, but the capacity to think critically and act strategically and meaningfully with and through digital media. In a world where every innovation reshapes what is asked of and what it means to be humans, developing digital skills is more than just preparation for the future. It is the key to shaping it.

Praise for *Digital Skills*

"Van Deursen and Van Dijk are widely published and influential scholars of information and communication technology, power, network society, and digital divides. Here they follow up their 2014 book *Digital Skills: Unlocking the Information Society* a decade later, with *Digital Skills: Key to a Smart Society*. While digital media and technologies, increasingly including AI, are pervasive, appropriate skills are not, representing another dimension of the digital divide. Thus this interdisciplinary book provides reviews, analyses, and measures of required and appropriate skills for equitable, responsible, effective, and participatory digital media use, from work to entertainment, economics to creativity, and health to relationships. Van Duersen and Van Dijk discuss implications for interventions, accessibility, and interface design; strategies for education and informal learning by students, adults, and workers; and policy implications that consider the multidimensional nature of the digital media environment. This exciting, detailed, and thoroughly grounded book should be required reading in all disciplines related to the contemporary digital technology world."

—Ronald Rice, *Distinguished Professor, Arthur N. Rupe Endowed Professor, Social Effects of Mass Communication*

"This excellent book combines wisdom from years of innovative research with insightful solutions to address the digital skills so critical for participation in society today, especially in an age of AI. With useful concepts and measures for future research, the authors also offer nuanced, evidence-based recommendations for human-centered design, education, and public policy, targeting diverse needs for different populations. This is a must-read for scholarship and practice."

—Karen Mossberger, *Professor Emerita, School of Public Affairs (SPA)*

"Digital skills determine who can participate, and who is left behind, in an increasingly digital society. This book shows how digital skills not only reflect social inequalities but actively amplify them, especially in the age of AI, where people no longer simply use tools but interact with agents. Rejecting one-size-fits-all solutions, it argues for targeted, context-sensitive interventions and sustained collaboration between researchers, practitioners, and policymakers. A must-read for anyone committed to inclusive and meaningful digital participation."

—Leen d'Haenens, *Professor, Institute for Media Studies (IMS)*

Contents

1 Introduction 1

1.1 Digital Inequality and the Appropriation of Technology 1

1.2 Digital Skills in the Media Landscape of Smart Societies 6

1.3 A Framework of Seven Digital Skills 11

1.4 From Orality to Algorithms: A Brief History of Media Skills 16

1.5 An Overview of Traditional and Digital Media Skills 20

1.6 Emerging Patterns of Digital Media Inequalities 33

1.7 Conclusions 37

References 39

2 Digital Skills for Internet and Intelligent Media 41

2.1 Introduction 41

2.2 Strategic Media Choice Skills 42

2.3 Operational Skills 45

2.4 Formal Skills 49

2.5 Information Skills 53

2.6 Communication Skills 56

2.7 Content Creation Skills 64

2.8 Strategic Media Use Skills 67

2.9 Conclusions 70

References 71

3 Digital Skills: Levels and Distribution 75
3.1 Introduction: Measuring Digital Skills 75
3.2 Level of Strategic Media Choice Skills 79
3.3 Level of Operational Skills 81
3.4 Level of Formal Skills 85
3.5 Level of Information Skills 88
3.6 Level of Communication Skills 93
3.7 Level of Content Creation Skills 97
3.8 Level of Strategic Media Use Skills 100
3.9 Differences across the Population 103
3.10 Conclusions 111
References 113

4 Impact of Digital Skills 117
4.1 Introduction: The Social Context of Digital Skills 117
4.2 What Is At Stake: Digital Skills as Enablers of Participation 122
4.3 Lacking Digital Skills: Such a Big Deal? 132
4.4 Unequal Digital Skills as Indicator of Broader Social Inequality 139
4.5 Conclusions: Digital Skills as Gateway to Participation 143
References 144

5 Enhancing Interfaces and Content 147
5.1 Introduction: The Role of Designers 147
5.2 Medium-Related Skill Design Improvements 148
5.3 Content-Related Skill Design Improvements 159
5.4 Conclusions 177
References 179

6 Fostering the Learning of Digital Skills 181
6.1 Introduction: Pathways of Learning 181
6.2 Learning by Doing and Learning from Others 183
6.3 Acquiring Digital Skills Through Formal Education 188
6.4 Learning Digital Skills in the Workplace 199
6.5 Learning in Adult and Distance Education 202
6.6 Learning in Public Access Centers and Communities 205
6.7 Learning among Disadvantaged Groups 207
6.8 Conclusions 217
References 218

7 Conclusions and Policy Perspectives 223
7.1 Conclusions 223
7.2 General Policy Perspectives 233
7.3 Policy Actors 235
7.4 A Synopsis of Strategies and Instruments 247
7.5 Closing Remark 253
References 254

References 255

Index 267

About the Authors

Prof. Dr. Alexander van Deursen holds the Chair of Digital Inequality at the University of Twente in The Netherlands. He serves as Director of the Centre for Digital Inclusion. In this role, he focuses on identifying and explaining mechanisms of digital inclusion, mapping both the benefits and risks of emerging technologies, pinpointing groups at risk of digital exclusion, and developing policy measures and interventions to address these challenges. He also evaluates best practices aimed at fostering equitable participation in a rapidly digitizing society. Alexander has published widely in scientific journals and popular media. He maintains active international collaborations and has held visiting positions at the London School of Economics and Political Science and Arizona State University. His research and leadership contribute to a deeper understanding of how digital transformation affects individuals and communities, and how inclusive strategies can ensure that no one is left behind.

Prof. Dr. Jan van Dijk is a Dutch emeritus professor of communication science and the sociology of the information society at the University of Twente in The Netherlands, where he continues to be active in research and teaching. He is internationally recognized for his pioneering work on the digital divide, the social aspects of digital media, and digital democracy. Van Dijk's influential books include The Network Society, The Deepening Divide, Digital Democracy, Digital Skills, and The Digital Divide, which explore how unequal access to technology and digital skills reinforces broader social inequalities. Throughout his career, he has advised various governments and the European Commission on information and communication technology policy and remains a leading voice in understanding the societal impacts of digitalization.

List of Figures

Fig. 1.1	Process of technology appropriation (after Van Dijk, 2005)	2
Fig. 1.2	Media landscape (after Van Deursen & Helsper, 2021)	9
Fig. 1.3	Digital skills process model	11
Fig. 3.1	Sufficient mastery of strategic media choice skills, % adult population	81
Fig. 3.2	Sufficient mastery of operational skills components, % of adult population. * asked to respondents using smart devices	83
Fig. 3.3	Sufficient mastery of formal skills components, % of adult population	86
Fig. 3.4	Sufficient mastery of information skills components, % of adult population	90
Fig. 3.5	Sufficient mastery of communication skills components, % of adult population	94
Fig. 3.6	Sufficient mastery of content creation skills components, % of adult population	98
Fig. 3.7	Sufficient mastery of strategic media use skill components, % of adult population	100
Fig. 3.8	Differences in sufficient mastery of strategic media choice skills, %	105
Fig. 3.9	Differences in sufficient mastery of operational skills, %	106
Fig. 3.10	Differences in sufficient mastery of formal skills, %	107
Fig. 3.11	Differences in sufficient mastery of information skills, %	107
Fig. 3.12	Differences in sufficient mastery of communication skills, %	108

Fig. 3.13 Differences in sufficient mastery of content creation skills, % 109
Fig. 3.14 Differences in sufficient mastery of strategic media use skills, % 110
Fig. 4.1 A causal model of resources and appropriation theory (after Van Dijk, 2005) 118
Fig. 7.1 Clusters of strategies and instruments for digital skills improvement 248

List of Tables

Box 1.1	Medium-related skills for traditional and digital media	22
Box 1.2	Content-related skills for traditional and digital media	24

CHAPTER 1

Introduction

1.1 Digital Inequality and the Appropriation of Technology

In the 1990s, researchers and policymakers began to draw attention to what became known as the *digital divide*: the gap between those who had access to computers and the internet and those who did not. At the time, simply having an internet connection was assumed to unlock numerous social and economic opportunities, whereas a lack of access was understood to place individuals at a substantial disadvantage. However, by the early 2000s, conversations surrounding the digital divide began to fade from the political spotlight. As internet access and device ownership expanded rapidly, especially in developed countries, many assumed that the core issue had been addressed. With the majority of people connected in some form, policymakers began treating the digital divide as a problem of the past.

The initial framing of the digital divide had a key limitation: it presented internet access as a binary condition and suggested a stark separation between two opposing groups ("haves" versus "have nots"). In reality, people engage with technology in very different ways. Some individuals use digital tools fluently and frequently across all aspects of daily life, whereas others use them only occasionally, superficially, or not at all. Recognizing this, scholars have increasingly moved away from the term digital divide in favor of *digital inequality*, a concept that better

A. van Deursen and J. van Dijk, *Digital Skills*, Digital Education and Learning, https://doi.org/10.1057/978-1-349-96162-7_1

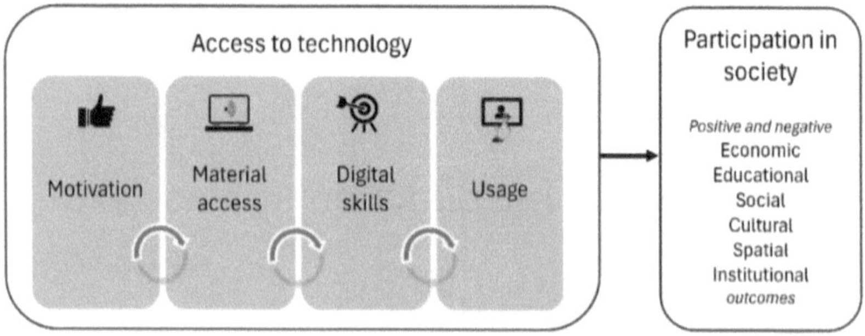

Fig. 1.1 Process of technology appropriation (after Van Dijk, 2005)

captures the nuanced spectrum of differences in how people use technology. Research over the past two decades has reignited concerns about these disparities, as they are aligned with existing social inequalities related to income, education, age, and race (Scheerder et al., 2017). In response, many national and international policy agendas now emphasize the importance of *digital inclusion* and focus not only on physical access to the internet, but also on improving digital skills or encouraging broad and beneficial use.

To illustrate the dimensions along which digital inequalities occur, we draw on the Resources and Appropriation Theory (Van Dijk, 2005, 2020). Chapter 4 discusses this macro-structural theory in detail. In general, the theory posits that categorical inequalities within society lead to an unequal distribution of resources, which in turn results in unequal access to technology. At the heart of the theory is the process of technology appropriation, which identifies four types of access with a successive and cumulative nature: motivational, material, digital skill, and usage access. See Fig. 1.1.

Motivational Access

Motivation is the first stage in the process of appropriating new technologies. It is not only crucial for the decision to purchase or start using technology but also influences the willingness to become familiar with it and invest effort in developing the necessary skills. In the 1980s and the 1990s, phenomena such as computer anxiety and technophobia were quite common. Fear of new technologies affected a significant portion of the population, and critical or negative views of their impact on individuals and society were widespread. In the second half of the 1990s, driven by the breakthrough of the World Wide Web, these fears began to subside. By the early 2000s, the internet established itself as a central feature of modern culture. Within the following decades, it became a familiar part of everyday life in developed nations. Even older adults, who often perceive the internet as difficult, are increasingly motivated to use digital media, recognizing its many benefits in their daily lives. Unfortunately, the rise of artificial intelligence (AI) seems to reinstate computer anxiety, as AI applications are often perceived as complex, opaque "black boxes" that generate uncertainty. In popular media, public figures frequently voice concerns that AI can spiral beyond human control and has devastating consequences for individuals and society. Consequently, motivation levels may diverge across different segments of the population, influencing both the use of technology and the process of becoming familiar with it. This, in turn, affects the next stages of appropriation: acquiring digital media depends on motivation, and developing digital skills requires sustained effort and persistence. When using digital media feels easy and helpful in meeting people's goals, motivation grows, creating a cycle of greater confidence and engagement.

Material Access

The second stage of appropriation, gaining material access, became the dominant focus of public opinion and policy discourse in the late 1990s and the early 2000s. With widespread campaigns to provide computers and internet connectivity to schools, libraries, and low-income households, many policymakers began to believe that the digital divide was on the verge of being resolved. This perception gained traction particularly after computer and internet ownership rates in many high-income countries surpassed 90 percent of the population. However, physical access is still far from universal as worldwide rates remain below 70 percent, ranging from 98 percent in Northern Europe to 29 percent in Eastern Africa (Statista, 2025). More importantly, this reductionist view of the digital divide neglects the other forms of access shown in Fig. 1.1 (motivation, digital skills, and usage) and overlooks that material access extends beyond mere physical connection to include the quality, functionality, and diversity of digital devices, as well as the types of software and connectivity that people use. These material access factors influence the depth and quality of digital engagement and, in turn, the outcomes that people derive (Van Deursen & Van Dijk, 2019). The ability to afford the costs associated with access to high-quality material, such as faster internet connections, updated hardware, premium software, and technical support, varies significantly across socioeconomic groups. Consequently, even among those with basic access, their actual experience of using digital media differs substantially. Furthermore, AI and Internet of Things (IoT) applications and devices have introduced new forms of material access inequality. New advanced technologies tend to be adopted first by higher-income populations, expanding material access differences, even as overall device ownership grows.

Digital Skills

The third stage of technology appropriation involves the digital skills necessary to master them. Various related terms, such as *digital literacy*, *media literacy*, *digital competence* (or combinations like *digital literacy skills*), are used in academic and policy discourse. *Literacy* is the most widely used in related compound nouns. In its classical form, "a literate person is able to read, write, and understand his or her native language and express a simple thought in writing" (Bawden, 2001, p. 220). Over time, this definition has expanded to encompass the wide range of abilities required to function effectively in information-rich environments. When the cultural and contextual dimensions of information use are considered, literacy assumes a deeper and more socially embedded meaning. De Castell and Luke (1988, p. 159), for example, define literacy as "having mastery over the process by means of which culturally significant information is coded." This view emphasizes that literacy is not merely a technical skill but also a means of participating in a broader social and cultural sense-making system. Building on this, Anttiroiko et al. (2001) distinguish between two dimensions: *knowledge* and *skills*. Knowledge refers to an individual's understanding of how the world is structured and how systems operate, whereas skills involve the practical application of this knowledge, consciously or unconsciously, in everyday life. From this perspective, knowledge provides a conceptual foundation, whereas skills enable individuals to navigate and act effectively in digital environments. In our view, skills capture the interactive, task-oriented, and procedural behaviors that characterize effective digital media use more accurately. Digital media use is not a passive activity; it requires individuals to navigate complex digital interfaces, interact with applications, communicate with others in real time, evaluate vast quantities of information or collected data, and perform tasks ranging from simple searches to financial transactions and content creation. A possible exception are smart devices equipped with autonomous or semi-autonomous functions. These technologies can update software, adjust settings, filter content, and implement personalized adjustments with minimal or no user intervention. Such automation may create the deceptive impression that digital skills are becoming less essential as devices increasingly manage tasks "in the background" and make decisions on our behalf (Van Deursen & Mossberger, 2018). However, as we will show later in this book, the absence of skills to operate these devices and interpret and use the data they generate limits the extent to which their advantages can be realized. Their use still stands in contrast to the relatively passive forms of media engagement, such as reading books or watching television, which rely primarily on cognitive and interpretive skills. This book identifies and focuses on seven distinct but interrelated types of skills that serve as the core analytical framework for the following chapters: strategic media choice, operational, formal, information, communication, content creation, and strategic media use skills. Each of these skills contributes to an individual's overall capacity to engage meaningfully and effectively with digital media.

Usage Access

The fourth and final stage of technology appropriation is *usage*, which refers to how individuals engage with digital media in their daily lives. Patterns of digital media use can vary widely, encompassing dimensions such as frequency and duration of use, type and diversity of the activities performed, and level of engagement (e.g., from passive consumption to active productive contributions). It is important to recognize that not all media use is conscious or active. In today's connected and intelligent media landscape, usage often involves automated or ambient interactions, such as personalized recommendations from streaming platforms and social media feeds, where AI determines which posts appear first, navigation apps that automatically reroute based on real-time traffic, smart home devices that continuously collect data, and fitness trackers that synchronize in the background.

Outcomes

The four stages of appropriation interact in complex and dynamic ways, ultimately leading to positive or negative outcomes of digital media use. These outcomes can enhance or diminish a person's position in society or access to resources, as captured by the term digital inequality. For example, a person might increase their financial resources by selling products online or lose them through online fraud, expand professional opportunities through networking on social platforms or damage their reputation with an ill-considered post, use AI tutors to learn new languages or develop unnatural speech patterns if the AI's training data is flawed, and become healthier by following a workout program recommended by a smartwatch or develop anxiety from obsessive health monitoring. As resources also influence each stage of access, traditional forms of inequality are closely intertwined with inequalities in digital media use, thus creating a recursive cycle of inequality. Economic resources are needed to purchase a tablet with internet access, social resources to receive support in using it, and cultural resources to navigate the overwhelming amount of online information. Individuals who fall behind in terms of motivation, material access, digital skills, and usage are likely to be disadvantaged in every societal domain (whether recognized or not). This is further discussed in Chap. 4.

1.2 Digital Skills in the Media Landscape of Smart Societies

The central message of this book is that digital skills are fundamental to the technology appropriation process. They enable the conversion of digital media use into meaningful and beneficial outcomes related to living, working, studying, and engaging in leisure activities. Digital skills act as a gateway to more complex, beneficial, and empowering forms of media use and shape how, why, and to what extent digital media are used. For example, individuals with only basic skills may limit their media use to routine tasks, such as checking emails, browsing news, or consuming entertainment. In contrast, users with more advanced skills, such as information evaluation, content creation, and strategic decision-making, are more likely to engage in high-value activities such as online learning, political participation, entrepreneurship, or professional networking. Furthermore, digital skills are necessary for active media use and maintaining agency in increasingly automated digital environments. Users with greater digital skills are more likely to recognize algorithmic bias, manage data flows, and configure intelligent systems to support decision-making processes to better serve their needs. In contrast, those with lower digital skills may become passive recipients of AI-driven decisions, potentially reinforcing their dependence or making misinformed choices. The importance of skills in such developments is reflected in the title of this book: *Digital skills as key to a smart society*.

A smart society (also referred to as an intelligent society, super-smart society, or Society 5.0) represents the vision of a society that harnesses digital technologies to enhance the quality of life across all areas. In this vision, data, AI, and smart technologies are embedded in infrastructure and services to support automated, adaptive, and intelligent decision-making. Beyond human information processing, such as searching for, interpreting, and communicating data, these systems can augment, guide, or replace human judgment in certain cases. AI can detect patterns and predict trends at a scale and speed beyond human capacity, whereas certain autonomous systems can make operational decisions without direct human intervention. The skills to use AI tools in ways that foster productive human-AI collaboration ensure that decision-making processes are not only more efficient but also align with the desired outcomes. Human-AI interaction requires advanced digital skills; individuals must understand how information is produced, curated, and potentially manipulated within algorithmic systems while exercising critical and ethical judgment regarding the appropriate scope of AI automation.

Given the complexity of a smart society, the necessary skills do not emerge spontaneously but require deliberate cultivation. Experience may contribute to the development of basic operational skills, but it does not adequately support the acquisition of more advanced information, communication, content creation, or strategic media use skills. These skills must be developed before meaningful engagement with digital media can begin. Once used, these skills must be continuously adapted to the requirements of each medium. For instance, searching for information in a library differs significantly from using a search engine or requesting information through conversational AI tools. As digital media become increasingly embedded in everyday life, differences in digital skills are magnified, reflecting and reinforcing existing social, economic, and cultural inequalities. The uneven distribution across demographic and social groups can create unequal opportunities for education, employment, civic participation, and social engagement, further entrenching disparities in smart societies.

With growing differences in digital skills and digital media use, scientific research has brought the issue of digital inequality back into focus. Many national and international policy agendas emphasize the importance of ***digital inclusion***. The term digital inclusion carries a more positive connotation than digital divide or digital inequality and highlights the importance of participation in a digital society. Similar to digital divide, this term should not be interpreted as a simple binary of inclusion or exclusion. Beyond inequalities in the ownership of devices and connections, the emphasis has shifted toward improving digital skills and encouraging use of the internet. Importantly, digital inclusion policy initiatives tend to frame the internet primarily in terms of websites and social media platforms. While these aspects are undeniably important, researchers and policymakers must recognize that society is experiencing rapid technological development. The media landscape in which we operate is becoming increasingly complex. Figure 1.2 simplifies the underlying layers of media to show the complexity and highlight the aspects that digital skills must address.

In Fig. 1.2, we distinguish between input, structure and texture, form, and media. Media refer to the material or method used to convey meaningful formats and platforms (forms). Formats and platforms are built on structure and texture that define the rules by which input is organized before being presented in a form. The bottom layers represent an analog media landscape and entail:

- *Input*: Text, numbers, audio, or video.
- *Structure and texture*: Rules that organize input, such as grammar for text or formulas for numbers.
- *Form*: Transmission of meaningful formats, such as speech, photographs, graphs, films, or written articles.
- *Media*: The way formats are shared, such as through television, radio, newspapers, or magazines.

The upper layers represent digital media. From the inside out:

- *Input*: Digits, pixels, and other raw digital data.

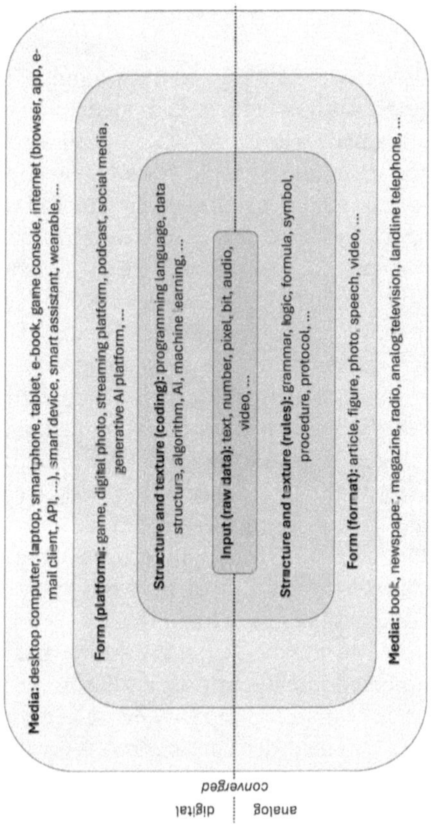

Fig. 1.2 Media landscape (after Van Deursen & Helsper, 2021)

- *Structure and texture*: Input is given structure through databases, programming languages, algorithms, AI, or machine learning.
- *Form*: Meaningful presentation of coded elements on platforms such as games, social media, podcasts, and streaming platforms.
- *Media*: The way platforms are shared, such as through computers, smart devices, or internet browsers.

In the media landscape, individuals are continuously exposed—consciously or unconsciously, willingly or unwillingly—to a constant stream of analog, digital, and/or converged media (an example of a converged medium is a smart television, where traditional broadcast is combined with internet streaming). While research on digital inequality and related policies often seems to underestimate the complexity of current media landscapes, audience and reception scholars have emphasized this through concepts such as *mediatization* (Madianou, 2014), *media ecologies* (Horst et al., 2010), and *polymedia* (Madianou & Miller, 2013). These concepts capture the implications of living in a deeply mediated world by considering the landscape as a composite in which each medium is understood in relation to the others. Within the media landscape, people develop *media repertoires*, patterns of media, platforms, and formats that they use together in meaningful ways (Hasebrink & Popp, 2006). A repertoire is not random; it reflects how people combine, prioritize, and sequence their media use to meet practical, social, and personal needs (Hasebrink & Hepp, 2017). Media repertoires are not only determined by media and platform availability or by needs and preferences, but also depend on the skills users possess. The following section briefly introduces the skills considered in this book (with a more detailed discussion about internet and connected intelligent media skills in the next chapter). The foundation lies in the strategic capacity to select media and platforms meaningfully. This also includes considerations for non-use, such as conscious decisions to avoid, limit, or stop using certain media when they no longer serve one's goals or values. Thus, media repertoires are actively created through interactions between the available media (and formats and platforms) and the skills people bring to their use. After choosing which media to engage with, digital skills remain crucial. They determine whether individuals can convert a wide array of options into coherent, effective, and empowering repertoires that support their daily goals.

1.3 A Framework of Seven Digital Skills

In this book, we propose seven types of digital skills, as shown in the process model in Fig. 1.3. The range of the seven skills is best characterized by the distinction between *medium*- and *content*-related skills. Medium-related skills account for the fundamental requirements of media use, apparent in strategic media choice, operational, and formal skills, whereas content-related skills account for essential requirements that relate to the content provided by the media, apparent in information, communication, content creation, and strategic media use skills. The top-to-bottom array illustrates skills as part of a process. They have a sequential and conditional nature: performing content-related skills requires the command of medium-related skills. Furthermore, strategic media use skills are ineffective without possessing sufficient levels of information, communication, or content creation skills. The sequential nature

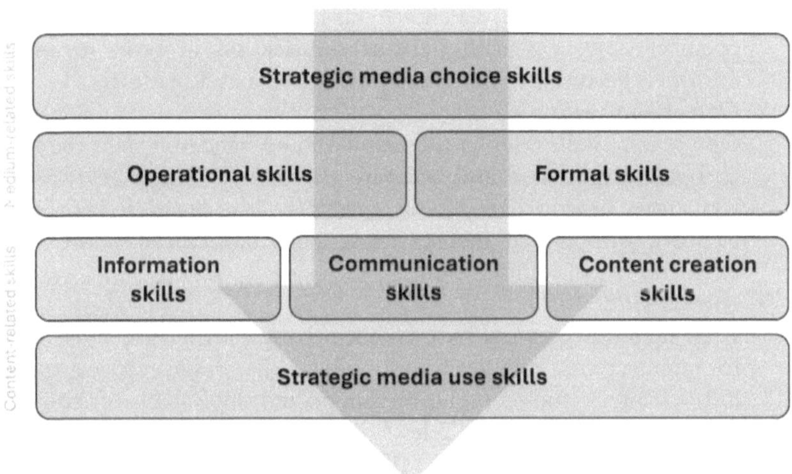

Fig. 1.3 Digital skills process model

of medium- and content-related skills aligns with the other three stages of appropriation, as illustrated in Fig. 1.1. After developing motivation and gaining material access, including the diversity and quality of digital media employed, individuals need strategic media choice skills to select the media and platforms that best help them achieve their goals or meet their emotional needs. On the other skill end, strategic media use skills play a crucial role in shaping the outcomes that result from engaging with media.

1. *Strategic media choice skills*
   The importance of this first skill follows the previous discussion on the role of digital skills in shaping media repertoires. It encompasses the skills to make deliberate and informed decisions when selecting digital media and platforms. This skill set has two key dimensions: (1) rational, goal-oriented decision-making, which includes defining objectives, comparing media and platforms, and selecting those that do or do not match the objective (e.g., learning, work, communication), and (2) emotional need satisfaction, which involves recognizing personal habits or desires (e.g., entertainment, social connection, personal well-being) that favor certain media. Mastering strategic media choice skills enables individuals to balance practical objectives with personal satisfaction in order to make informed decisions about the selected media and platforms
2. *Operational skills*
   Operational skills refer to the technical and hands-on skills required to operate hardware and software. In popular language they are sometimes described as *button knowledge*, the practical know-how to work with digital media. These skills have received the most attention in policy discussions
3. *Formal skills*
   Each medium presents its own formal logic that users must learn to interact with effectively and efficiently. Books are organized into chapters and paragraphs, supported by tables of content, indexes, and references. Television relies on the channels, schedules, and program formats. The internet is structured through websites, menus, (hyper)links, and navigation bars. AI tools introduce complex and often hidden structures that rely on algorithms and multimodal interactions (e.g., text, voice, and images). Formal skills refer to the skills to navigate and understand these structural and organizational features. They involve acting within the structural rules of a medium, such as clicking hyperlinks to move across websites or crafting prompts to navigate an AI system's logic. Users

must learn the specific characteristics of the medium. For instance, many older adults or those with limited reading skills struggle with menu structures and hyperlinks because these organizational logics are not intuitive to them

4. *Information skills*
   Unlike medium-related strategic media choice, operational, and formal skills, information skills are content-related. They originally referred to the skills to search, select, organize, and evaluate information in digital media. They help users understand the vast amount of information available on digital platforms. With AI-driven tools, the challenge of information skills has evolved into managing data-intensive and algorithmically curated content, which involves knowing how to phrase questions ("prompting") and understanding that AI outputs are generated based on data patterns. Furthermore, these skills extend to reading and interpreting sensor-driven data (e.g., health metrics from wearables or energy consumption patterns from smart meters)
5. *Communication skills*
   Contemporary media environments revolve around interactions and exchanges. Digital platforms, such as e-mail, instant messaging, social networking, online dating, and community forums, require effective and responsible communication. These practices demand skills such as adapting tone and style to different audiences, managing digital identity, interpreting subtle cues in written or multimodal interactions, and resolving misunderstandings without face-to-face communication. Furthermore, people interact not only with other humans through digital media but also with AI-driven chatbots, voice assistants, and automated customer service agents. Effective communication in these contexts requires the skills to critically interpret responses and adapt language to maximize the usefulness of AI interactions. Moreover, individuals must be aware of how their phrasing, tone, and information disclosure shape the outputs they receive while recognizing the limitations, biases, and potential misinterpretations inherent in AI systems. Despite the growing importance of communication skills, there is no formalized curriculum or universal training that addresses these challenges
6. *Content creation skills*
   Content creation skills have become increasingly vital as the internet has shifted from a medium of passive consumption to one centered

on active user participation and user-generated content. Content creation encompasses a wide range of practices, such as writing blogs or forum posts, recording and editing photos, videos, and audio, curating and remixing digital materials, and producing and sharing messages, images, and profiles on social networking platforms. Activities that require professional expertise have become broadly accessible owing to user-friendly tools and platforms. Algorithmic recommendation engines and generative AI further reduce the technical barriers to create digital content and enable individuals to quickly produce outputs that would have previously required advanced design, writing, or editing skills. Generative AI refers to systems that learn from data to produce new content that mirrors the style, structure, or meaning of the input data (Jovanovic & Campbell, 2022). These systems are capable of generating original outputs (such as text, images, audio, software code, or video) by learning statistical patterns from large-scale training data. Recent advances in machine learning, particularly in deep learning architectures and large language models, have substantially expanded the scope and sophistication of generative AI. As a result, these systems now support complex forms of text generation, creative assistance, and decision support (Bommasani et al., 2021; Dwivedi et al., 2023). Although generative AI can make content creation appear straightforward, potentially leading users to overestimate their ability to produce high-quality outputs, effective use still requires a well-developed set of digital skills. Content creation extends beyond producing output to include considerations of authenticity, originality, and ethical responsibility. When working with generative AI, creators must learn to balance automation with their own voices, integrating these systems as creative partners while maintaining human agency

7. *Strategic media use skills*
   Strategic media use skills refer to the purposeful use of digital media and platforms to achieve specific personal and professional goals. In practice, this involves continuous decision-making in various applications. For instance, users may compare prices in e-commerce environments, select the most effective workout program based on data collected by a smartwatch, or choose the cheapest and most convenient flight when planning travel. These processes require the

capacity to critically evaluate options, weigh trade-offs, and anticipate consequences. These skills rely heavily on judgment and critical thinking. The integration of AI into media landscapes has intensified the importance of strategic media use skills. AI tools increasingly mediate decision-making by providing recommendations, predictions, and automated solutions, ranging from personalized shopping suggestions and fitness guidance to AI-generated travel itineraries and medical diagnoses. The use of these tools requires a strategic combination of the generated insights, personal knowledge, preferences, and objectives. Mastering strategic media use skills allows individuals to harness AI as a tool for informed, purposeful, and goal-oriented actions, transforming the abundance of mediated options into coherent, effective, and empowering strategies rather than passively accepting automated guidance. Crucially, AI tools function through collaboration between users and AI systems. Strategic media use skills enable users to determine the next step in the decision-making process and ultimately make the final decision. This partnership is at the core of strategic media use skills

In this book, our discussion of skills focuses primarily on digital skills related to the internet and connected intelligent media for two fundamental reasons.

1. The internet serves as the central infrastructure and connective backbone for a wide array of online services. Popular activities such as web browsing, email, social networking, file sharing, streaming, and cloud storage require skills that users need to participate in society. Second, the internet alone is no longer sufficient to capture the complexities of today's digital environment, which increasingly includes intelligent media—content and platforms powered by AI, machine learning, or other forms of computational intelligence. They can adapt, respond to, and interact with users in novel ways. Consequently, developing skills that allow individuals to navigate both internet infrastructure and intelligent media layered on top of it has become essential for effective and meaningful engagement with digital media.
2. Internet and intelligent media provide a comprehensive lens through which the full spectrum of digital skills can be observed and

analyzed, from basic operational tasks to advanced content creation and strategic media use. Within this context, we can see a clear manifestation of the seven digital skills.

While our primary emphasis will remain on digital skills for the internet and connected intelligent media, in Sect. 1.5, we will also include a discussion of skills relevant to traditional analog media and computer media, acknowledging their continued relevance and evolving relationships with newer intelligent media.

1.4 From Orality to Algorithms: A Brief History of Media Skills

The history of media skills that people require to function in society is marked by three epochal tendencies: (1) the expansion and accumulation of required skills, (2) ever-larger sections of the population that require these skills, and (3) a transition in how these skills are taught, from private instruction to public education systems. This section offers a snapshot of how these trends developed over time.

During the European Middle Ages, society was largely oral in nature. Most people lived within rigid structures dominated by religious authorities and economic necessity. The church exerted control over spiritual life and education, which was minimal and primarily reserved for training the clergy. Instruction focused on rote memorization and recitation of religious texts in Latin, a language inaccessible to the general population (Ong, 1984). Even as written documents began to circulate widely in administrative and legal contexts, their presence did not necessitate widespread literacy. Awareness of the power of the written word grew, but active literacy was still limited to a small fraction of the population, likely no more than ten percent by 1500 (Mizrach, 1998). For the majority, reading and writing were neither necessary nor expected, and oral traditions were sufficient for everyday communication, cultural transmission, and economic activities.

The invention of the Gutenberg printing press in 1439 revolutionized the production and distribution of written content (Briggs, 2000). For the first time, books were mass-produced, breaking the monopoly of handwritten manuscripts controlled by religious institutions. This shift paved the way for new formats and formal structures in texts, such as chapters, indexes, and page numbers, which required new reading and writing conventions to accommodate them. Despite these advancements, literacy remained concentrated among the bourgeois and the educated elite. They held the power to record, interpret, and preserve knowledge, while the rest of society functioned effectively within the oral traditions of storytelling, memory, and direct interpersonal communication (Briggs & Burke, 2009). Lack of literacy was not perceived as a disadvantage; rather, it was irrelevant to the daily lives of the general population, whose tasks and responsibilities did not require the use of written texts.

At the end of the eighteenth century, the Age of Enlightenment marked a profound shift in the way societies thought about knowledge, progress, and human development. Thinkers championed the values of freedom, democracy, and universal education as tools to liberate individuals from ignorance and enable societal advancement (Stone, 1969). These ideals have inspired significant reforms in education. In 1779, Thomas Jefferson proposed his "Systematic Plan of General Education." His vision emphasized the role of public education in cultivating informed citizens capable of participating in democratic governance (Stone, 1969). Shortly afterward, the first publicly funded and state-supervised schools emerged in the United States and Europe. These institutions represent a historical turning point. Until then, formal education was largely a private affair organized by churches, local guilds, and small-scale workshops in rural and early industrial economies (Collins, 2000). The shift toward publicly organized schooling laid the groundwork for more systematic and equitable access to education, gradually extending learning opportunities to broader segments of the population (Rury & Rury, 2005).

Between the seventeenth and nineteenth centuries, most people continued to lack basic literacy. Economic structures relied heavily on manual labor, particularly in agriculture and emerging industrial sectors. However, as European economies began to shift toward more complex systems of trade, governance, and early forms of industrialization, the demand for clerical skills, record-keeping, and bureaucratic administration grew. Consequently, elementary schooling began to expand, particularly among urban middle-class and merchant families. However, education remained a privilege, and the ruling elite often resisted reforms. There was widespread fear that educating people in poverty would encourage rebellion and disrupt the existing social order (Stone, 1969).

Following the industrial revolution and rapid urbanization, reading and writing gained new and heightened importance. The industrial economy demanded a workforce capable of operating machinery and understanding technical manuals, following written instructions, managing inventories, and performing administrative tasks. The growing complexity of production, distribution, communication, and consumption systems created a pressing need for mass literacy. This era marked the beginning of a *control revolution*, in which the flow of information became as vital as the flow of goods and labor (Beniger, 1986). This transformation prompted societies to invest more heavily in public education, and, throughout the second half of the nineteenth century, many developed countries began to introduce compulsory schooling laws. These mandates represent another historic milestone: for the first time, literacy and basic education became legal requirements for the entire population. Reading and writing were no longer optional or limited to social elites. They became essential tools for economic participation, civic engagement, and personal autonomy. The industrial age laid the foundation for a modern information society in which knowledge-based work, bureaucratic systems, and increasingly complex communication networks demanded a literate citizenry. By the mid-twentieth century, this commitment to universal education was globally recognized. The United Nations Declaration on the Rights of the Child, adopted in 1959, explicitly affirmed every child's right to receive free and compulsory education, at least at the elementary level. This declaration acknowledged not only the practical necessity of education but also its role in promoting dignity, equity, and opportunity worldwide. Literacy was no longer merely a gateway to employment; it was declared a fundamental human right and a cornerstone of human development.

In the communication revolution at the turn of the twentieth century, society's growing complexity demanded new forms of coordination and information management (Beniger, 1986). A range of new media emerged, including photography, film, the gramophone, radio, and television. Audio, visual, and audiovisual media communicate through sound and images, requiring users to develop auditory and visual literacy in addition to textual literacy. However, despite the increasing presence of such media in daily life, schools largely ignored the need to teach students how to interpret or critically engage with audiovisual content (Goldfarb, 2002). It was assumed that because everyone could speak, hear, and watch, no formal instruction was necessary. The use of these media was considered either intuitive or a domain of professionals, such as film-makers, sound engineers, or broadcasters. This widespread assumption left a significant gap in formal education, where students were taught to decode written texts but not visual or auditory languages that increasingly shaped public discourse and cultural life.

However, this perception changed dramatically with the introduction of personal computers in the 1970s. Unlike radio or television, computers were not considered intuitive or self-explanatory. Instead, they were perceived as complex tools that required mastery of operational skills, such as commanding hardware, using software, navigating file systems, and understanding basic programming. The advent of the internet further expanded these skills. Initially, the internet was viewed as an extension of computers, demanding the same operational skills with some additional networking and information retrieval challenges. With the launch of the World Wide Web in the 1990s, a graphical interface was placed on top of the internet's technical infrastructure. This interface, with its clickable icons, images, and multimedia features, provided the illusion that anyone could easily use the web. The idea emerged that the internet was more accessible than previous technologies and that even those with minimal education could participate by simply clicking their way through digital spaces. However, this assumption proved misleading. In our prior book, "Digital skills, unlocking the information society" (Van Dijk & Van Deursen, 2014), we argued that the internet does not require fewer skills than previous media; it actually demands more skills. To use the internet effectively, users must combine traditional literacy (reading, writing, and understanding textual and numerical data) with operational skills (using browsers and online applications), formal skills (navigating digital structures such as menus and hyperlinks), information skills (searching and evaluating sources, as well as interpreting graphics, video, and sound), communication skills (exchanging meaning online, networking, managing identity), content creation skills (producing quality textual or visual content), and strategic media use skills (using the internet to achieve personal or professional goals). Even touch screens and simplified user interfaces on tablets and smartphones, while reducing operational barriers, cannot replace the foundational skills required for meaningful participation. Without the skills to critically interpret and strategically use text, visuals, sounds, and other data, users are at risk of becoming passive consumers rather than empowered participants. To fully leverage the opportunities presented by the internet, individuals must develop an extensive skill set that bridges traditional and digital skills.

The evolving skill set becomes even more crucial as we witness a profound transformation in the media landscape, fueled by the rapid rise and integration of AI. Generative AI tools, such as large language models, image generators, synthetic voice technologies, and deepfake applications, have altered the ways in which content is produced, distributed, and engaged with. Unlike previous media, which primarily serve to store or transmit human-created content, AI-driven systems actively generate, personalize, and curate content in real time. This shift blurs the boundaries between authorship and automation of consumption and creation. As a result, users are no longer passive recipients or active participants; they are co-creators in media environments increasingly governed by algorithmic logic and machine learning models. AI interfaces are designed to appear simple and intuitive, echoing the early promises of the graphical web: simply type a prompt, click a button, or speak a command, and content emerges. However, this seamless user experience is extremely complex. To use AI in a collaborative manner to improve responsible decision-making, individuals must develop a critical understanding of how algorithms function, how they are trained, what data they rely on, and how that data may encode societal biases, inequalities, or misinformation. Unlike earlier technologies that transmitted information in relatively static forms, AI can dynamically simulate human conversation, creativity, and decision-making. Users must learn to question the apparent neutrality of outputs, recognize manipulation, and understand how their data are used to influence or tailor their experience.

1.5 An Overview of Traditional and Digital Media Skills

In Sect. 1.3, we introduced seven key skills: strategic media choice, operational, formal, information, communication, content creation, and strategic media use skills. Here, we apply them to different media types. For simplicity, we have consolidated these types into:

1. Print media
2. Audio, visual, and audiovisual media
3. Computers, including desktops, laptops, tablets, and (smart)phones

4. Internet media, including web browsers, online applications (apps), and accessible platforms
5. Connected intelligent media, including AI platforms and smart devices

The formats and platforms, and the ways in which they are structured, accessible through these media co-define the required skills (see Fig. 1.2). Boxes 1.1 and 1.2 present comparative summaries of the five media categories. We organized the comparison according to medium-related skills (strategic media choice, operational, and formal) and content-related skills (information, communication, content creation, and strategic media use). Medium-related skills refer to foundational aspects related to the use of the medium, whereas content-related skills concern content conveyed through the medium. Despite the differences between the media categories, the required skills share common features. All media use begins with defining the objective that the medium or platform is meant to achieve. Across all media and platforms, users need the skills to read, write, and interpret texts and figures; navigate text structures; interpret and evaluate content; and communicate by encoding and decoding messages to exchange meaning. They must also be able to compose.or adapt texts and visuals according to a specific design, understand copyright and licensing, represent others with fairness and respect, and decide, act, and reflect upon information in texts and visuals to achieve a specific goal.

Print Media

Even in an era dominated by print media, people required *strategic media choice skills* to select among the available options. For example, if someone wants to discover interesting local events, they can consult newspapers, flyers, pamphlets, and brochures. Each medium offers a distinct format, level of detail, and convenience, making the act of choosing the most appropriate option a skillful process. *Operational skills* reflect the technical skills required to use a medium. In the context of print, this includes reading and writing texts and visuals, including analog design elements such as illustrations, charts, tables, symbols, or icons. *Formal skills* relate to the structures that users must learn. For print, this means navigating

Box 1.1 Medium-related skills for traditional and digital media

	Print media	*Audio, visual, and audiovisual media*	*Computers (desktop, laptop, tablet, smartphone)*	*Internet (browser, apps, and digital platforms)*	*Connected intelligent media*
Strategic media choice skills	• Define the objective that the medium should achieve • Identify, evaluate, and select media	• Define the objective that the medium should achieve • Identify, evaluate, and select media	• Define the objective that the medium should achieve • Identify, evaluate, and select media	• Define the objective that the medium should achieve • Identify, evaluate, and select media and platforms	• Define the objective that the medium should achieve • Consider whether to engage with an intelligent agent or act independently • Identify, evaluate, and select media and platforms
Operational skills	• Read and write texts, visuals, and design elements	• Read and write texts, visuals, and design elements • Watch, listen, record, and edit audio, video, and audiovisuals	• Read and write texts, visuals, and design elements • Watch, listen, record, and edit audio, video, and audiovisuals • Manage toolbars, buttons, and menus • Manage installation, settings, and updates • Manage file formats	• Read and write texts, visuals, and design elements • Watch, listen, record, and edit audio, video, and audiovisuals • Manage toolbars, buttons, and menus • Manage installation and settings • Manage user input • Manage file formats • Share files and documents	• Read and write texts, visuals, and design elements • Watch, listen, record, and edit audio, video, and audiovisuals • Manage toolbars, buttons, and menus • Manage installation and settings • Manage user input • Manage file formats • Share files and documents • Integrate across devices

	Print media	*Audio, visual, and audiovisual media*	*Computers (desktop, laptop, tablet, smartphone)*	*Internet (browser, apps, and digital platforms)*	*Connected intelligent media*
Formal skills	• Navigate text structures	• Navigate text structures • Navigate the (temporal) structures of audio, video, and audiovisuals	• Navigate text structures • Navigate the (temporal) structures of audio, video, and audiovisuals • Navigate and edit (temporal) computer structures: Drives, folders, and files • Maintain a sense of location while navigating computer structures (folders and files)	• Navigate text structures • Navigate the (temporal) structures of audio, video, and audiovisuals • Navigate text and multimodal hypermedia and app structures • Navigate interactive hypermedia • Maintain a sense of location while navigating	• Navigate text structures • Navigate the (temporal) structures of audio, video, and audiovisuals • Navigate text and multimodal hypermedia and app structures • Navigate interactive hypermedia • Navigate adaptive/ intelligent hypermedia • Maintain a sense of location while navigating

Box 1.2 Content-related skills for traditional and digital media

	Print media	*Audio, visual, and audiovisual media*	*Computers (desktop, laptop, tablet, smartphone)*	*Internet (browser, apps, and digital platforms)*	*Connected intelligent media*
Information skills	• Define information problem • Search and select information from text and visuals • Interpret and evaluate information	• Define information problem • Search and select information from text and visuals, and from audio, video, and audiovisuals • Interpret and evaluate information	• Define information problem • Search and select information from digital text, visuals, sounds, or videos • Interpret and evaluate information	• Define information problem • Search and select information from online text, visuals, sounds, or videos • Interpret and evaluate information	• Define information problem • Search and select information (data) from online text, visuals, sounds, videos, data flows, AI generated output, or sensors • Interpret (and visualize) and evaluate information and data (critical awareness of algorithmic influence)

	Print media	*Audio, visual, and audiovisual media*	*Computers (desktop, laptop, tablet, smartphone)*	*Internet (browser, apps, and digital platforms)*	*Connected intelligent media*
Communication skills	• Encode and decode messages to construct, understand, and exchange meaning in text and visuals	• Encode and decode messages to construct, understand, and exchange meaning in audio, video, or audiovisuals, possibly guided by text or visuals	• Encode and decode messages to construct, understand, and exchange meaning while interacting with computer interfaces and software	• Encode and decode messages to construct, understand, and exchange meaning in interactive web applications	• Encode and decode messages to construct, understand, and exchange meaning in interactions with dynamic multimodal AI applications
Content creation skills	• Compose or adapt texts or visuals according to a specific design: A letter, article, book, review, … • Understand copyright and licenses • Represent others with fairness and respect	• Create or adapt audio, visual, or audiovisual materials according to a specific design: sound, video, film, … • Understand copyright and licenses • Represent others with fairness and respect	• Create or adapt software according to a specific design: program or app, template, macro, … • Understand copyright and licenses • Represent others with fairness and respect	• Create or adapt online applications according to a specific design: website, blog, post, short/reel, video, profile • Understand copyright and licenses • Represent others with fairness and respect	• Create or adapt materials in collaboration with generative AI according to a specific plan • Understand copyright and licenses • Represent others with fairness and respect

(continued)

Box 1.2 (continued)

	Print media	*Audio, visual, and audiovisual media*	*Computers (desktop, laptop, tablet, smartphone)*	*Internet (browser, apps, and digital platforms)*	*Connected intelligent media*
Strategic media use skills	• Decide, act, and reflect upon information in texts and visuals to achieve a specific goal	• Decide, act, and reflect upon textual, audio, visual, or audiovisual information to achieve a specific goal	• Decide, act, and reflect upon textual, audio, visual, or audiovisual information in computers to achieve a specific goal	• Decide, act, and reflect upon online textual, audio, visual, or audiovisual information to achieve a specific goal	• Decide, act, and reflect upon textual, audio, visual, or audiovisual information or data from intelligent media to achieve a specific goal • Integrate AI tools/sensor data in the decision-making process to optimize results

structural elements, such as chapters, sections, headings, references, or tables of content.

Information skills involve searching, selecting, processing, and evaluating information. This can be demanding because print is largely text-based and requires significant cognitive effort to extract meaning. *Communication skills* in print involve encoding and decoding meaning through written texts, such as writing and interpreting letters, memos, articles, books, and other printed formats. *Content creation skills* involve the effective and purposeful production of written materials following a specific plan or design. This goes beyond simply writing—it includes carefully selecting the language, applying the correct spelling and grammar, and choosing a style that suits the intended audience and medium. Furthermore, content creation requires the skills to understand copyright and licenses and represent others with fairness and respect. Finally, *strategic media use skills* concern the purpose of using print media. The information obtained can inform decisions, guide actions, and provide personal and professional benefits. Importantly, the purpose is not limited to information in a narrow sense; entertainment can also be a legitimate goal.

Audio, Visual, and Audiovisual Media

Media such as radio and television originally provided sounds, videos, or images that could be largely processed without print media skills (Reeves & Nass, 1996). Audiences were mainly required to listen and watch attentively. However, over time, audiovisual media have become increasingly text-rich, incorporating introductions, subtitles, captions, text boxes, and scrolling banners. *Strategic media choice skills* are required to decide when certain audio, visual, or audiovisual media are more effective than written media (e.g., using a video tutorial instead of a written manual). These skills are also important when selecting audio, visual, or audiovisual options. For instance, if someone wants to learn how to cook a new recipe, they might choose a culinary radio show or television program, depending on their preferences and objectives. *Operational skills* still include reading and writing texts and analog design elements but extend to watching, listening, recording, and editing audio, video, and audiovisual elements such as voice, music, compositions, and imagery. *Formal skills* involve navigating and, when necessary, editing the underlying structures of audio, video, and audiovisuals. This includes understanding how scenes, shots, sequences, openings, and endings are organized to create meaning.

The application of *information skills* to audio, visual, and audiovisual media requires mental processes distinct from those used in text-based contexts. In addition to finding and selecting information from texts and visuals, information is conveyed through sounds, videos, or a combination of both. Nevertheless, the fundamental tasks of problem definition, searching, selecting, interpreting, and evaluating information remain the same. For example, distinguishing between factual reporting and entertainment or evaluating the reliability of visual sources are essential. *Communication skills* for audio, visual, and audiovisual media differ substantially from those of print. Encoding and decoding meaning through images, sound, speech, and body language requires both an awareness of how these elements convey emotion and intent, and the skills to use them effectively. For instance, gestures and tone of voice can strongly influence how messages are received and understood. *Content creation skills* are also more complex because audiovisual production combines multiple modes (text, sound, image, and/or motion). Framing shots, using microphones and cameras effectively, and applying basic editing techniques are just a few examples of the skills required. Regarding *strategic media use skills*, it is important to understand which audio, visual, and audiovisual information can be used to act upon and make beneficial decisions. For instance, the actions involved differ based on whether the intended purpose is information retrieval or entertainment.

Computers

The characteristics of traditional analog media, such as their limited selectivity and lower accuracy (as compared to digital media), tend to encourage relatively passive use, despite arguments for the notion of an active audience. While analog media allow active mental processing, digital media require a basic level of active engagement and provide opportunities for interaction, transaction, and real-time interpersonal communication.

In the context of computers, *strategic media choice skills* extend to media that facilitate access to digital content, such as laptops, tablets, desktops, and smartphones. Understanding the capabilities and limitations is a key aspect of strategic media choice as it directly affects how effectively a user can create and process digital information. *Operational skills* are similar to those required for print and audiovisual media. Users must read and write texts, visuals, and design elements as well as watch, listen, record, and edit audio, video, or audiovisual content. However, additional skills are required to operate computers. Software operations include the use of toolbars, buttons, menus, and installation and handling (firmware) updates. Other skills are those required to manage different file formats, depending on the device and software. Unlike traditional media, *formal skills* for computer use are distinct because they involve navigating a structural (and temporal) system. Users must not only know how to open folders, save files, or move content between drives and folders but also maintain orientation within complex folder and file hierarchies. Formal skills entail understanding where files are stored, organizing and retrieving them efficiently, and maintaining a logical structure for future access.

Content-related skills for using computers are largely similar to those used with analog media but involve digital formats and tools. *Information skills* include problem definition, searching, selecting, interpreting, and evaluating information from a combination of digital texts, visuals, sounds, or videos. For example, information skills are required to search for local documents or collections, filter content by file type, date modified, or folder location, or to check the source and authorship of documents (e.g., metadata in PDFs or Word files). *Communication skills* involve encoding and decoding messages to construct, understand, and exchange meaning while interacting with computer interfaces and software. Think of following prompts or feedback from software interfaces. *Content creation skills* refer to the production of digital artifacts, such as computer programs, software applications, templates, macros, or presentations, each requiring a specific design or plan. Finally, *strategic media use skills* involve making informed decisions based on computer calculations, aggregations, and statistical analyses to compare options with the aim of achieving a particular goal (e.g., saving for a vacation).

Internet Media

As shown in Fig. 1.2, internet media include web browsers and applications that provide access to a wide range of online platforms such as social media and networking, e-commerce, streaming services, online games, collaborative cloud-based productivity tools, and user-generated participatory platforms such as Wikis. These all convey both verbal and nonverbal meanings and require skills to manage both. The next chapter extensively discusses these skills. The rapid growth of online platforms has emphasized the importance of *strategic media choice skills*. Users must decide which browser or application to use and choose between a vast number of platforms that serve similar purposes. Selecting a platform that best fits a specific goal or task can therefore be challenging and involves rational (e.g., when a student selects a particular app because it allows real-time collaboration and offline access) and emotional (e.g., if someone selects a particular music-streaming service because they like the interface, playlist suggestions, or brand identity) considerations. Accessing online platforms requires the use of a web browser or dedicated application, both of which demand *operational skills*. These skills include operating taskbar buttons, toolbars, menus, handling downloads and uploads, and sharing files and documents, among others. *Formal skills* in online environments are required for the effective use of temporal hypermedia structures. Hypermedia consists of interconnected text, images, audio, and video that users explore in a non-linear and interactive manner. Unlike traditional linear media, it allows users to create their own pathways based on individual interests or needs, moving forward, backward, or branching into new sections. This high degree of user control enables a flexible and personalized experience. However, this freedom also introduces challenges: without a strong sense of spatial orientation—understanding location, distance, and direction—users can easily become disoriented and lose track of their location (Kwan, 2001; Lee, 2005).

The *information skills* required for the internet resemble those required for traditional media and computers. The process begins with formulating a clear and focused question. Yet even with well-defined queries, search engines often return hundreds or thousands of results, many of which are irrelevant. The sheer volume of online content places greater demands on users when selecting, interpreting, and evaluating information. The latter involves assessing accuracy, validity, and reliability, for example, by verifying the author's credibility, the publication date, and whether the information is supported by data or expert evidence. *Communication skills* in online environments differ from those in traditional media because nonverbal cues are often reduced. This requires people to find new ways to express meaning clearly and appropriately. In addition, online interaction often involves asynchronous communication and the management of a high volume of messages and challenges, which are less common in face-to-face or print-based communication.

As a result, it is essential to develop practices suited to online contexts, such as writing professional and concise emails, using instant messaging with clarity and tone awareness, composing accurate and engaging online profiles, and participating constructively in online debates and discussions. *Content creation skills* enable users to actively contribute to the internet rather than simply consuming information. Content creation often requires careful planning and design because different types of contributions have distinct requirements. Examples include building a personal website, writing a blog, posting on a forum or online newspaper, shooting and editing a video for a video-sharing platform, and creating a personal profile on social networking sites. Mastering content creation skills also involves understanding how to present information clearly, attractively, and responsibly to an online audience. This includes understanding licensing and copyright, ensuring that content respects legal boundaries, and acknowledges the intellectual property of others. On the internet, where voices and perspectives are amplified and widely shared, representing others fairly and respectfully carries even greater weight. *Strategic media use skills* require users to distinguish between goals and means, as well as between what is more or less important for achieving these goals. Once the priorities are clear, users must make informed decisions regarding the most suitable course of action. Acquiring and applying these skills online requires a critical and analytical mindset supported by strong information and communication skills.

Connected Intelligent Media

With the rise of AI and smart systems in the media landscape, *strategic media choice skills* have gained increasing importance. The first decision to make before selecting a medium or platform is whether to rely on an intelligent, partly autonomous agent or act yourself. For instance, when in need of information, a user may decide between a traditional search engine, conversational AI tool, or voice-operated smart assistant. Intelligent tools are most valuable when they clearly improve outcomes, for example, using predictive text to take notes efficiently or deploying real-time machine translation to overcome language barriers. Simultaneously, there are situations in which avoiding AI applications is the more responsible choice. For instance, AI-generated text may not be suitable when accuracy, accountability, and ethical responsibility are critical, such as in legal or medical contexts where verified human expertise is essential.

Similarly, a student might choose to avoid automated writing assistance to strengthen their own critical thinking skills rather than outsourcing the task to a tool. Likewise, a user may opt out of a wearable device's health monitoring features if it collects sensitive biometric data without adequate privacy safeguards. When a user decides to use intelligent media or platforms, selecting the right option requires further consideration of characteristics such as functionality, security, and reliability. This also means evaluating which features best support the specific objective. In the context of connected intelligent media, *operational skills* that come on top of the aforementioned skills in other media include the skills to adapt and personalize performance, manage user input (e.g., text or voice), connect AI tools with other software and systems, export or convert AI or smart device output into usable formats, and manage the settings, permissions, and connectivity of smart devices to ensure they function effectively and securely. *Formal skills* for navigating online contexts remain essential but extend to navigating dynamic, multimodal interface structures in complex smart environments. To navigate effectively, users must understand how data are structured, organized, and presented and must handle system-driven adaptive behaviors such as prompts, alerts, and personalized recommendations.

Content-related *information skills* in intelligent media follow the same basic processes as those in traditional media—searching, selecting, interpreting, and evaluating—but the presence of AI introduces important differences. In intelligent media, user prompting plays a central role, with systems suggesting queries and highlighting relevant results based on past user behavior. Interpreting information becomes more complex as AI dashboards or smart device applications often combine charts, predictive analytics, and narrative summaries, requiring users to understand not only the data itself but also how the system presents and structures it. An accurate interpretation depends on recognizing patterns, trends, and relationships within these dynamic multimodal displays. Notably, evaluating information in intelligent media requires a critical assessment of both content and algorithmic behavior. AI-generated outputs are based on patterns in the data, which means that they can be flawed, biased, or misleading. Therefore, users must evaluate not only the credibility of the information but also how recommendations, predictive results, and personalization mechanisms may introduce errors, incomplete coverage, or systematic bias. *Communication skills* are required to interact effectively using multiple modalities, including voice commands, text input, and gestures. These skills further involve managing digital collaboration within smart environments, such as cloud-based shared dashboards, while remaining aware of the limitations of automated communication, such as when AI-generated responses may lack nuance or context. *Content creation skills* are similarly extended. Users must design prompts to optimize the outputs of generative AI. Finally, *strategic media use skills* involve integrating AI and smart devices in a manner that supports personal objectives, ensuring that technology enhances rather than complicates human decision-making. Central to human-AI collaboration is that users work alongside intelligent systems to optimize outcomes. To achieve this, users must understand the capabilities and limitations of AI, know when to rely on AI-generated suggestions, and know when to apply human judgment. These skills require informed decisions that leverage automation, while maintaining human oversight, critical thinking, and accountability. In essence, strategic media use in intelligent systems involves balancing the efficiency of AI with careful human decision-making.

1.6 Emerging Patterns of Digital Media Inequalities

For many years, we have been conducting extensive empirical studies to measure digital skills across diverse population segments. These studies relied on a combination of large-scale surveys and task-based performance tests, most of which were conducted in a media lab in the Netherlands. The performance tests required participants to complete a variety of internet-based tasks, such as searching for and evaluating information, engaging in online communication, and creating digital content. In addition, we conducted performance tests in which participants were asked to interact with emerging technologies, including wearable devices and simulated smart home environments. They were asked to interpret the data generated by smart systems and act appropriately. The findings of these studies have been published in numerous articles and reports, consistently demonstrating substantial inequalities in digital skills among different groups. Chapter 3 elaborates on the levels of digital skills measured and examines how they differ across population groups. However, whenever we present these findings, we are often confronted with the question *of why these inequalities are so important.* Critics have pointed out that disparities in skill levels have always existed among media. For instance, differences in educational backgrounds have long shaped how people navigate print media or understand audiovisual content. From this perspective, one may ask what is genuinely new in our observations. Our response begins with a distinction between traditional media, such as print and audiovisual formats, and digital media, particularly the internet. Furthermore, the evolution of intelligent media has introduced an additional layer of complexity. Below, we argue that these impose new barriers to participation that extend beyond the traditional internet and amplify inequalities for those lacking the advanced skills needed to engage effectively with intelligent media.

Comparing Skill Inequalities in Analog and Internet Media

As illustrated in Boxes 1.1 and 1.2, the skills required for using analog print and audiovisual media share some fundamental similarities with digital skills required for internet media. Individuals must be able to locate, interpret, and communicate their information. However, the transition from analog to digital media has amplified pre-existing differences in these skills and has introduced new forms of inequality. On the one hand, the internet has simplified many tasks that were more demanding in the analog era. For instance, systematic information retrieval—once dependent on physically navigating a library, mastering classification systems, and relying on a limited set of sources—can be performed in seconds with the help of search engines that rank, filter, and prioritize results automatically. Similarly, online communication through email, instant messaging, and social networking platforms allows people to connect and exchange information more quickly and effortlessly than traditional correspondence or face-to-face interaction. On the other hand, the internet has introduced additional complexity beyond the skills required to handle books, newspapers, and audiovisual media. Online environments demand operational and formal skills to use digital interfaces, navigate hyperlinks, manage multiple platforms, and understand the structures of websites and databases. These requirements have created new barriers that extend beyond traditional literacies of reading and writing. Moreover, internet media place a premium on advanced information, communication, content creation, and strategic media use skills, which only partially overlap with the skills associated with traditional analog media. Without such skills, individuals risk becoming overwhelmed in the vast and unfiltered ocean of digital information and interaction.

In this book, we argue that, while operational and formal skills are often acquired relatively quickly through computer training, workplace practice, or even personal trial and error, most content-related digital skills are not learned automatically. The skills to critically evaluate online information, communicate effectively in diverse digital contexts, create content that is both meaningful and socially impactful, and use media strategically for personal, professional, or civic goals require structured learning and targeted guidance. Unfortunately, such instructions are not yet common and widespread. Generally, schools do not equip students with communication skills required to participate in online communities or social networks. Strategic media use—deploying digital tools to achieve broader personal or societal goals, such as advancing one's career, engaging in political participation, or building social capital—is typically addressed only in specific professional or educational contexts in which internet media are used instrumentally to achieve narrowly defined outcomes. However, where should individuals learn to search systematically for information tailored to their unique personal or professional needs? Where do they gain the skills to interpret online voting guides, locate peers on social networking sites, or engage responsibly and effectively in online dating? At first glance, some forms of digital participation, such as creating a personal profile, posting a message, editing a wiki, and uploading content to video-sharing or knowledge exchange platforms, appear straightforward because they are heavily structured by the platforms themselves. However, a closer examination raises questions about the quality and effectiveness of most of this user-generated content, at least from the perspective of professionals who evaluate communication in terms of its accuracy, coherence, and impact. Taken together, the inequalities already visible in the realm of traditional media have not only persisted but have also deepened in the transition to internet media.

Comparing Skill Inequalities in Internet and Intelligent Media

Inequalities are likely to widen further with the rise of intelligent media. On the surface, such technologies create new opportunities and convenience. Recommendation algorithms suggest content tailored to personal preferences. AI assistants can summarize long texts or generate preliminary drafts of emails and reports, and smart home devices can monitor energy use, adjust lighting, or even reorder groceries. Complex tasks appear to be more manageable even for users with moderate digital skills.

Paradoxically, intelligent media again introduce new layers of complexity. Beyond the skills needed to operate computers and navigate the internet, individuals must now engage in environments in which intelligent media actively generate data, make recommendations, and sometimes take autonomous action. AI-driven platforms, wearables, and smart homes require users to interpret feedback, configure settings, and make informed decisions regarding functionality, privacy, and security. Moreover, users must evaluate the reliability of the AI-generated outputs, recognize algorithmic biases, and reflect on the ethical implications of automated decisions. In this context, strategic media choice skills have become increasingly important. Users must decide which AI applications are best suited to particular goals; for instance, selecting between conversational AI platforms, wearable devices, and home assistants. Furthermore, intelligent media demand specialized information, communication, content creation, and strategic media use skills that differ in important ways from those needed for traditional internet media. Beyond finding and interpreting information, users must now design precise prompts to optimize AI outputs; critically assess whether AI-generated texts, recommendations or predictive analytics are accurate and trustworthy; interact effectively with automated systems; adapt their workflows to effectively integrate AI or IoT; and consider the long-term social and ethical consequences of relying on them.

As with the earlier transition to internet media, skills for intelligent media are not automatically acquired. Understanding the reliability of AI-generated summaries or recommendations requires additional skills. It demands critical thinking, knowledge of algorithms, and awareness of potential biases. Communication in AI-mediated environments—where chatbots filter messages, automated assistants propose responses, or collaborative AI applications shape group work—requires new skills that are not systematically taught. When it comes to the strategic use of intelligent media, individuals are largely left to learn and experiment on their own. People must determine, often inefficiently, how to use AI for personal decision-making, leverage social networking strategies for career advancement, manage AI-driven dating platforms, and curate AI-generated content for personal branding. As with earlier media shifts, the outcomes are uneven. The results presented in Chap. 3 indicate that some individuals quickly develop sophisticated strategies in AI-enhanced environments, whereas others struggle immensely, leading to an even wider skill gap.

1.7 Conclusions

This chapter explains that digital skills represent a critical phase in the overall process through which people appropriate and make beneficial use of digital media. The process begins with motivation: individuals must first be motivated to obtain digital media and platforms. Motivation is also required to learn how digital media work and to develop the skills needed to use them. These skills enable meaningful uses of digital media, after which individuals can begin to realize beneficial outcomes of their use. We deliberately use the term digital *skills* rather than alternatives such as digital literacy or competence. The use of digital media, particularly internet and intelligent media, involves far more than mental operations, such as reading, writing, or acquiring knowledge. It requires interactive operations, such as working with software, navigating complex interfaces, communicating with others, generating content, and performing online transactions. We introduced a framework of seven digital skills. The first three are medium-related skills:

- *Strategic media choice skills* to select the most appropriate medium or platform for a specific task, such as deciding whether to use a search engine, smart assistant, or specialized app.
- *Operational skills* to operate digital media and platforms (including devices, software, and interfaces).
- *Formal skills* to navigate and orientate in hypermedia environments, including Web browsers and complex dashboards.

The other four are content-related skills, which have parallels in traditional media, but take unique forms in digital media:

- *Information skills* to search for, evaluate, and select information from digital platforms, including critically assessing AI-generated outputs.
- *Communication skills* to interact through digital media, ranging from email and social media to AI-mediated collaboration tools.
- *Content creation skills* to produce, adapt, and share digital content, including using AI prompts, curating media, or developing user-generated content.

- *Strategic media use skills* to employ digital media to achieve broader personal, professional, or societal goals, such as career advancement, civic participation, and health improvement.

These seven skills are both sequential and conditional: content-related skills build on the successful mastery of medium-related skills. However, medium-related skills on their own are not enough to generate meaningful outcomes. All skills share commonalities and distinctions across analog and digital media. For instance, every medium requires the skills to read and write texts and visuals, search for and select relevant information, interpret and evaluate content, communicate by encoding and decoding messages to create, understand, and exchange meaning, and make decisions or take action based on the information obtained. This is illustrated in Boxes 1.1 and 1.2.

From a historical perspective, media skills have continually evolved alongside technological change, and an ever-growing portion of the population has needed to acquire them. Each new medium expanded the range of skills required for full participation. Digital media, in particular, have created a dual effect. On the one hand, they have simplified tasks such as searching, immediate communication, or sharing content. On the other hand, they have made meaningful participation more demanding by assuming additional and more complex skills. Although critics argue that skill disparities have always existed—for example, in navigating print or audiovisual media—digital landscapes, especially those involving internet and intelligent media, introduce new layers of complexity that intensify these inequalities. Internet and intelligent media require a broader, more advanced skill set that does not develop automatically. Individuals must be able to search effectively across vast amounts of information, communicate on platforms with specific encoding and decoding requirements, and create and manage digital content in strategic and responsible ways. Without sustained support, inequalities in digital skills deepen with each technological shift—from analog to internet-based media, and now to intelligent media—leading to growing barriers to social participation, opportunity, and empowerment. By contrast, those who are able to develop and integrate the seven digital skills will be best positioned to participate fully in a smart society and adapt successfully to future media developments.

References

Anttiroiko, A. V., Lintilä, L., & Savolainen, R. (2001). Information society competencies of managers: Conceptual considerations. In P. Eero, R. Savolainen, & P. Tynjälä (Eds.), *In search for a human-centred information society* (pp. 27–56). Tampere University Press.

Bawden, D. (2001). Information and digital literacies: A review of concepts. *Journal of Documentation, 57*(2), 218–259.

Beniger, J. R. (1986). *The control revolution: Technological and economic origins of the information society*. Harvard University Press.

Bommasani, R., Hudson, D. A., Adeli, E., Altman, R., Arora, S., von Arx, S., ..., & Liang, P. (2021). *On the opportunities and risks of foundation models*. arXiv preprintarXiv 2108.07258.

Briggs, C. F. (2000). Literacy, reading, and writing in the medieval West. *Journal of Medieval History, 26*(4), 397–420.

Briggs, A., & Burke, P. (2009). *A social history of the media: From Gutenberg to the Internet*. Polity.

Collins, R. (2000). Comparative and historical patterns of education. In M. T. Hallinan (Ed.), *Handbook of the sociology of education* (pp. 213–239). Springer.

De Castell, S., & Luke, A. (1988). Defining "literacy" in North American Schools. In E. R. Kingten, B. M. Kroll, & M. Rose (Eds.), *Perspectives on literacy* (pp. 159–174). Southern Illinois University Press.

Dwivedi, R., Dave, D., Naik, H., Singhal, S., Omer, R., Patel, P., et al. (2023). Explainable AI (XAI): Core ideas, techniques, and solutions. *ACM Computing Surveys, 55*(9), 1–33.

Goldfarb, B. (2002). *Visual pedagogy: Media cultures in and beyond the classroom*. Duke University Press.

Hasebrink, U., & Hepp, A. (2017). How to research cross-media practices? Investigating media repertoires and media ensembles. *Convergence, 23*(4), 362–377.

Hasebrink, U., & Popp, J. (2006). Media repertoires as a result of selective media use. A conceptual approach to the analysis of patterns of exposure. *Communications, 31*(3), 369–387.

Horst, H. A., Herr-Stephenson, B., & Robinson, L. (2010). Media ecologies. In M. Ito et al. (Eds.), *Hanging out, messing around, and geeking out: Kids living and learning with new media* (pp. 29–78). MIT Press.

Jovanovic, M., & Campbell, M. (2022). Generative artificial intelligence: Trends and prospects. *Computer, 55*(10), 107–112.

Kwan, M. P. (2001). Cyberspatial cognition and individual access to information: the behavioral foundation of cybergeography. *Environment and Planning B: Planning and Design, 28*(1), 21–37.

Lee, M. J. (2005). Expanding hypertext: Does it address disorientation? Depends on individuals' adventurousness. *Journal of Computer-Mediated Communication, 10*(3), JCMC1036.

Madianou, M. (2014). Polymedia communication and mediatized migration: An ethnographic approach. In K. Lundby (Ed.), *Mediatization of communication* (pp. 323–346). De Gruyter Mouton.

Madianou, M., & Miller, D. (2013). *Migration and new media: Transnational families and polymedia*. Routledge.

Mizrach, S. (1998). *From orality to teleliteracy*. Retrieved from http://www2.fiu.edu/~mizrachs/orality.htm

Ong, W. J. (1984). Orality, literacy, and medieval textualization. *New Literary History, 16*(1), 1–12.

Reeves, B., & Nass, C. (1996). *The media equation: How people treat computers, television, and new media like real people*. Cambridge University Press.

Rury, J., & Rury, J. L. (2005). *Education and social change: Themes in the history of American schooling*. Routledge.

Scheerder, A., Van Deursen, A. J. A. M., & Van Dijk, J. A. G. M. (2017). Determinants of Internet skills, uses and outcomes. A systematic review of the second-and third-level digital divide. *Telematics and Informatics, 34*(8), 1607–1624.

Stone, L. (1969). Literacy and education in England 1640–1900. *Past & Present, 42*, 69–139.

Van Deursen, A. J. A. M., & Helsper, E. J. (2021). *Mediawijsheid: Conceptualisering en belang in een gemedieerde samenleving. Lacunes in bestaand onderzoek en beleid*. Universiteit Twente.

Van Deursen, A. J. A. M., & Mossberger, K. (2018). Any thing for anyone? A new digital divide in Internet-of-Things skills. *Policy & Internet, 10*(2), 122–140.

Van Deursen, A. J. A. M., & Van Dijk, J. A. G. M. (2019). The first-level digital divide shifts from inequalities in physical access to inequalities in material access. *New Media & Society, 21*(2), 354–375.

Van Dijk, J. A. G. M. (2005). *The deepening divide: Inequality in the information society*. Sage.

Van Dijk, J. A. G. M. (2020). *The digital divide*. Polity Press.

Van Dijk, J. A. G. M., & Van Deursen, A. J. A. M. (2014). *Digital skills: Unlocking the information society*. Palgrave Macmillan.

CHAPTER 2

Digital Skills for Internet and Intelligent Media

2.1 Introduction

In the prior chapter, we introduced a set of seven digital skills: strategic media choice, operational, formal, information, communication, content creation, and strategic media use skills. These skills were outlined in relation to both analog and digital media, establishing a comparative foundation for understanding how media shape the skills that individuals need. In this chapter, we examine the seven skills in greater depth in the context of the internet and connected intelligent media. Our goal is not only to refine the conceptual framework but also to propose skill indicators that allow us to measure them in practice. Each skill is grounded in a broad interdisciplinary research tradition, drawing on scholarship from media and communication studies, computer science, information science, and literacy and education studies. This interdisciplinary basis ensures that the framework captures both the skills required to operate and navigate digital media and platforms and the substantive skills necessary to interpret, evaluate, and strategically apply digital content. Our framework explicitly recognizes that engagement with internet and intelligent media and platforms encompasses more than technical operations and necessitates skills that users need to effectively convert their use into personal benefits. The proposed definitions are deliberately designed for ordinary users to derive the greatest possible benefit. This focus reflects

A. van Deursen and J. van Dijk, *Digital Skills*, Digital Education and Learning, https://doi.org/10.1057/978-1-349-96162-7_2

our larger concern with equity: identifying the skills essential for meaningful participation in a smart society and understanding where and why inequalities emerge.

2.2 Strategic Media Choice Skills

Figure 1.2 in the previous chapter illustrates a landscape in which individuals are continuously exposed, willingly or not, to analog, digital, and converged formats and platforms, along with the media through which these formats and platforms are shared. Furthermore, the chapter discussed the concept of media repertoires, patterns of use that reflect how people combine, prioritize, and sequence media to meet their needs. Digital skills are a key determinant of media repertoires, as they influence whether and how a platform or digital medium can be effectively used. Importantly, these skills also encompass deliberately avoiding certain media or platforms when they no longer align with one's goals or values. At its core, strategic media choice skills involve the capacity to make intentional, goal-oriented decisions about which media and platforms to engage with and which to reject. To better understand what this entails, it is helpful to turn to media choice theories that explore how and why individuals select media for specific tasks. *Media Richness Theory* (Daft & Lengel, 1984) proposes that people select media based on their richness, that is, their ability to transmit multiple cues, handle ambiguity, provide feedback, and convey emotions. Richer media (e.g., video conferencing) are better for complex or uncertain tasks, whereas leaner media (e.g., email) are more suitable for straightforward exchanges. *Uses and Gratifications Theory* (Katz et al., 1973) emphasizes the active role of users in choosing media to satisfy specific needs, such as seeking information, maintaining social connections, entertainment, or self-expression. *Media Synchronicity Theory* (Dennis et al., 2008) argues that different tasks require different levels of synchronicity. Synchronous platforms or media (e.g., video calls, instant messaging) are most effective for interactive, time-sensitive collaboration, whereas asynchronous platforms or media (e.g., email, forums) support reflective communication and documentation. Specifically applied to digital contexts are *affordance-based views* that highlight that media are chosen for specific features such as anonymity, persistence, reach, and editability (Treem & Leonardi, 2013). *Polymedia theory* (Madianou & Miller, 2013) emphasizes the relational and moral dimensions of media choice. In an environment where multiple media and platforms are available, the choice itself carries meaning. For example, a text message instead of a call can signal a particular relational stance.

To frame media choice as a skill, we can understand it as a structured decision-making process. See Box 2.1.

Box 2.1 Strategic media choice skills in internet and intelligent media

The skills to…

1. Define the objective to be achieved. This includes purpose, reach, outcomes, and constraints.
2. Evaluate options in terms of:
   (a) Technical affordances (e.g., functionality, accessibility, synchronicity).
   (b) Emotional resonance (e.g., social context, relational cues, personal satisfaction).
   (c) Ethical responsibility (e.g., privacy, fairness, social norms).
3. Select the medium and platform that best aligns with the objective, relational context, and ethical considerations.

1. The process begins with *defining one's objective*, that is, clarifying what to achieve through the use of a particular medium or platform. This first step requires asking fundamental questions: What is the purpose of my media use? Who am I trying to reach? What outcome do I want to achieve? What constraints do I face? Constraints may take many forms: the availability of devices, the amount of time one has, the costs of a platform, privacy concerns, or the possession of operational and formal skills. An important consideration is whether to perform a task manually or delegate parts of it to an intelligent semi-autonomous system. For example, one person might choose to use a traditional search engine to manually conduct a search and review the results, while another might prefer to use an AI-powered agent that can quickly summarize and contextualize

relevant content. Several factors shape this choice. One is the sensitivity of the data; entering confidential or personal information into an external system may create privacy or security risks. Another is the system's interpretive capacity: while AI can be efficient, it may overlook nuances or misinterpret context in ways that a human would not. At the heart of this step lies agency, the ability to deliberately decide between personal effort and AI assistance, weighing efficiency against control, speed against precision, and convenience against trust. This reflective process is at the core of strategic media choice skills, ensuring that use serves clearly defined goals rather than occurring by default.

2. After defining the objective, potential media choices are *evaluated* along three dimensions. From the *rational* dimension, a user should evaluate available media or platforms by examining technical characteristics such as synchronicity, richness, accessibility, and security and assess whether these features align with the objective. Even everyday choices, such as deciding between a messaging app, social media platform, or AI chatbot for quick advice, involve weighing the features of each medium against the task at hand. The second dimension is *emotional and relational* in nature. Certain platforms may resonate better with the social context, either because they are commonly used among friends or family or because they signal relational intentions. For instance, posting a story on social media instead of sharing a private photo via chat can indicate a desire for broader social connections or affirmation. Choosing a voice note over text may convey warmth, tone, or emotional nuance, whereas selecting a smart home device with shared access, such as a family calendar assistant, can reflect care and coordination within the household. In such cases, emotional and relational considerations can be as decisive as technical features in shaping media choices. The third dimension is that media choice can also have *ethical* implications. Users may deliberately avoid certain tools or platforms because they conflict with their personal norms. For example, someone might choose not to use a social media platform known for spreading misinformation, avoid a messaging app that lacks strong privacy protection, limit the use of AI applications that rely on biased

algorithms, or refuse to adopt a voice assistant that continuously collects data.

3. The final step is then to *select the medium or platform* that best aligns with the objective and fits the rational, emotional and relational, and ethical considerations. This selection is the outcome of a skill-based reflective process rather than a matter of habit (including mindless scrolling) or convenience.

2.3 Operational Skills

Shortly after personal computers became widespread, in 1981 the concept of *computer literacy* was introduced in the Washington Post (Warschauer, 2004). At that time, the term referred to a limited set of basic skills such as turning on a computer, opening folders, and saving files. For years, this narrow understanding shaped both research and education, where computer literacy education often meant tool-oriented instruction focused on simple software operations (Hoem & Schwebs, 2005). As technology advanced, scholars proposed alternative terms to capture similar ideas while emphasizing technical skills in different ways. Examples include *technical competence* (Mossberger et al., 2003), *technological literacy* (Carvin, 2000), and *technical proficiency* (Søby, 2003). All these terms highlight the skills required to use everyday digital tools and applications. In common language, this is often described as *button knowledge*. Building on earlier definitions, in our prior book, we introduced an inventory of operational skills for internet media (Van Dijk & Van Deursen, 2014). As the media landscape has evolved significantly over the past decade, we update the original inventory accordingly. This definition extends beyond basic websites and social media to encompass popular platforms, AI applications, and smart devices. However, we limit our definition to software, excluding skills related to hardware, such as pressing physical buttons or placing smart devices in a room. Box 2.2 presents the inventory of operational skills.

Box 2.2 Operational skills in internet and intelligent media

The skills to...

1. Recognize and operate toolbars, buttons, and menus.
2. Manage installation, settings, and updates.
3. Manage user input.
4. Manage file formats.
5. Share files and documents.
6. Integrate across media and platforms.

1. First, we consider the basic skills of *recognizing and operating toolbars, buttons, and menus*. Every web browser encompasses a set of recognizable functions, such as home, back, and refresh buttons, along with options for bookmarking pages. Although these features may seem straightforward, their complexity increases as users transition from browsers to a diverse array of online applications. Each application presents its own design style, and although there are established guidelines and principles from user experience research aimed at creating intuitive and consistent interfaces, designers' compliance with these standards varies widely. They employ various visual styles, including icons, colors, shapes, and placements, to signal the importance or functionality of a button. Similarly, menus may be concealed behind icons (e.g., behind the "hamburger" menu: ☰) or replaced by gesture-based navigation on mobile devices. This variability poses challenges for users, as they must recognize functional elements across different conventions. Furthermore, they must be adept at operating these elements effectively—whether by clicking, tapping, swiping, dragging, or long-pressing—depending on the device and application.
2. The second set of operational skills focuses on *managing installations, settings, and updates*. At a basic level, users need to install, open, close, and uninstall applications to enable their functioning. Adjusting settings is essential, as it determines how media behave

and ensures it operates according to the user's needs. Examples of such adjustments include selecting language options, choosing visual themes, personalizing features, adjusting notification preferences, setting privacy levels, changing passwords, activating two-factor authentication, or resetting to the default state. Users need to adapt to the variability of settings across different media and platforms. With smart devices in particular, effective use necessitates the optimization of system preferences, such as adjusting volume, brightness, or display modes on devices ranging from smart speakers to wearable fitness trackers. Equally important are the skills to maintain software and firmware updates, thereby ensuring security, functionality, and access to the latest features.

3. The third set of operational skills pertains to *managing various input options*, including text boxes, pull-down menus, check boxes, radio buttons, and list boxes, as well as more advanced forms, such as image uploads, voice commands, and biometric authentication. Users must be able to identify such input elements and comprehend how to interact with them. An obvious example is the traditional search engine, where users need to locate the search bar on a webpage, click on the field to activate it, input their query, and then either press the Enter key or click the search button to commence the process. Similarly, when completing an online form, such as when creating an account or ordering a product, users must understand how to input their email addresses, select an option from a dropdown menu, or attach a document or image in the appropriate field. Many AI-integrated platforms provide voice-based input, enabling users to dictate search queries, compose messages, or issue commands. In these scenarios, operational skills encompass knowing how to activate the microphone, articulate commands in a manner that the system can recognize, and rectify errors when speech recognition fails. With smart devices, the input fields are no longer restricted to screens. A smart thermostat may require users to adjust temperature settings via a touch interface, whereas a wearable fitness tracker might prompt users to enter weight, height, or activity goals through a combination of swipes, taps, and synchronized voice commands. The operational skill challenge lies in identifying the appropriate input mode for each device and applying it correctly.

4. *Managing different file formats* constitutes the fourth set of operational skills. Users frequently encounter a broad spectrum of file types across various media and platforms. To utilize these effectively, individuals must be able to open, save, and convert files into the formats required for their tasks. This entails recognizing file types based on their extensions (for example, docx, pdf, jpg, mp4) and their associated icons and default applications. Users should also comprehend compatibility issues, such as instances where certain formats may not be accessible on specific devices or software versions, and how to resolve these issues by converting or exporting files into alternative formats (or downloading programs to open them). Furthermore, users require skills to identify suspicious file types, avoid unverified downloads, and apply basic security practices, such as verifying files for threats before opening them.
5. *Sharing files and documents* is an operational skill that facilitates effective information exchange and collaboration across media and platforms. This encompasses actions such as attaching files to emails or messaging applications and uploading documents to cloud-based services. Numerous applications offer integrated "Share" functions, enabling users to transmit files directly without navigating complex folder structures. Effective file sharing extends beyond merely sending a document; it involves generating shareable links within cloud services and configuring permissions appropriately. Mismanagement of these permissions can result in accidental data loss, privacy breaches, and unintended edits. In this context, AI-powered collaboration platforms can automatically synchronize files across applications or generate shared spaces for projects. Operational skills are necessary to manage these automated processes and ensure that files are shared intentionally rather than indiscriminately.
6. The sixth set of skills involves the *integration of media and platforms*, which requires skills in configuration, maintenance, and troubleshooting. For instance, AI assistants may require users to link various applications to ensure that reminders, notifications, and tasks are synchronized across smartphones, smart speakers, and wearable devices, thereby maintaining continuity of experience across different contexts. Similarly, integrating a smart thermostat with a voice assistant and mobile application requires more than mere

installation. Users must establish and link accounts across platforms, create automated routines (e.g., adjusting the temperature based on the time of day or occupancy), and address connectivity issues. The initial step in successful integration is the recognition of compatibility. Users must comprehend the communication methods employed by different devices, such as Bluetooth, Wi-Fi, NFC, and cloud-based synchronization, as these protocols determine the flow of information between components. Furthermore, understanding the permissions, account-linking requirements, and interoperability rules of each platform is crucial. Beyond technical configuration, users must assess how interactions affect privacy, security, and overall system reliability. For example, linking a health tracker to a cloud service might offer valuable insights but also introduce risks if sensitive health data are not adequately protected from unauthorized access.

2.4 Formal Skills

Each medium and platform possesses unique formal characteristics that necessitate the acquisition of specific skills. These formal skills pertain to the foundational structures upon which they are constructed. The internet, particularly the Web, serves as the most prominent example of *hypermedia*, characterized by multiple representations of information and non-linear branching from one location to another. Hypermedia, for example, allows users to explore a website where text, images, videos, and audio are all interconnected, allowing them to navigate freely between articles, tutorials, and multimedia content based on their interests. We consider two dimensions pertaining to formal skills. See Box 2.3.

Box 2.3 Formal skills in internet and intelligent media

The skills to...

1. Navigate:
   (a) Text and multimodal-based hypermedia.
   (b) Interactive hypermedia (that offer paths based on user input).

(c) Adaptive /intelligent hypermedia (that adapts content and navigation based on user's profile, behavior, or goals).

2. Maintain orientation and a sense of location while navigating text and multimodal-based, interactive, and adaptive/intelligent hypermedia.

1. The first dimension concerns ***navigating hypermedia*** through hyperlinks and textual, image, audio, and video elements. Over time, hypermedia has evolved from simple text-and-image websites into more adaptive and intelligent systems. In general, three major forms of hypermedia can be distinguished, all of which remain widely used and require particular skills from users.

   (a) *Text- and multimodal-based hypermedia* represent the most traditional forms. Originally, it comprised written content interconnected through hyperlinks, facilitating non-linear navigation between documents, topics, or data entries. In contrast to a book, which presents information in a fixed sequence, text-based hypermedia (or hypertext) allows readers to traverse related information nodes, thereby constructing their own exploratory paths. Typical examples include encyclopedias, where users click through internal links to follow chains of related concepts, academic databases, or blogs that enable non-linear movement from one topic to another. Text-based hypermedia can be augmented by incorporating multimodal elements, such as images, videos, audio, graphics, and animations, into a cohesive structure. Consider an online news site that provides a text article alongside an embedded video report, interactive graphics, and a photo slideshow.

   (b) *Interactive hypermedia* represents sequences of information or outcomes of an experience contingent upon the user's decisions, inputs, or actions. Rather than merely browsing linked content, users actively shape the flow through branching narratives, simulations, or responsive applications. This non-linearity is both structural and experiential, as subsequent events are determined by the user's actions. Such interactivity renders hypermedia highly engaging, as users are not merely selecting links but are dealing with sequences where their decisions influence the outcome. They must navigate decision trees, handle dead ends or looping sequences, anticipate the consequences of choices, and backtrack or adapt if a chosen path does not lead to the desired result. Examples include interactive documentaries where viewers select story paths, video games with branching storylines, or online quizzes or surveys where responses determine the subsequent question or result.

(c) *Adaptive or intelligent hypermedia* advances further by customizing pathways, recommendations, and interfaces based on the user's profile, objectives, or previous interactions. These systems are driven by algorithms or AI that monitor user behavior, preferences, and performance, and subsequently adjust the hypermedia structure accordingly. Each pathway is individualized to optimize its relevance, efficiency, and engagement. The system autonomously determines the information presented, often imperceptibly, based on user profiles and historical activity. Examples include playlists and personalized recommendations such as "because you watched/listened to…" or "customers also bought…". Navigation is partially automated, with the system personalizing pathways and recommendations frequently without the user's conscious awareness. Users may perceive themselves as merely scrolling, but the content they encounter is algorithmically determined. Navigation involves managing personalization by comprehending how algorithms shape pathways and exercising control to prevent excessive dependence.

2. The second dimension pertains to a commonly cited issue in hypermedia usage: disorientation (Lee, 2005). *Maintaining orientation and having a sense of location* is challenging across all three hypermedia forms.

   (a) In text- and multimodal-based hypermedia, disorientation primarily involves path overload or sensory/attention overload. Users have the option to select non-linear paths, as opposed to the fixed formal structures of print media, such as chapters, paragraphs, and references (Kwan, 2001; Coiro & Dobler, 2007). Users can navigate forward, backward, to known and unknown locations, and to other services. Given the lack of a sense of location, distance, and necessary direction, it is unsurprising that users experience a sense of disorientation (Kwan, 2001). This can occur even when the users possess sufficient domain expertise. Disorientation should be conceptualized in terms of structure, links, and design, independent of the information topics being navigated (Danielson, 2003; Webster & Ahuja, 2006). Users may lose track of their path while following a chain of hyperlinks and forget how to return to their starting point. Consider a news site where a user reads part of an article, becomes distracted by an autoplay video, and then scrolls through a photo gallery without noticing an interactive map that actually contains the most pertinent data.

(b) In interactive hypermedia, disorientation might arise from decision path confusion. Users may select an option that leads them down an unexpected pathway, lose track of the decisions that brought them to a certain point, or struggle to find their way back to a missed option. For example, in a recommendation tool, a user might answer several prompts or questions to refine suggestions (e.g., travel planning). If the interface does not clearly show the decision path, the user may forget earlier selections or how to adjust previous choices, leading to confusion regarding how the recommendations were generated.

(c) In adaptive intelligent media, disorientation might occur when users lose awareness of why certain content is being shown to them. As the system adapts invisibly, users may feel confused when the sequence no longer aligns with their intentions or when relevant information is obscured. This makes it difficult to navigate automated and personalized system behaviors (prompts, alerts, or performance indicators). For example, a user searching for tutorials on "basic video editing" may gradually be directed toward algorithmic recommendations for advanced editing, unrelated software, or even unrelated entertainment content. The adaptive personalization shifts them off-course without their noticing.

2.5 Information Skills

In Chap. 1, we defined information skills as the capacity to search, select, process, and evaluate information. This definition aligns with the original vision of the internet: "once someone somewhere made available a document, database, graphic, sound, video, or screen at some stage in an interactive dialogue, it should be accessible by anyone, with any type of computer, in any country" (Berners-Lee, 2000, p. 37). Since that vision was articulated, digital media have advanced considerably, and the scope and nature of information skills have evolved. Previously, users were required to meticulously define queries and navigate multiple sources. Currently, AI-powered search tools, recommendation engines, and conversational assistants retrieve, filter, and even generate information on behalf of the user. This transition not only supports some steps in the search process but also amplifies the need for interpretive and evaluative skills. Users must not only identify appropriate information but also assess the reliability of AI-generated outputs, comprehend the biases inherent in algorithms, and remain cognizant of the influence of training data. Despite these advancements, Marchionini's (1995) recursive framework, comprising problem definition, source selection, query formulation, information selection, and evaluation, remains relevant. However, in a smart society context, problem definition may be influenced by AI's predictive suggestions, source selection may be constrained by algorithmic filtering, and information evaluation may necessitate critical awareness of both the content and the system generating it. Consequently, information skills extend beyond mastering search engines; they encompass the skills to interact intelligently with AI while balancing efficiency and skepticism. Moreover, several steps can be applied to data collected by smart devices. Box 2.4 lists the five steps.

Box 2.4 Information skills in internet and intelligent media

The skills to...

1. Define the information problem.
2. Choose a website or a search system to seek information.
3. Define search options or queries.

4. Select information (on websites or in search results).
5. Evaluate information sources.

1. *Developing a comprehensive problem definition* requires a clear description of the issue and specification of the type and amount of information needed to address it. In practice, this can be challenging because users are often confronted with a surplus of information from multiple sources, including search engines, databases, social media, and AI applications. The abundance of potentially relevant materials makes it difficult to identify what is needed. AI can support this step by asking guided questions to help users clarify what they are looking for. Furthermore, AI-powered search engines can analyze user inputs and propose related terms, topics, or sub-questions, which can help users better articulate their information requirements. This step is also applicable to smart systems that collect large amounts of data. Users need to define what question they want to answer or what problem they want to solve with the data to be collected, for example, monitoring energy consumption patterns or tracking personal fitness progress.
2. Once the information problem is defined, users must identify the appropriate options and *choose a search system* from which information can be obtained. In addition to traditional search engines that utilize keyword-based queries or direct website navigation, users can turn to specialized databases that provide curated or peer-reviewed content, meta-search engines that query multiple engines simultaneously, social media or user-generated platforms, conversational tools such as voice assistants that offer summarized answers or direct users to pertinent sources, or AI search applications that interpret natural language queries and generate summaries or answers. The quality of the options needs to be evaluated based on criteria such as precision, completeness, accuracy, timeliness, accessibility, novelty, and cost (Brand-Gruwel et al., 2005).
3. *Formulating search queries* constitutes the third step in the information retrieval process, which involves designing queries to obtain relevant and useful information. The efficacy of the entire search process is contingent on the quality of these queries. Beyond

keyword-based queries, which may include words or phrases specified by Boolean operators (e.g., AND, OR, NOT), AI applications provide the capability to autofill search terms and employ natural language queries, voice searches, or conversational assistance to interpret ambiguous questions and generate potential answers. Although these features may initially render query formulation seemingly straightforward, they necessitate users' comprehension of how the inputs are interpreted.

4. The fourth stage involves discerning useful results and *selecting information*. Broad search strategies often yield an overwhelming volume of results, including irrelevant, low-quality, and misleading data, thus complicating the task of effective selection. This challenge is frequently exacerbated by user behavior such as reviewing only a few initial search results or neglecting to explore beyond the first results page, potentially leading to the omission of highly relevant or high-quality sources. The utilization of AI can assist in this stage, as machine learning algorithms can categorize search results, highlight content deemed most pertinent, filter out duplicates, and summarize information for an expedited assessment. However, AI introduces new challenges. Users must comprehend the operation of algorithmic ranking systems and remain vigilant of the potential biases inherent within them, which may prioritize certain sources, perspectives, or commercial content. For example, an algorithm used to recommend products on a website may show users products that are more likely to appeal to them, even if they are not needed. This can lead to impulse purchases which they later regret. Effective selection requires balancing AI guidance with human judgment to identify relevant information. This principle is particularly important in the context of smart systems, where devices and sensors generate large amounts of data. When selecting data, users must focus on metrics that align with their objectives and filter irrelevant or redundant information. For example, a fitness tracker may collect sleep, heart rate, and activity data, but a user analyzing sleep quality should prioritize sleep-related metrics over steps or calorie consumption. Visualization tools such as dashboards, charts, and graphs can greatly support this process by highlighting patterns, trends, and anomalies, making it easier to identify meaningful insights without being overwhelmed by the full dataset.

5. The final stage, ***information evaluation***, entails skills to make informed judgments regarding the credibility, accuracy, and relevance of retrieved information. The quality of online information varies considerably, necessitating meticulous assessment, as poor information quality may lead to decision-making errors. Tate and Alexander (1996) identified five essential evaluation criteria: accuracy (reliability and correctness of the content), authority (author or creator of the information and their credentials), objectivity (fair and unbiased presentation of information), currency (timeliness of the information), and coverage (scope and completeness of the information). AI both facilitates and complicates the evaluation process. On the one hand, it can flag potentially unreliable sources and highlight discrepancies in information. On the other hand, users must critically evaluate AI-generated outputs, recognizing that algorithms may encode biases, omit context, or emphasize certain perspectives disproportionately. The evaluation of data collected by smart devices is equally critical. Sensors can produce inaccurate readings, algorithms interpreting data may be designed with assumptions that do not fit all users (e.g., sleep trackers may misclassify quiet wakefulness as sleep), and concerns regarding data ownership arise. Evaluation, therefore, requires comparing data to previous measurements and personal experiences (Karvalics, 2014; Van Deursen & Mossberger, 2018).

2.6 Communication Skills

During its initial two decades, the internet primarily served as a medium for information retrieval. Following the turn of the century, the internet began to evolve into a major communication platform, largely propelled by the emergence of social media and interactive applications. Today, the majority of internet activity is devoted to communication and the number and diversity of services supporting online interactions continue to expand. The following categories of online communication services illustrate the breadth of digital communication:

- World Wide Web: Threaded discussions and topic-based exchanges.
- E-mail: Personal messaging.

- Chat and instant messaging: Real-time text, voice, and multimedia communication.
- Online telephony /Video conferencing: Voice and video interaction.
- Blogs and microblogging: Publishing content and interaction via comments or threaded discussions.
- Social networking sites: Platforms for creating profiles, sharing content, and interacting with others.
- Online dating platforms: Communication and interaction for digital matchmaking.
- Collaborative knowledge platforms: Platforms for co-creation, learning, and problem-solving.
- Virtual social worlds and immersive communities: Interaction in virtual or augmented environments.
- Collective online games: Communication and coordination during gameplay.

To qualify as a communication service, a platform must support the regular exchange of messages, with the meaning encoded by the sender and interpreted by the receiver. This encompasses traditional text-based tools, such as email, chat boxes, and instant messaging, as well as social media networks, collaborative workspaces, video conferencing, and live-stream interactions. AI-driven communication applications, including chatbots and virtual assistants, can facilitate and participate in conversations, thereby extending the possibilities of communication in digital contexts. We present ten communication skills in the progression from basic to advanced. The first six skills are essential for the effective use of online communication services. The final four are advanced skills that require strategic thinking, drawn in part from the framework for participatory online culture of Jenkins (2009): users must consider their goals, the intended audience, and the desired outcome of their communication. The skills are listed in Box 2.5.

Box 2.5 Communication skills in internet and intelligent media

The skills to...

1. Search, select, evaluate, and act upon contacts.

2. Encode messages to construct meaning.
3. Decode messages to understand meaning.
4. Exchange messages to share meaning.
5. Attract attention.
6. Manage identities.
7. Adopt alternative identities for discovery or improvisation.
8. Experiment for better decision-making.
9. Pool knowledge in peer-to-peer networking (collective intelligence).
10. Negotiate to reach decisions while understanding others' viewpoints.

1. Effective communication begins with networking, which involves *searching for, selecting, evaluating, and engaging with contacts*. Online applications have greatly expanded the range of potential connections, from professional relationships and casual acquaintances to algorithmically suggested matches on dating platforms. This expansion creates new opportunities but also challenges individuals to manage increasingly large and diverse networks. Unlike face-to-face interactions, online networking requires skills to search for, select, and engage with contacts through email, chat, social networks, professional platforms, and AI-mediated systems. Without these skills, people can quickly become overwhelmed by the sheer volume of connections. Effective networking also involves continuous evaluation of contacts. Social networking sites illustrate this well, as users must create, expand, maintain, and sometimes reduce their lists of "friends." Online dating provides another clear example in which users acquire, organize, and pursue potential partners by choosing selectively.
2. The second communication skill is the ability to *encode messages to construct meaning*. Speaking and writing skills provide the foundational means for input in online communication, whereas gesture-based input for individuals with limited literacy remains relatively scarce (Chap. 6 discusses the challenges faced by users with low reading and writing skills). The conventions for communication vary widely across platforms. Some encourage the use

of emojis, GIFs, stickers, and concise messages, whereas others promote creativity through short-form videos, layered texts, or sound effects. Users must strategically select and combine these symbol systems to convey their meanings clearly. Writing assistants, including predictive text, autocorrect, and generative AI applications, can further support users by helping them compose messages, refine their tone, and translate content across languages.

3. After encoding, individuals also need the skill to *decode messages to understand their meaning*. Strong reading skills developed for traditional texts remain essential for effective digital communication. However, more is needed to understand the tone of communication in distinct norms and symbolic languages where contextual cues, such as facial expressions, are absent. Consider abbreviations, emojis, GIFs, memes, short videos, livestreams, and interactive stories that combine captions, soundtracks, filters, and visual effects; interpreting their intended meaning can be challenging. For less experienced internet users, these forms of communication may feel like a chaotic, overwhelming set of cryptic codes, where meaning relies heavily on shared cultural references. Generative AI platforms add even more complexity, as they automatically produce emails, social media posts, and multimedia content. Users must be able to distinguish between human- and AI-generated material while remaining vigilant about bias, inaccuracies, and potential manipulative uses of synthetic media.
4. *Exchanging meaning* is the next aspect of communication skills. Many online communication platforms, such as email, social networking, microblogging, forums, and dating apps, are asynchronous by nature. Users often face uncertainty about when and how to respond because these platforms lack nonverbal cues, such as tone, gestures, and facial expressions, which typically signal urgency or emotional intent. While informal norms around response times exist, conventions remain fluid and context-dependent: replies to professional emails may be expected within 48 h, whereas dating apps often invite faster replies. This uncertainty can lead to unclear expectations regarding etiquette and timing. Although many platforms provide AI-generated prompts to encourage interaction, meaningful connections continue to depend on the subtleties of human communication. Furthermore, users

need to be mindful of how AI-generated or automated content affects meaning.

Related to the exchange of meaning is knowing how to conduct oneself as a communicator. Online interactions differ significantly from face-to-face conversations and often lack nonverbal cues (tone of voice, facial expressions, and body language) that help signal politeness or soften directness. As a result, online communication is frequently short, abrupt, and at times perceived as impolite. In extreme cases, this can escalate to rude, aggressive, or inflammatory language. To address these challenges, users must develop an awareness of *netiquette*, the informal rules and norms that govern respectful behavior online. Unlike traditional etiquette, which may be explicitly taught through family, education, or cultural rituals, netiquette is rarely included in formal curricula. Instead, it should be learned through practice, observation, and community feedback in digital environments.

Finally, exchanging meaning involves understanding the ethical and social implications of sharing the various forms of media. For instance, posting photos, videos, or voice notes requires sensitivity to issues of consent, privacy, and ownership. A photo shared casually in one context may expose another individual to unwanted visibility or harm in another context. Therefore, users must balance self-expression with awareness of the rights, expectations, and vulnerabilities of others.

5. The fifth communication skill is *attracting and maintaining attention* through messages, profiles, and online identities. Although it is easy to speak online, being heard remains a challenge. The sheer volume of content results in most posts, videos, or profiles receiving minimal engagement. Numerous personal blogs remain unread, posts on discussion forums remain unanswered, and most social media updates are lost in the incessant flow of digital noise. This issue is not merely a reflection of individual deficiencies but a structural characteristic of the platforms themselves: the ease of publishing creates an overwhelming surplus of content while human attention remains limited. To distinguish themselves, users must not only excel in concise and compelling communication—akin to the rhetorical skills of journalists, influencers, or politicians—but also adeptly navigate algorithms that determine

visibility. Success on social media platforms often hinges on alignment with algorithmic trends, hashtags, and engagement metrics. Although generative AI lowers the barrier to creating attention-grabbing content, it also increases competition for visibility and raises questions about authenticity. AI-generated images or posts may quickly draw attention, but risk losing trust if they are revealed to be artificial.

6. The importance of online profiles and digital identities has grown significantly in today's individualized networked society (Van Dijk, 2020). Social networking sites, professional networking platforms, dating apps, and virtual worlds now serve as key arenas where individuals present themselves, connect with others, and cultivate their reputations. Here, some form of impression management is unavoidable. Users need skills to *construct profiles and identities:* personal profiles, digital representatives, or avatars that not only convey who they are but also strategically highlight aspects of their identity to achieve specific goals, whether building professional credibility, attracting followers, or creating a trustworthy persona. Many platforms provide ready-made templates and design aids, such as suggested prompts, default avatars, or AI-generated bios and profile pictures. While these features make it easier to build a profile, they also produce a homogenizing effect, resulting in a sea of lookalike accounts and generic self-presentations where few stand out.
7. The next communication skill involves *adopting alternative identities for discovery or improvisation.* Online profiles and identities are not static entities; rather, they are dynamic and evolving constructs shaped by continuous interactions. Each post, comment, and shared image contributes to an identity refined through feedback from others. The skills to interpret and respond constructively to feedback, whether affirming, critical, or algorithmically generated, are essential. Young individuals in particular frequently utilize digital spaces as arenas for identity exploration and experimentation. Through social media platforms or multiplayer gaming environments, they test different versions of themselves, experiment with new styles of self-presentation, and learn how their choices resonate with peers (Jenkins, 2009). This identity play can foster creativity and self-discovery but also requires skills when

confronted with people with harmful intentions or manipulative feedback systems shaped by algorithms. While younger users integrate experimentation into their personal growth, older users may focus more on professional credibility, personal branding, and trustworthiness (e.g., when selling items in online marketplaces). Across all forms of profiling and self-presentation, recommendation algorithms, automated comment systems, and AI-driven content curation shape how users perceive themselves and others. Generative AI can create avatars, profile pictures, and fully developed personas, blurring the line between authentic self-expression and synthetic identity. Communication skills involve critically assessing authenticity, managing online reputation, and safeguarding personal integrity.

8. *Experimenting for better decision-making* through play and simulation is the next aspect of communication skills. The internet hosts a diverse array of game-like and simulation-based applications that extend beyond mere entertainment. These digital environments are progressively being utilized for educational purposes, training, and decision-making, offering immersive methods for exploring complex scenarios and practicing problem-solving. Particularly for young individuals, games serve as a potent medium for learning, experimentation, and knowledge acquisition, not only because of their engaging nature but also because they promote active participation and interactive exploration (Jenkins, 2009). Multiplayer environments require collaboration, negotiation, and conflict resolution. Participants are required to coordinate their actions, build trust, and manage group dynamics, often transcending cultural and linguistic boundaries. The skills required to effectively engage in serious games and simulations can be acquired through practice or trial and error, with the exception of the most challenging applications. Individuals who do not enjoy playing or have not cultivated communication skills in collaborative play may encounter difficulties.
9. *Pooling* knowledge *and exchanging meaning through peer-to-peer networking,* or collective intelligence, represents the ninth aspect of communication skills. In peer-to-peer networks, online knowledge communities, and collaborative platforms, the continuous exchange of information, expertise, and experience is prevalent. This exchange is contingent on online cooperation skills

that extend beyond message exchange. Effective cooperation necessitates the skills to recognize and utilize the expertise of others, appropriately assign roles or functions, and coordinate activities respectfully and efficiently (Jenkins, 2009). These skills are critical in workplaces where distributed teams, cross-border collaboration, and hybrid work environments are the norm. However, despite their increasing importance, formal education systems continue to emphasize individual achievement and autonomous problem-solving over collective and networked knowledge creation. Students are often assessed based on their skills to complete tasks independently, whereas contemporary digital workplaces increasingly value team-based creativity, collaborative problem-solving, and interdisciplinary knowledge sharing. Consequently, most individuals informally acquire online cooperation skills through trial and error in their participation in digital communities. Children and adolescents learn these skills independently within their online culture, which is characterized by the extensive exchange of nearly everything.

10. Finally, we consider *negotiating to reach decisions while understanding others' perspectives.* This communication skill pertains to the art of online negotiation, which has become increasingly essential in a diverse array of digital interactions. Online negotiation transpires within online communities, peer-to-peer networks, email exchanges, e-commerce transactions, collaborative projects, and dating platforms, among others. Effective negotiation requires advanced skills, including clarity, persuasion, empathy, and conflict management. The demands on negotiation skills are intensified in heterogeneous digital environments that are characterized by social, cultural, and linguistic diversity. While early observers often presumed that online communities were relatively homogeneous, connecting individuals with similar interests, the reality is considerably more complex. Long-distance, international, and cross-cultural interactions bring together individuals and groups that rarely encounter each other in the physical world. In such environments, it is crucial to develop skills to understand multiple perspectives, respect diversity, and negotiate conflicting opinions (Jenkins, 2009). Modern online negotiations encompass more

than merely reaching a compromise. They also involve cultural sensitivity, intercultural communication, and strategic adaptability. Despite its significance, online negotiations remain largely absent in formal education and training. These skills are mostly acquired informally through experience in social media communities, workplace collaborations, online marketplaces, or dating environments.

2.7 Content Creation Skills

Content creation skills are essential for producing online materials that meet acceptable quality standards for publication. The internet thrives on user-generated content, ranging from websites, blogs, and forums to podcasts, videos, music, and social media posts. An extensive range of tools and platforms now makes content creation and publishing far more accessible than in the past, and the barriers to entry for content creation seem to be continuously decreasing. A decade ago, uploading a video online required knowledge of compression formats, codecs, and resolution standards. Today, users no longer require extensive technical knowledge to share their work. For instance, with smartphones, it has become easier to film videos and upload them directly to a platform that automatically handles publications. Similarly, editing software allows creators to add professional effects, captions, and transitions; writing and blogging tools enable users to publish blogs without requiring coding knowledge; AI assistants can be used to improve clarity, grammar, and styles; graphic and visual tools support non-designers in creating images by generating illustrations from text prompts; Audio platforms allow users to record, edit, and publish podcasts; AI platforms allow creators to compose and produce original tracks without advanced knowledge of music theory; and website-building platforms use AI to enable users to create personal websites within minutes, eliminating the need for coding expertise. Our notion of content creation skills comprises three dimensions. However, despite the low barriers to content creation, digital skills for producing high-quality content remain essential. Box 2.6 outlines three key aspects.

Box 2.6 Content creation skills in internet and intelligent media

The skills to...

1. Create content (textual, musical, visual, video, multimedia, or remixed) that meets minimum quality standards and is effective or engaging.
2. Understand licenses and copyright.
3. Represent others with fairness and respect.

1. Content creation skills first encompass the skills to produce online *content of acceptable quality*, whether text, images, short-form videos, interactive infographics, podcasts, photo essays, or remixed content. The latter involves reworking or combining existing content into new creations (Seneviratne & Monroy-Hernandez, 2010). The growing availability of tools that support content creation has fueled the explosion of online content. However, despite the apparent ease of creation, the quality varies widely. At one end of the spectrum, we find carefully crafted blog posts, professional-grade photography, and polished video productions. At the other end, the web is saturated with poorly written articles, blurry images, and hastily edited videos. This inconsistency often determines whether the content fulfills its intended purpose or whether its message becomes diluted, overlooked, or even misinterpreted. Low-quality work can hinder communication, damage credibility, and reduce engagement (although it may still go viral if it captures a funny accident, an unexpected moment, or breaking news). Notably, those who possess the skills to consistently create and share high-quality content are more likely to shape not only the conversation but also the agenda of online discussions. However, most contributions remain amateur in nature, which is not inherently negative. On the contrary, much of digital culture thrives on the creativity, spontaneity, and relatability of non-professional creators. Amateur content can be powerful when it resonates with audiences by informing, entertaining, and fostering emotional connections. However, challenges arise when contributions fall

below the basic quality threshold. In writing, this may take the form of poor structure, frequent errors, or unclear phrasing. In videos, this often appears as shaky footage, uneven pacing, or abrupt transition. In photography, it can refer to images that are blurry, poorly framed, or lack focus. Despite the rise of generative AI platforms that can create websites or polished content within seconds, human skills remain indispensable. Narrative design, audience alignment, and communicative intent require human judgment. Effective content, whether professional or amateur, achieves its goals and sometimes even unexpected effects by resonating with the audience. In this sense, content creation skills are inseparable from communication skills: understanding audience expectations, managing form and style, and ensuring that messages achieve their intended purpose.

2. The second dimension of content creation skills involves *understanding copyright and licensing*. In a digital environment in which images, text, music, and videos are easily shared, remixed, and repurposed, creators must respect the rights and efforts of others. This requires users to recognize when content is protected by copyright and when it is in the public domain. Many users assume that the material found online is free to use, but this is rarely the case. Content creators must learn to identify protected works and distinguish them from open access or public domain resources. Furthermore, content creators need to be skilled in interpreting different types of licenses. For instance, Creative Commons licenses specify whether material can be reused, modified, or shared commercially, and under what conditions attribution must be provided. Proper attribution involves not only citing the original source but also doing so accurately, visibly, and in line with license requirements.
3. A third dimension of content creation skills concerns *ethical awareness and the responsibility to represent others with fairness and respect.* Creating and sharing digital content is never a neutral act; every image, message, or video conveys meaning that can shape how individuals, groups, or communities are perceived. Therefore, content creators must cultivate skills to critically reflect on how people are portrayed and avoid material that could embarrass, stereotype, or misrepresent others. These skills also involve sensitivity to cultural, social, and religious contexts. A created meme, symbol, or phrase that seems harmless in one setting may be offensive or harmful in another. Content creators therefore need the skills to anticipate

diverse interpretations and adapt their material accordingly. Equally important is the skill of ensuring ***authenticity and transparency***. Photos, videos, and text can be easily manipulated through subtle editing or advanced techniques, such as deepfakes. Presenting staged or artificially generated content as real undermines trust and can have serious consequences. Creators should therefore disclose when content has been altered or produced with AI, maintaining honesty in how material is framed and shared.

2.8 Strategic Media Use Skills

Our earlier work identified strategic media use skills as essential for using digital media to achieve specific goals and, more broadly, to improve one's position in society. Strategic media use skills are the most advanced digital skills. To receive the greatest benefits of internet and intelligent media, users must be able to translate information, communication, or content creation into beneficial outcomes. This requires decision-making and involves the skills to plan, implement, and evaluate digital actions in a purposeful, goal-oriented manner. In this process, users must be critical, analytical, reflective, and capable of assessing whether information, communication, or content creation aligns with their goals. In a digital environment saturated with data, algorithms, and automated recommendations, strategic media use skills determine whether a person merely consumes content passively or actively shapes outcomes, from personal growth and career advancement to community engagement and societal contribution. In this section, we propose a definition based on four analytically distinct steps in the context of classical decision-making frameworks. These frameworks emphasize systematic procedures for achieving optimal solutions in the most efficient manner (Miller, 2006). In the context of a smart society, this process must also account for AI collaboration, in which efficiency concerns critical discernment, ethical reflection, and long-term impact. The strategic media use skills indicators are orienting objectives, taking required actions, making decisions, and implementing decisions (Miller, 2006). See Box 2.7.

Box 2.7 Strategic media use skills in internet and intelligent media

The skills to…

1. Develop an orientation toward a particular objective.
2. Take appropriate actions to reach this objective.
3. Make informed decisions to reach this objective.
4. Reflect and gain the benefits derived from the objective.

1. The initial phase of the decision-making process involves *developing an orientation toward a particular objective*. This entails awareness of the opportunities presented by the internet and connected intelligent media. This awareness must be translated into clear and actionable objectives. Maintaining focus on the objective is challenging, particularly within a digital media landscape replete with distractions, including targeted advertisements, incessant notifications, algorithm-driven recommendations, and a continuous influx of attention-grabbing content. In such an environment, sustaining focus requires discipline and strategic awareness. A well-defined objective serves as a guiding principle for activities such as acquiring knowledge, building professional networks, exerting influence, enhancing productivity, and improving personal well-being. Some examples: A city commuter who wants to minimize travel time and fuel consumption could rely on AI-based traffic apps that aggregate real-time data. A homeowner may set the goal of reducing energy consumption by integrating data from a smart thermostat with an AI-powered energy optimization platform that predicts usage patterns and suggests efficient schedules. A fitness enthusiast may set personalized exercise objectives using an AI-enabled smartwatch to monitor health metrics and receive adaptive training recommendations.
2. The second phase of the decision-making process involves *taking the correct action to achieve the objective*. Building on the objective identified in the initial phase, this stage necessitates the collection, evaluation, and integration of online information or communication

to ascertain the most effective strategy for achieving the specified objective (Miller, 2006). For instance, an individual seeking a hospital with the shortest waiting list and the best user reviews for a particular medical treatment should not depend solely on a single hospital's website or anecdotal recommendations from an online forum. Instead, they should consult official government health portals, cross-reference patient review platforms, and utilize AI-driven health navigation services that aggregate data on waiting times, treatment outcomes, and patient satisfaction. In this way, the actions taken are informed by a synthesis of diverse, credible sources rather than a singular, potentially biased perspective. This phase extends to strategic publication decisions. Creators aiming to maximize the reach of a new video or article must judiciously decide whether to share it on a certain social media platform or personal website, contingent upon the target audience and the intended impact. In this second phase, users integrate data with prior knowledge, experience, and other information to assess the feasibility of the objective and the progress that can be made toward it (Filonik et al., 2013).

3. Following appropriate online actions, the subsequent phase in the decision-making process involves *making the right decision to reach the objective*. This phase involves formulating a set of decision options and evaluating them based on carefully considered criteria, ultimately leading to the identification of an optimal solution and implementation of the selected course of action (Miller, 2006). The decision-making process concludes when an optimal decision is identified, allowing for the commencement of decision implementation (Miller, 2006). This process encompasses data interpretation, recommendation assessment, and informed decision-making, which integrates automated insights with personal goals. For instance, when an individual's objective is to enhance career visibility, AI-supported tools can suggest strategies for networking and content creation. Users must evaluate which actions—such as posting articles, commenting on discussions, or participating in online panels—will most effectively advance their professional objectives. In cases where the goal is to reduce energy consumption, observations of smart thermostat heating and occupancy data may reveal that a house is heated while unoccupied or during sleep. Decisions could involve manually adjusting the heat via an app, modifying the

heating schedule for efficiency, or employing AI-enabled automation features such as geofencing to adjust the temperature when the house is unoccupied. The critical aspect of this third step is balancing automated recommendations with critical goal-oriented judgment. Although algorithms and AI tools can provide valuable options, users must determine actions that genuinely advance their objectives.

4. The fourth and final stage entails *reflecting on and gaining the benefits that result from the objective.* Here, users implement the decisions formulated in the preceding phase to achieve their objectives while simultaneously monitoring and reflecting on the outcomes of both their actions and automated systems. This stage is crucial for realizing the benefits of optimal decision-making. As elaborated in the subsequent chapter, internet and intelligent media can generate significant and quantifiable outcomes across several domains. This step underscores the iterative nature of decision-making. As data are continuously collected from wearables, IoT devices, online analytics, or AI recommendations, users acquire increasingly detailed insights into their progress toward their objectives. For instance, a user equipped with an AI-enabled smartwatch may monitor their activity pattern, heart rate, or sleep quality. If step counts or activity objectives are not met, the user can modify routines, set reminders, or employ AI-driven coaching applications to propose more effective exercise schedules. In all instances, this step encompasses both action and reflection. Users not only execute decisions but also critically evaluate outcomes, assessing whether AI recommendations, IoT automation, or their interventions genuinely align with the objective. Based on these insights, goals may be refined, new strategies adopted, or entirely new objectives pursued.

2.9 Conclusions

In this chapter, we elaborated the seven digital skills as introduced in Chap. 1, situating them specifically within the context of internet and connected intelligent media. The proposed definitions are grounded in the skills of individual users necessary for socially accepted, responsible, and effective engagement with internet and intelligent media. These skills are not exclusive to experts or professionals; they are essential for the general population to participate meaningfully, make informed decisions, and maintain agency in a digital media landscape. This emphasis reflects our broader commitment to equity—identifying the skills required for meaningful participation in a smart society and understanding the origins and dynamics of emerging inequalities.

The framework covers medium- and content-related skills. Medium-related skills encompass strategic media choice, operational, and formal skills, that is, the skills to critically select appropriate media and platforms, as well as to operate and navigate them effectively. Content-related skills include information, communication, content creation, and strategic media use skills. The framework avoids a technologically deterministic perspective that reduces digital skills to mere technical skills. It acknowledges that digital skills involve not only using digital media and platforms, but also involve aspects such as understanding and evaluating information, exchanging meaning, collaboration and negotiation, producing content in a responsible manner, and achieving personal, professional, and societal goals. Importantly, the skills framework is sequential and conditional rather than strictly hierarchical. While content-related skills partly depend on the mastery of medium-related skills, the acquisition of medium-related skills does not automatically guarantee success in content-related domains. Similarly, skill development does not follow a linear path. For example, an individual may have a conceptual understanding of how algorithm-driven social media platforms operate, yet lack operational and formal skills to adjust privacy settings, control recommendations, or navigate online interfaces to maintain autonomy in use.

References

Berners-Lee, T. (2000). *Weaving the web: The original design and ultimate destiny of the world wide web*. Harper Business.

Brand-Gruwel, S., Wopereis, I., & Vermetten, Y. (2005). Information problem solving by experts and novices: Analysis of a complex cognitive skill. *Computers in Human Behavior, 21*(3), 487–508.

Carvin, A. (2000). More than just access: Fitting literacy and content into the digital divide equation. *Educause Review, 35*(6), 38–47.

Coiro, J., & Dobler, E. (2007). Exploring the online reading comprehension strategies used by sixth-grade skilled readers to search for and locate information on the Internet. *Reading Research Quarterly, 42*(2), 214–257.

Daft, R. L., & Lengel, R. H. (1984). *Information richness: A new approach to managerial behavior and organizational design*. JAI Press.

Danielson, D. R. (2003). Transitional volatility in web navigation. *It & Society, 1*(3), 131–158.

Dennis, A. R., Fuller, R. M., & Valacich, J. S. (2008). Media, tasks, and communication processes: A theory of media synchronicity. *MIS Quarterly, 32*(3), 575–600.

Filonik, D., Medland, R., Foth, M., & Rittenbruch, M. (2013). A customisable dashboard display for environmental performance visualisations. In S. Berkovsky & J. Freyne (Eds.), *Persuasive technology: 8th International conference* (pp. 51–62). Springer.

Hoem, J., & Schwebs, T. (2005). *Personal publishing and media literacy: Designing a virtual learning arena based on weblogs and wikis*. Paper presented at the IFIP World Conference on Computers in Education (WCCE), Cape Town, South Africa.

Jenkins, H. (2009). *Confronting the challenges of participatory culture: Media education for the 21st century*. MIT press.

Karvalics, L. Z. (2014). Emerging new information literacies: A conceptual outlook. In S. Kurbanoğlu, S. Špiranec, E. Grassian, D. Mizrachi, & R. Catts (Eds.), *European conference on information literacy* (pp. 37–46). Springer.

Katz, E., Blumler, J. G., & Gurevitch, M. (1973). Uses and gratifications research. *The Public Opinion Quarterly, 37*(4), 509–523.

Kwan, M. P. (2001). Cyberspatial cognition and individual access to information: the behavioral foundation of cybergeography. *Environment and Planning B: Planning and Design, 28*(1), 21–37.

Lee, M. J. (2005). Expanding hypertext: Does it address disorientation? Depends on individuals' adventurousness. *Journal of Computer-Mediated Communication, 10*(3), JCMC1036.

Madianou, M., & Miller, D. (2013). *Migration and new media: Transnational families and polymedia*. Routledge.

Marchionini, G. (1995). *Information seeking in electronic environments* (Vol. 9). Cambridge University Press.

Miller, K. (2006). *Organizational communication: Approaches and processes*. Thomson Wadsworth.

Mossberger, K., Tolbert, C. J., & Stansbury, M. (2003). *Virtual inequality: Beyond the digital divide*. Georgetown University Press.

Seneviratne, O., & Monroy-Hernandez, A. (2010). Remix culture on the web: A survey of content reuse on different user-generated content websites. In W. Nejdl, F. Abel, K. Tochtermann, & H. Sack (Eds.), *Proceedings of the WebSci10: Extending the frontiers of society on-line* (pp. 26–27).

Søby, M. (2003). *Digital competence: From ICT skills to digital "bildung"*. University of Oslo.

Tate, M., & Alexander, J. (1996). Teaching critical evaluation skills for World Wide Web resources. *Computers in Libraries, 16*(10), 49–55.

Treem, J. W., & Leonardi, P. M. (2013). Social media use in organizations: Exploring the affordances of visibility, editability, persistence, and association. *Annals of the International Communication Association, 36*(1), 143–189.

Van Deursen, A. J. A. M., & Mossberger, K. (2018). Any thing for anyone? A new digital divide in Internet-of-Things skills. *Policy & Internet, 10*(2), 122–140.

Van Dijk, J. A. G. M. (2020). *The network society*. Sage.

Van Dijk, J. A. G. M., & Van Deursen, A. J. A. M. (2014). *Digital skills: Unlocking the information society*. Palgrave Macmillan.

Warschauer, M. (2004). *Technology and social inclusion: Rethinking the digital divide*. MIT Press.

Webster, J., & Ahuja, J. S. (2006). Enhancing the design of web navigation systems: The influence of user disorientation on engagement and performance. *MIS Quarterly, 30*(3), 661–678.

CHAPTER 3

Digital Skills: Levels and Distribution

3.1 Introduction: Measuring Digital Skills

In the previous chapter, we outlined seven types of digital skills required for using internet and connected intelligent media. In this chapter, we examine how the general population performs across these skills and identify the most important contributors. Our goal is to identify bottlenecks and provide insights that can guide policy efforts to overcome them. The following methods are commonly employed to assess digital skills (Van Deursen & Helsper, 2020):

- *Indirect measurements*. Various benchmarks rely on surveys that ask respondents which activities they have ever carried out online. The assumption is that the more activities someone reports, the more skilled they are. The advantage of such measurements is that large-scale surveys can be conducted efficiently. However, performing an activity does not automatically imply skilled performance, and not performing an activity does not imply that someone is incapable of doing so. The problem lies in limited validity, as no direct measurement or observation of actual digital skills takes place.
- *Self-assessments*. Studies using self-assessments typically ask participants to rate their skills, for example using scales ranging from "very poor" to "excellent." Self-reports are cost-effective and allow researchers to gather data quickly and easily. However, they are not

A. van Deursen and J. van Dijk, *Digital Skills*, Digital Education and Learning, https://doi.org/10.1057/978-1-349-96162-7_3

reliable indicators of actual digital skills. Perceptions of skill can vary depending on context and personal factors. For instance, gender and age influence self-assessments, with men and younger individuals tending to overestimate their skills (Palczyńska & Rynko, 2021). Self-assessments might also be shaped by the comparison group; using colleagues in a technology-intensive environment as a reference may result in lower ratings than comparing oneself with family members or friends, even when actual skill levels are similar.

- *Task-based performance tests*. This is the most valid method for obtaining a realistic view of digital skills. The method is used to assess someone's skills by having them perform actual tasks. Instead of asking participants to rate themselves, the test directly measures their skills through observable actions. However, their high cost poses a major limitation for large-scale implementation. These tests require the design of realistic tasks, monitoring of participants, and evaluation of results, which makes them more difficult to scale for large populations.
- *Interactive standardized measurements*. These are conducted in secure test environments where participants must solve problems using software simulations. This method is frequently used in educational settings but applying it to broader populations is labor-intensive and requires on-site testing.
- *Counterfactual measurements*. These do not directly measure skills but instead examine the effects of interventions. For example, differences in the outcomes of internet use are compared between people with similar backgrounds but different skill levels. Such studies provide valuable insights for intervention evaluations.

These methods stipulate that measuring digital skills across populations in a valid manner is not straightforward. Existing studies on digital skills often originate from fields such as library science, computer science, or education, and typically focus on specific groups, such as students in training programs. While these studies offer meaningful insights into performance within controlled environments, they seldom capture skill levels or demographic variations across the general population. To assess digital skills on a larger scale, most research and benchmarking initiatives rely on indirect measures (such as frequency or type of use) or self-assessment questionnaires. This chapter presents findings from three complementary sources. The two main sources are a survey with self-assessments and a series of seven task-based performance tests. The survey and performance tests are conducted in the Netherlands, a highly digital society supported by extensive and fast broadband infrastructure, including robust fixed and mobile networks and a strong national push for fiber-optic deployment. 99 Percent of households have broadband internet access (Statistics Netherlands, 2024). Dutch policy recognizes the importance of high-speed internet for all citizens, and the country was an early adopter of net neutrality legislation, reflecting a commitment to equitable digital access. International benchmarks, although often relying on less reliable or indirect measures, indicate that the Netherlands has the highest proportion of residents aged 16 to 75 years with at least basic digital skills (Statistics Netherlands, 2023). Given this highly developed digital country, it is likely that the levels of digital skills presented in this chapter represent an optimistic scenario. In other national contexts with lower broadband penetration, less developed digital infrastructure, or fewer initiatives to promote digital inclusion, the overall skill levels can be expected to be similar or lower. Consequently, the presented findings can be viewed as a benchmark for understanding digital skills in countries with advanced digital infrastructure, while also underscoring the challenges faced by countries with a less mature digital landscape.

The first main source is a large-scale *survey* conducted among adults aged 18 years and older in January 2026. Respondents were recruited from a national online panel designed to represent the Dutch population. Panel members received an email invitation detailing the survey topic and estimated completion time. The survey was designed to take approximately 15 minutes, and the software used automated prompts to encourage respondents to complete missing items. Data collection lasted for three weeks, during which the sample composition was continuously monitored and adjusted to maintain representativeness. The background characteristics of the respondents (gender, age, and education) were compared with the most recent data from Statistics Netherlands. Of 2000 randomly selected individuals, a total of 1311 responses were received, of which 115 were incomplete. Consequently, 1236 valid responses were included in the final analysis. This sample closely aligned with the national population distribution in terms of gender, age, and education, requiring minimal post-hoc adjustments. The figures presented in the following sections are based on this survey; however, they should be interpreted as indicative estimates of digital skills rather than precise measurements, as self-assessments are not fully reliable indicators of actual skills. The skill items were originally adapted from the Internet Skills Scale (ISS; Van Deursen et al., 2016) and the Youth Digital Skills Indicator (yDSI; Helsper et al., 2020). However, the ISS and yDSI include fewer items per skill type and are grounded in somewhat different conceptual frameworks, as they do not account for strategic media choice, formal, and strategic media use skills. Consistent with the ISS and yDSI, all items were rated on a five-point scale. The scale ranged from 1 ("Not at all true of me") to 5 ("Very true of me"), with an additional option, "I do not understand what you mean by that." Cognitive interviews conducted during the pilot phases of the ISS and yDSI development indicated that the wording of these items elicited neutral and objective responses. The phrasing was carefully designed to prompt respondents to reflect on their own skills rather than compare themselves to others and to avoid terms such as "expert" that might introduce bias. The figures presented indicate the percentage of respondents who provided positive responses to the statements.

The second main source consists of a series of *seven task-based performance tests* conducted in a media lab at the University of Twente. These tests aimed to assess how individuals apply various digital skills in real-world contexts. The first three tests focused on online governmental, general leisure, and health-related activities and measured operational, formal, information, and strategic media use skills. More than 300 internet users participated in these studies. Each participant completed task-based assignments reflecting common online activities, allowing for an accurate assessment of their digital skills (for detailed descriptions, see Van Deursen, 2012, Van Deursen & Van Dijk, 2009, 2011a, 2011b; Van Deursen et al., 2011). A fourth performance test evaluated operational, formal, information, and strategic media use internet skills among primary school children (Van Deursen et al., 2014), and a fifth test measured information and strategic media use skills among 54 students from nine secondary school classes (Van Deursen & Van Diepen, 2013). Two additional tests specifically investigated digital skills in intelligent media contexts, particularly the IoT. The first examined the use of health-related wearables (De Boer et al., 2020, 2023). In this study, 100 participants were introduced to an activity tracker and, following a one-week familiarization period, completed task-based assessments of their information and strategic media use skills. The second test evaluated operational, information, and strategic media use skills in a smart home environment (De

Boer et al., 2024; Van Deursen et al., 2025). A total of 101 participants performed tasks related to energy management, comfort, and lighting control, which reflected common smart home scenarios.

A third source used to enrich the presented findings consists of *task-based performance tests* conducted among children in six countries (Estonia, Finland, Germany, Italy, Poland, and Portugal). These tests, which are part of the ySkills project (yskills.eu), were specifically designed to measure information, communication, and content creation skills. Publications on the development of the tests (Van Laar et al., 2025) and the results (Van Deursen et al., 2023) contain details on samples, measurement, and procedure. The development of the tests included an iterative process encompassing pilot studies, cognitive interviews with children, and regular feedback provided by the research team from six country partners. The tests were split into two modules to limit the cognitive load on the children. The first module focused on information and content creation skills and the second on communication skills. In total, 772 children aged 13–18 participated in the tests.

3.2 Level of Strategic Media Choice Skills

Findings

Strategic media choice skills begin by defining clear objectives: identifying the purpose of media use, the intended audience or reach, the desired outcomes, and constraints that may influence the choice. This reflection helps ensure that digital media and platforms are used effectively and ethically to achieve specific goals. Encouragingly, Fig. 3.1 shows that 76 percent of the respondents in our survey indicate that they consciously link the platform they chose to their intended objective. However, maintaining this awareness over time appears to be challenging. Once people start using a particular platform, 65 percent continue to do so without exploring alternatives. This suggests a tendency toward habitual use rather than reflective decision-making, a pattern that may limit efficiency, innovation, and privacy protection.

When evaluating potential media and platforms, many users appear to demonstrate some degree of critical thinking. Figure 3.1 shows that 74 percent of the respondents report checking whether a platform is decent and fair, and 72 percent says they actively weigh the pros and cons before adopting one. Yet, the survey also reveals important areas for improvement as 30 percent of the respondents admit that they do not know how to make a well-considered choice among the vast range of available online platforms. AI adds more complexity as its use involves opaque algorithms and data-sharing risks that are not immediately visible to the average user. Only 48 percent of the respondents claim that they carefully consider the decision to use AI, and more than half do not know what aspects to pay attention to before choosing to engage with AI.

The survey also included two statements that, while not directly reflecting skills, provided insight into participants' media choice skills. Remarkably, 40 percent of respondents prefer calling a service provider rather than visiting their website. This highlights the significant value of human interaction and personal communication. It suggests that online platforms cannot fully replace the reassurance, trust, and immediacy that come from speaking directly with another person. For many users, a phone call offers greater clarity, faster problem resolution, and a sense of personal connection that automated systems or websites often fail to provide. Additionally, 41 percent of respondents report using certain platforms primarily because everyone else did. This reveals the strong influence of social norms and peer behavior on the choice of media or platforms. Rather than making a deliberate or critical choice, many users adopt popular platforms to stay connected, maintain convenience, or avoid feeling excluded from common digital practices. While this can facilitate social belonging, it also underscores the importance of fostering independent and informed decision-making in media use, encouraging users to evaluate whether widely used media and platforms truly meet their needs, values, and objectives.

Conclusions

Strategic media choice skills center on making conscious, goal-oriented, and ethical choices regarding which media and platforms to use, considering the purpose, audience, and desired outcomes. The findings present a mixed picture. Although many individuals reflect on their media choices, critical evaluation and sustained awareness remain challenging. Habitual use, social influence, and convenience often guide decisions more than deliberate or informed reasoning. The growing presence of AI further complicates these choices as users seem to miss clarity regarding issues such as transparency, privacy, and bias.

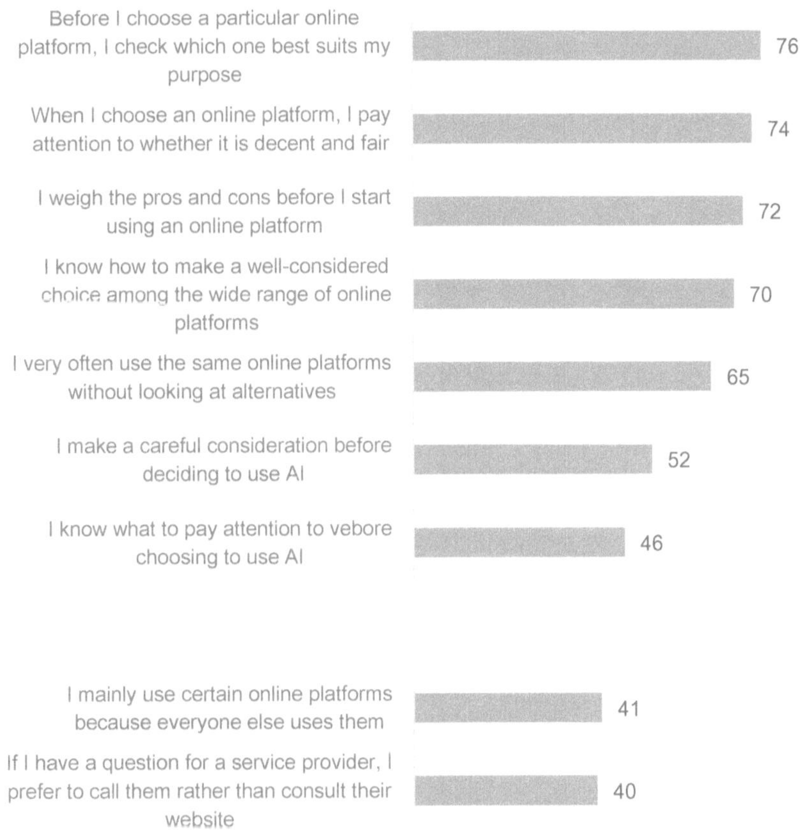

Fig. 3.1 Sufficient mastery of strategic media choice skills, % adult population

3.3 Level of Operational Skills

Findings

The first set of operational skills focuses on recognizing and operating toolbars, buttons, and menus. These can be considered fundamental actions required for the effective use of digital media and platforms. In the performance tests, we found that the levels of operational skills among the Dutch population were quite high. Figure 3.2 shows the survey results and confirms that a large majority of respondents possess basic operational skills: 85 percent know how to open a new browser window, 77 percent can bookmark a website, and 76 percent know how to turn off the location function on their smartphone. These figures suggest that although most people are comfortable with routine browser and device operations, a substantial number are less certain about performing related actions. The findings also reveal that 28 percent of respondents do not know the functions of all browser buttons. In the performance tests, we found that the use of an internet browser is often not straightforward, particularly for older adults. Some of them did not even recognize the browser if Google was not displayed on the screen. They did not seem to have any clues about how to proceed and seemed unfamiliar with the use of the browser's address bar. In some cases, they did not recognize the address bar at all. While completing tasks in the smart home environment, some participants struggled with simple button-related interface interactions; for instance, when attempting to turn on a dimmable floor lamp at half brightness. Most of those who failed did so because they clicked the button instead of holding it to adjust the light level.

When it comes to managing settings, 79 percent of the survey respondents report knowing how to secure their devices, for example, by setting up a PIN code, unlock pattern, or facial recognition. Additionally, 70 percent indicate that they know how to adjust privacy settings in their web browser. These results suggest that most users possess at least a basic understanding of personal security and privacy management. However, the fact that approximately one in five respondents lacked knowledge of fundamental device security practices and nearly one in three were unfamiliar with browser privacy settings implies that many individuals may still struggle to effectively implement protective measures or adapt their settings to evolving privacy risks.

With respect to user input, completing online forms remains a challenge for a small proportion of the population. Approximately 16 percent of the respondents report finding it difficult to fill out forms online. The performance tests, which included a range of tasks involving different types of online forms and input fields, revealed similar results. Most participants were able to complete the forms successfully, although minor difficulties were observed. A few participants forgot to complete all the required fields, which triggered warning messages that caused confusion. Others encountered more technical input-related problems, for instance, entering search keywords without spaces or typing "www." before the keywords in the search bars. Some participants, particularly older adults, exhibited difficulties with basic interaction patterns, such as using the

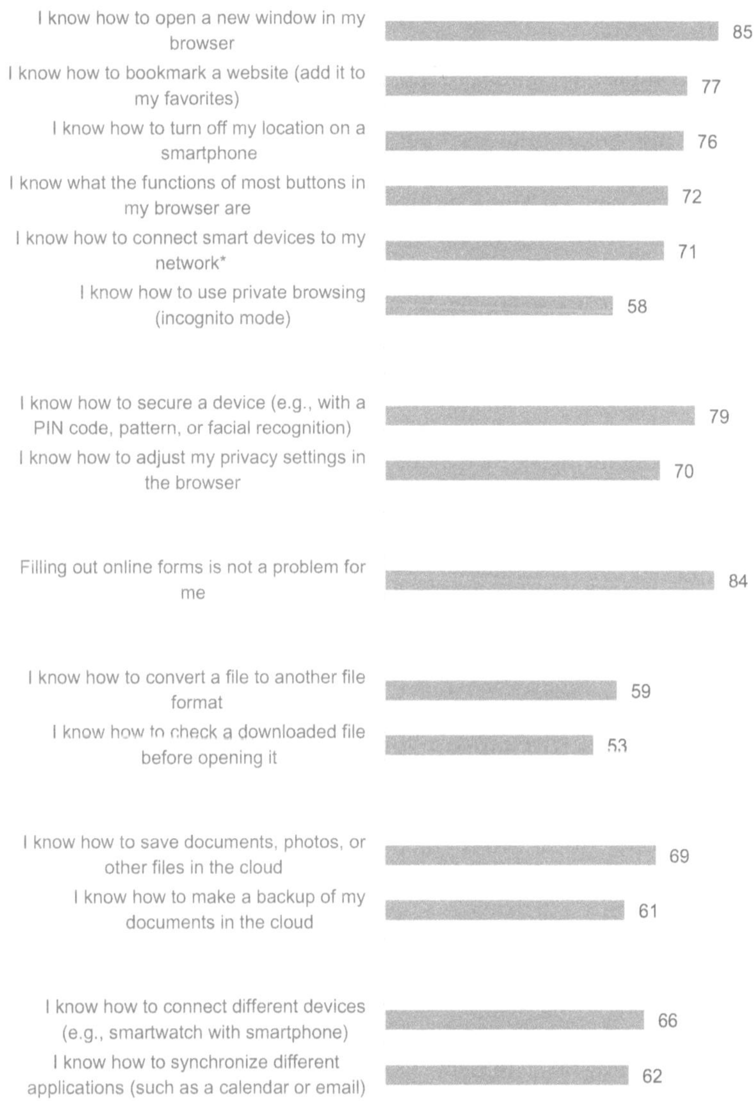

Fig. 3.2 Sufficient mastery of operational skills components, % of adult population. * asked to respondents using smart devices

right mouse button instead of the left when attempting to type into a text box.

More complex operational tasks, such as managing file formats, present substantial challenges. The survey results reveal that 41 percent of respondents do not know how to convert a file to a different format when necessary, and 47 percent are unaware of how to check a downloaded file before opening it. These difficulties were also reflected in our performance tests. Nearly half of the participants were unable to successfully save a PDF to the desktop. Many struggled to distinguish between saving an individual file via a download link and saving an entire webpage or website. Some participants appeared completely unsure of how to handle tasks such as saving a brochure, music file, or video clip. Common errors included assuming that a file was automatically saved after opening the save dialog, creating desktop shortcuts to websites or bookmarking a page instead of saving the actual file, and becoming confused about folder locations and file-naming conventions.

Operational skills related to file sharing were assessed in the survey by asking users about their cloud-based activities. The results indicate that a majority of respondents possess basic skills: 69 percent report knowing how to save documents, photos, or other files to a cloud service, while 61 percent indicate that they know how to create a backup in the cloud. These findings suggest that most users are familiar with fundamental cloud storage functions. However, the difference between general file saving and creating backups indicates that while users can store files, fewer fully understand or routinely implement practices that ensure data security and redundancy.

Finally, operational skills that involve connecting or integrating multiple devices and services appear to be less widespread among users. Only 66 percent of the survey respondents report knowing how to link different devices (e.g., connecting a smartwatch to a smartphone), while 62 percent say they know how to synchronize applications such as calendars or email across devices. These tasks require not only basic operational skills but also an understanding of device compatibility, app settings, and data synchronization processes, which can present challenges for less-experienced users. Interestingly, in the smart home performance test, connecting a device proved to be relatively straightforward. Only a few participants were unable to connect the designated smart light bulb to the IoT platform. This might indicate that while many users may theoretically lack confidence in their skills to integrate media, they might still be able to successfully complete such tasks when given clear instructions. It also highlights the potential benefits of intuitive design and step-by-step guidance for promoting the broader adoption of connected intelligent media.

Conclusions

Most users have an adequate understanding of basic digital operations including routine browser use, device management, and basic security practices. Many are comfortable performing everyday tasks, such as opening browser windows, bookmarking websites, adjusting privacy settings, and managing straightforward cloud storage or file-sharing activities. However, certain groups, particularly older adults, continue to struggle with basic interface elements and routine form-filling tasks, often finding interface conventions and error messages challenging. In addition, a notable portion of users experience considerable difficulty when performing more complex operational skills.

3.4 Level of Formal Skills

Findings

Formal skills refer to using hypermedia in internet and intelligent media. These skills encompass an understanding of online structures, interpretation of design conventions, and maintenance of orientation while browsing. Users who struggle with navigation and orientation often attribute their difficulties to design issues. Indeed, many studies focus primarily on the technical perspective, testing platforms for navigational flaws, while overlooking deficiencies in users' navigation and orientation skills. Figure 3.3 shows that most survey respondents indicate confidence in finding information on a website regardless of its design. However, significant challenges remain. Approximately a quarter of the respondents reported that they often do not know where to click on a website, suggesting that navigation is not always intuitive. Similarly, 29 percent state that the wide variety of website layouts makes it difficult to use the internet effectively. In line with this, 31 percent of respondents disagree with the statement that the websites they use are clear and easy to understand. The performance tests revealed similar patterns. When participants were asked to find a simple piece of information (for example, a street address) on websites with different layouts and design features, many

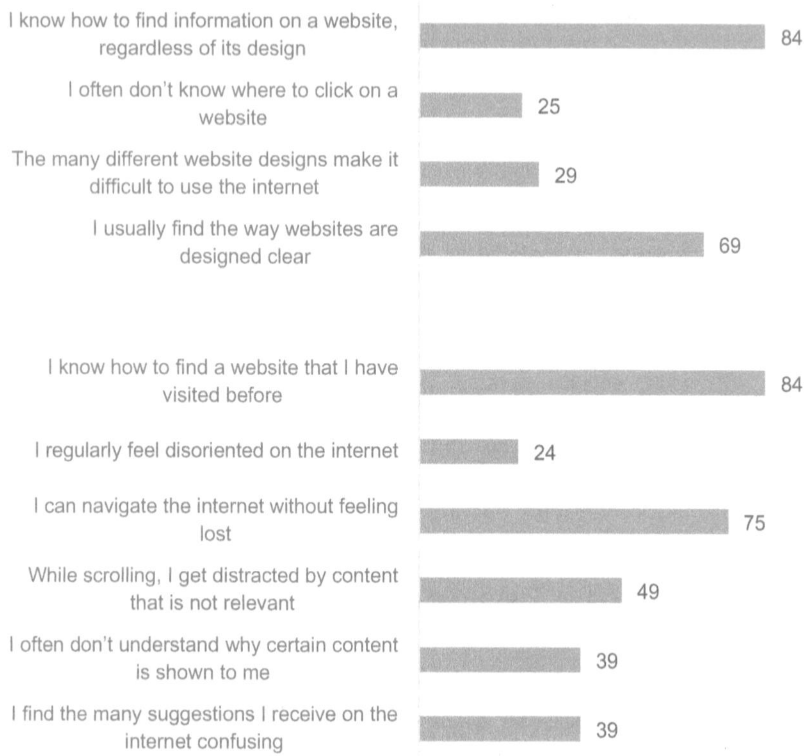

Fig. 3.3 Sufficient mastery of formal skills components, % of adult population

overlooked options or links in the main menus or ignored the menus entirely. Roll-over menus were especially problematic for older adults, who did not understand why a menu disappeared when their mouse pointer inadvertently moved outside the menu area.

Regarding orientation, most respondents indicate to know how to return to a website they have previously visited. Yet, about one in four report feeling disoriented on a regular basis while browsing and disagree with the statement that they can navigate the internet without getting lost. This highlights the absence of a confident and structured understanding of the online environment. A related challenge is distraction: half of the participants report being distracted while scrolling, reflecting the fragmented and attention-demanding nature of online environments. Confusion also arises from the increasing prevalence of personalized content and recommendation systems, which are often apparent in interactive or adaptive hypermedia environments. Of the survey respondents, 39 percent find the suggestions or recommendations they receive confusing, and a similar share often do not understand why certain types of content are being displayed to them. These findings indicate that for many users, the internet remains a complex and sometimes opaque environment where navigation and orientation are not straightforward. Users with lower levels of formal skills seem to be more dependent on clear and predictable design conventions. They tend to struggle when these differ between sites or applications. Performance tests confirmed these difficulties. Participants were asked to navigate to a page within a large website and return to the homepage. More than 25 percent of the participants experienced problems. Some believed they were already on the homepage, clicked "Up" instead of "Home," or clicked a link to the current page. Many users were unfamiliar with the convention that a small home icon or company logo would typically lead back to the homepage. Additionally, several participants did not recognize image links if they were not explicitly labeled as links. Orientation issues also occurred between websites. Approximately 21 percent of the performance test participants lost their orientation when a new browser window was opened. They did not understand why the back button in the new window was inactive and overlooked the original website, even when it was visible in the background. When asked to open the first and fourth search results after performing a search, one-third of the participants experienced difficulties. The primary problem was that after opening the first search result, participants mistakenly chose the fourth option in a nearby menu unrelated to the search results, believing that they had opened the correct result. Some participants did not return to the original search results; instead, they navigated back to the homepage, retyped the search query, and opened the fourth result.

Conclusions

Although many users report confidence in browsing websites, a substantial proportion still experience difficulties with navigation and orientation. Common challenges include interpreting diverse website layouts, managing complex menus, returning to previously visited pages, and understanding interactive or adaptive content such as personalized recommendations. Performance tests confirmed these issues, revealing that users frequently overlook important links, misinterpret navigation icons, and become disoriented when navigating multiple pages or search results. Older adults and less-experienced internet users are particularly affected, as they tend to rely on consistent and predictable design cues. For these groups, distractions, fragmented online environments, and opaque interface conventions complicate navigation. Moreover, website structures can sometimes create misleading orientation cues, causing users to make errors without realizing it.

3.5 Level of Information Skills

Findings

Among all the digital skills discussed in this book, information skills have received the most attention in scientific research. They are particularly well studied in educational contexts where researchers have investigated how students seek information and what strategies they use. Most studies consistently reveal that the average internet user has a limited understanding of how search engines function and often lacks the skills to conduct a systematic, goal-oriented information search. Our survey and task-based performance tests corroborate these findings and raise concerns regarding whether users possess sufficient skills to fully benefit from online information resources.

The first and arguably most critical step in the information search process is defining the information problem, that is, clearly determining what information is needed, for what purpose, and under what constraints. Many individuals struggle during this initial stage. Figure 3.4 shows that 29 percent of respondents report that they do not explicitly define what they are looking for, and 32 percent fail to consider the type or amount of information required. Encouragingly, 47 percent indicate that they know how to use AI tools to clarify or refine their information needs, suggesting that technological support may help compensate for weaknesses in this phase. Defining the information problem is often accompanied by feelings of uncertainty or confusion, as individuals may only have a vague or general understanding of the topic. These early ambiguities are a natural part of the search process but can hinder efficiency and accuracy if not addressed properly. The performance tests highlight clear age-related differences: younger participants tend to begin searching immediately, often typing a query into a search engine without prior reflection, whereas older participants are more likely to pause, consider the task, and articulate their objectives before initiating the search. This contrast suggests that metacognitive skills, such as planning and self-regulation, play a key role in effective information searching and may develop with age and experience.

The second step in the information search process involves deciding where to search for information, that is, selecting the most appropriate platforms or resources for the task at hand. Of the survey respondents, 55 percent report consciously reflecting on which platform to use, for example, whether to consult an AI-based platform or rely on a traditional search engine. However, task-based performance tests revealed that most participants consistently defaulted to one search engine as their primary source, regardless of the nature or complexity of the task. A smaller proportion of respondents employed alternative strategies, such as revisiting familiar websites or attempting to locate information by guessing URLs. These methods were typically unsystematic and inefficient, often resulting in trial-and-error behavior and incomplete search outcomes. Once a search platform is selected, the next step is to formulate effective search queries. According to the survey, approximately 70 percent of the respondents believe that they know how to phrase effective queries, 69 percent report understanding how to use advanced search options, and 55 percent claim to know how to instruct AI systems to retrieve relevant information. However, the performance tests reveal a substantial gap between perceived and actual skills. Over half of the participants (56 percent) used search terms that were overly general or poorly aligned with their information problem, and most queries contained only one or two keywords. Search engines often compensate for users' limited search skills by offering auto-suggestions and related keywords; however, when initial searches fail, many users make only minor adjustments to their queries, changes that are typically insufficient to improve the results. More effective strategies, such as using Boolean operators (e.g., AND, OR, NOT) to refine searches or leveraging advanced search options (e.g., specifying date ranges, locations, or formats), were rarely used. Some search engines also allow users to search within the search results, a feature that the participants in the performance tests did not utilize. These findings suggest that most users tend to accept the default settings provided by search systems instead of actively refining their queries. This behavior was also evident

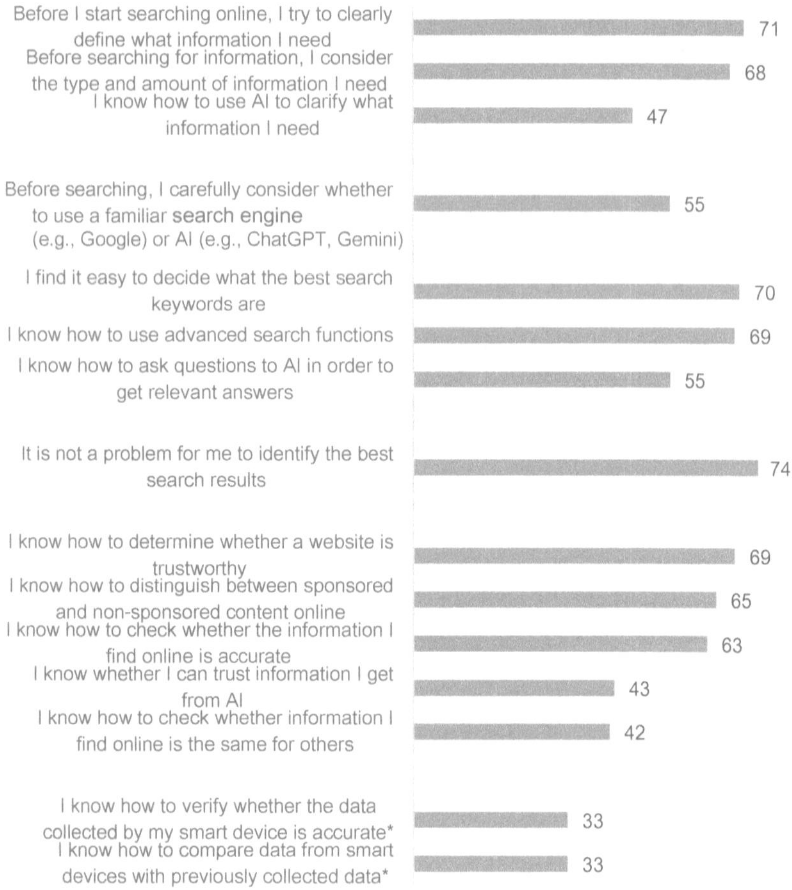

Fig. 3.4 Sufficient mastery of information skills components, % of adult population

among children, who rarely used advanced search tools to narrow results by criteria such as time range while completing search tasks.

The fourth step in the information search process involves selecting relevant information from the search results. According to the survey, 74 percent of respondents report knowing how to identify the best results. However, performance test data revealed a discrepancy between perceived and actual skills. Many participants tended to rely heavily on the top-ranked results, that is, those positioned highest by the search algorithm, without critically assessing their relevance. This behavior suggests a dependence on algorithmic rankings as proxies for trustworthiness. The performance tests among younger users indicate that this tendency is even more pronounced. Most children extracted answers directly from the Google search results page without visiting the original source of information. As a result, they often lacked awareness of the sources of their information. Notably, only 27 percent of the children were able to accurately identify the source of their answers.

The final, and perhaps most challenging, stage of the information search process is evaluating the quality and credibility of the information obtained. Traditionally, media literacy has emphasized the importance of adopting a critical stance toward media content. However, several studies have raised concerns regarding the questionable reliability of online information and the widespread inability of users to validate or evaluate the information they find. In the survey, approximately two-thirds of the respondents claim to know how to assess a website's trustworthiness, distinguish between commercial and noncommercial sources, and verify the accuracy of the information presented. However, the performance tests revealed a stark contrast between this perceived skill and actual behavior. Few participants paid attention to the sources of the information they encountered. Most appeared satisfied simply by locating an answer, regardless of its origin or authorship. For example, during one test involving government information, several participants mistakenly believed that they had found the correct answer on a website featuring class presentations by primary school students. Even when information was used to make strategic decisions, very few participants attempted to crosscheck or verify the results on other websites. The performance tests among children revealed an even more troubling pattern. Tasks requiring participants to identify the least reliable website or rank search results based on credibility produced similarly weak results. Further analysis revealed that children possess only a limited understanding of what makes a source trustworthy, which contributes to their difficulty in recognizing intent or bias in online content. Consequently, most children struggled to identify whether social media posts were advertisements, fake news, or phishing attempts, underscoring their vulnerability to misinformation. Overall, their performance indicates a clear deficit in evaluation skills, particularly in distinguishing reliable from unreliable sources. The evaluation of information generated by AI presents additional complexities. The majority of the survey respondents acknowledge that they do not know how to verify the credibility of AI-generated content. A similar uncertainty applies to data produced by smart devices—only about one-third of the respondents claim to verify the accuracy of such data or compare it meaningfully with previously collected information.

Conclusions

Information skills encompass problem definition, source location, query formulation, information selection, and evaluation. Users encounter challenges at nearly every stage. The initial step, defining the information need, is particularly problematic. Many users struggle to articulate their objectives, specify the type or scope of information required, and develop a clear search strategy. Although AI tools can assist with this stage, effective search planning and metacognitive strategies remain underdeveloped among a large proportion of users. Selecting appropriate sources also presents a major challenge. While many users claim to reflect on which platforms to use, in practice, most default to familiar search engines and seldom adapt their strategies to specific tasks or explore specialized resources. This suggests a limited understanding of the diversity of information sources available—such as academic repositories, data portals, or AI-assisted query tools—and an inability to align search strategies with task requirements. Strengthening users' source selection skills could therefore play a pivotal role in improving information search effectiveness. Query formulation skills are similarly limited. Searches are often overly broad, and users tend to rely on default system suggestions rather than employing advanced search functionalities. The results highlight the need for instruction in query design and the strategic use of search tools—skills that are critical for conducting accurate, efficient, and goal-oriented information searches. This also includes the skills to formulate effective prompts or instructions for AI systems to retrieve relevant information. Identifying relevant information from search results and assessing credibility present further difficulties. Users frequently depend on top-ranked results without critical evaluation, and younger users, in particular, often fail to verify sources. Evaluating the trustworthiness of content, including AI-generated outputs or information from smart devices, remains a significant challenge. Many users do not crosscheck information, detect bias, or distinguish between reliable and unreliable sources, leaving them vulnerable to misinformation and disinformation.

3.6 Level of Communication Skills

Findings

Our definition of communication skills begins with contact management, which encompasses the skills to curate and maintain online networks. Figure 3.5 shows that a large majority of the survey respondents (86 percent) report that they consider carefully before adding someone to their contact list, reflecting a cautious and deliberate approach to online networking. Similarly, 88 percent of the respondents report knowing how to remove a contact from their list. However, a notable proportion of users still seem to lack these basic functions. Lacking skills to effectively manage contacts can have practical and social consequences, from maintaining outdated or irrelevant connections to being exposed to unwanted interactions or content.

When it comes to encoding messages, nearly one in four respondents report difficulty in expressing themselves clearly in online communication. Furthermore, 27 percent indicate that they do not know how to ensure their messages do not have a negative impact on others, highlighting an incomplete understanding of tone, context, and audience sensitivity online. These findings suggest that many users may struggle to adapt their language, style, and emotional cues to the nuances of online communication, where misunderstandings can easily arise because of the absence of nonverbal signals. Comprehension also presents a significant challenge in decoding messages. Over one-third of adult users report frequent difficulties in understanding others when abbreviations, emojis, or memes are used. This indicates that the symbolic and visual elements of digital communication, which often carry cultural, contextual, or emotional meanings, are not fully understood by all users.

When examining the exchange of meaning, a concerning picture emerges: although over 80 percent of the survey respondents claim to understand online etiquette (netiquette) and reported knowing what types of information can or cannot be shared, performance tests among children aged 13 to 18 revealed a different picture. While they generally performed reasonably well in identifying situations in which sharing others' information would be inappropriate, approximately one in four still could not correctly determine when social media posts should not be shared without permission. Also troubling are the findings related to how children respond to negative or harmful online interactions. Approximately one-third did not consider blocking an unknown person who sent

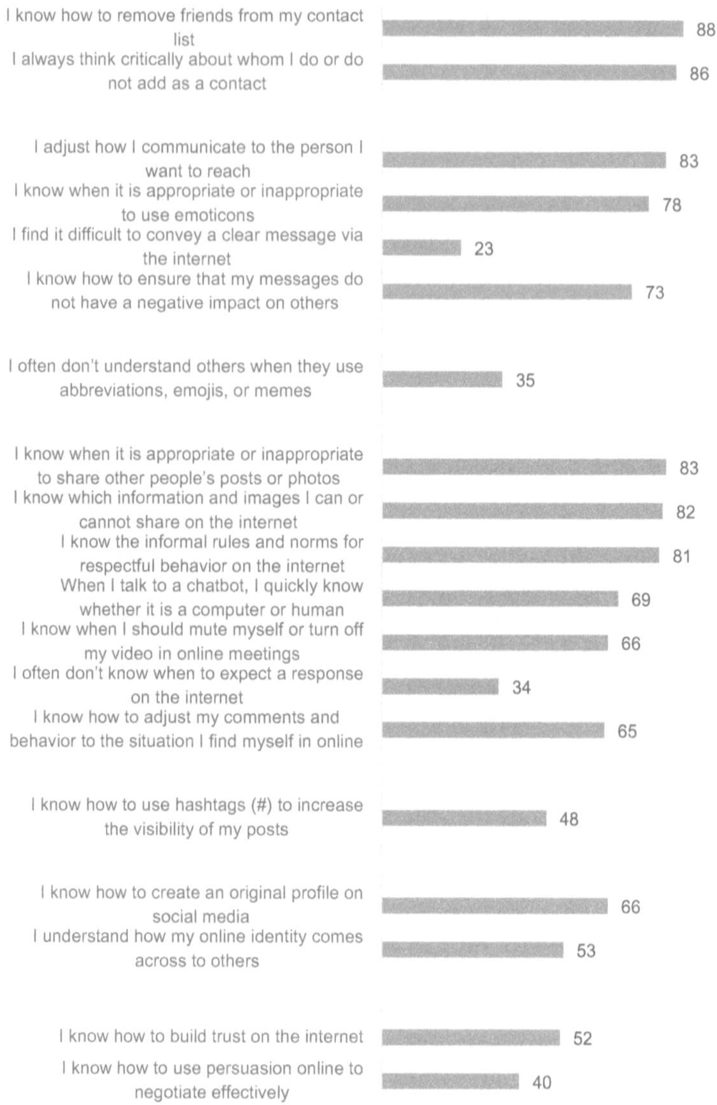

Fig. 3.5 Sufficient mastery of communication skills components, % of adult population

unpleasant or harmful messages, indicating a lack of protective behavioral strategies. Alarmingly, more than 40 percent of the children did not perceive name-calling in group chats as problematic, highlighting significant gaps in their understanding of respectful and courteous online behavior. Similar challenges arise in the context of online meetings and chats, where many children struggle to apply netiquette: they often failed to choose appropriate settings for virtual meetings or to adapt their communication style to the situation. Finally, the survey revealed that approximately one-third of the respondents are unable to quickly recognize whether they are communicating with a chatbot or human.

The skills to increase message visibility represent another important area for development. For example, hashtags can help reach a broader audience and enhance engagement across social media platforms. However, the survey revealed that fewer than half of the adult users appear to know how to use them effectively, suggesting that many users struggle to strategically amplify their messages. This can limit the reach and impact of online communication. Similar patterns emerged in the performance tests among children, many of whom were unaware of which options were most likely to increase the online visibility of a created presentation.

Skills related to online identity construction also showed considerable room for improvement. Only about 66 percent of the survey respondents indicate that they know how to create an original profile on social media, and half of the survey respondents report that they understand how their online identity is perceived by others. The latter suggests a limited awareness of how personal identities can shape others' impressions.

Finally, trust and persuasion remain underdeveloped aspects of digital communication skills. Only about half of the respondents report knowing how to build trust online, and only 40 percent indicate that they can use persuasive techniques effectively in online negotiations.

Conclusions

Communication skills encompass managing contacts; encoding, decoding, and exchanging messages; applying netiquette; increasing message visibility; constructing an online identity; and fostering trust and persuasion. A notable proportion of users still lack effective contact management skills. In practice, this can lead to practical and social consequences, such as maintaining outdated or irrelevant connections, or increased exposure to unwanted interactions and content. Furthermore, while many users are able to engage in routine digital exchanges, challenges persist in adapting messages to tone, context, and audience, as well as in interpreting symbolic or visual elements such as emojis, memes, or abbreviations that often convey cultural, contextual, or emotional meaning. Applying netiquette in online interactions also remains difficult, revealing a lack of awareness of appropriate digital behavior. Another challenge in exchanging meaning emerges from conversations with AI-driven tools and conversational agents that are increasingly integrated into everyday communication. The findings suggest that many users lack the skills to correctly identify the nature of their interlocutors, making them vulnerable to misleading information, manipulative content, or inadvertent sharing of personal data. This highlights the need for education on source recognition and critical engagement with online communication platforms.

Other important challenges include gaining attention online, handling harmful interactions, maintaining privacy, constructing and managing online identities, and understanding how one is perceived by others. A lack of awareness in these areas can undermine social credibility, personal branding, and online safety. Strengthening skills related to gaining and maintaining attention would not only improve individuals' skills to disseminate information effectively but also enhance their capacity for strategic engagement and meaningful participation within online communities. The limited skills related to trust-building and persuasive communication reduce effectiveness in collaboration and negotiation contexts. These skills require a nuanced understanding of the social and ethical dimensions of online interactions, such as distinguishing between sponsored and non-sponsored content, recognizing framing techniques, and anticipating the potential consequences of sharing personal information. The influence of algorithms, influencers, and targeted advertising further amplifies the need for awareness, reflection, and discernment in digital communication. As more aspects of daily life, work, and social interactions shift online, users increasingly need to establish trust, coordinate actions, and negotiate outcomes across cultural and linguistic boundaries.

3.7 Level of Content Creation Skills

Findings

Content creation skills refer to the ability to produce high-quality digital materials, including text, images, videos, and music. These skills are among the least developed in the general user population. As illustrated in Fig. 3.6, fewer than half of the survey respondents report knowing how to edit multimedia content such as images, videos, or music, and a similar proportion report being capable of creating remixed media, that is, combining or adapting existing materials to produce something new. Approximately 40 percent feel confident making meaningful adjustments to others' creations, indicating limited skills in creative adaptation and transformation. The task-based performance tests conducted among children highlight similar insufficiencies. Among those tasked with creating a presentation slide, 83 percent added the requested title and bullet points, 70 percent inserted a provided video, 64 percent successfully used an image as a background, and 68 percent changed the color of an image to black and white. The use of AI for content creation is relatively uncommon among the respondents. Approximately 32 percent of the survey respondents report knowing how to use AI to produce high-quality digital materials, while fewer than one in four are able to use AI to design or build websites.

Copyright awareness also remains a significant challenge for many internet users. Fewer than half of the survey respondents report to understand how to use copyrighted material appropriately or are aware of which copyright protections apply to different types of content. This lack of knowledge can lead to unintentional infringement when text, images, videos, or music are reused. Furthermore, approximately 60 percent of the respondents are unaware of how to correctly attribute materials created by others, indicating widespread gaps in the understanding of proper citation practices and intellectual property norms. The emergence of AI-generated content makes copyright awareness even more complex. Fewer than one in four users understand the copyright implications of using AI-generated materials, including questions about ownership, licensing, and ethical use.

Finally, approximately 60 percent of respondents report that they know how to represent others fairly and respectfully in their creative work. This suggests a moderate level of awareness of ethical and inclusive communication principles. However, it also highlights considerable room for

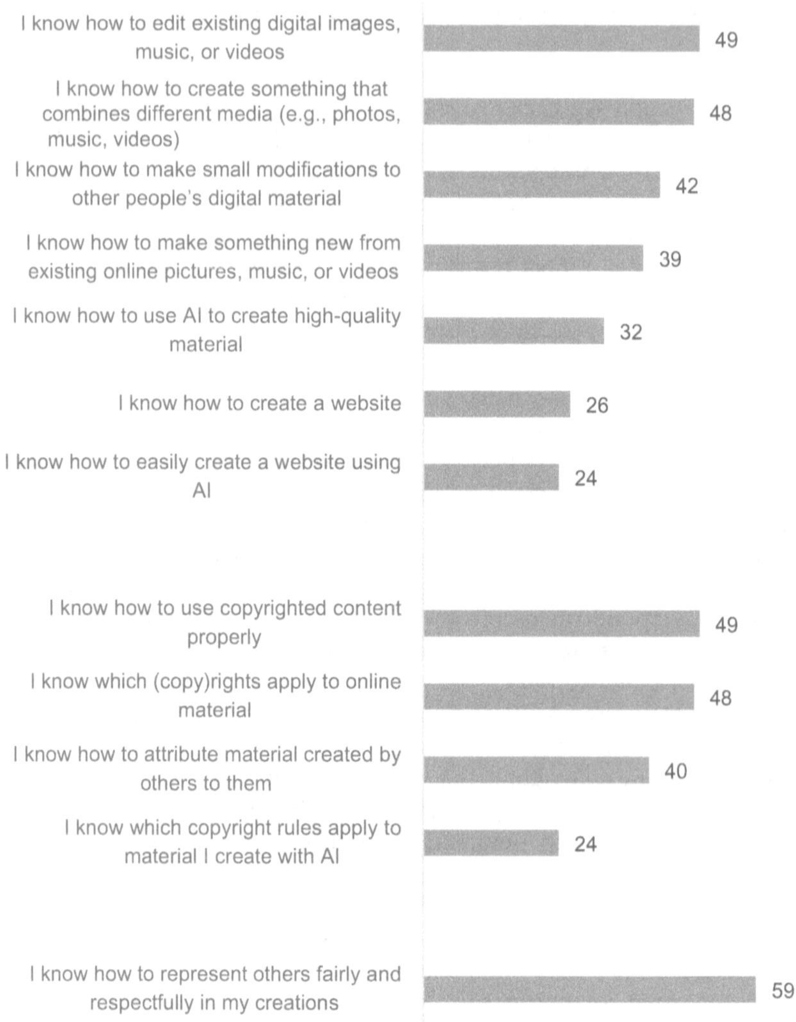

Fig. 3.6 Sufficient mastery of content creation skills components, % of adult population

improvement, as a substantial portion of users may not fully appreciate the social and cultural implications of the portrayal of individuals and groups in digital media. Ethical representation encompasses not only avoiding harmful stereotypes or biased depictions, but also actively promoting diverse, accurate, and respectful portrayals. Inadequate attention to these principles can lead to unintended harm, perpetuate misinformation, and marginalize underrepresented groups.

Conclusions

The importance of content creation skills has grown considerably in recent years. The skills to produce engaging and effective digital content, whether by writing a blog post, designing visuals, or creating videos, have become vital components of participation. Content creation is not only a means of personal expression but also a form of civic engagement; those who can publicly share their ideas, experiences, and creative output actively contribute to shaping online discourse and influencing public opinion. However, content creation skills remain among the least developed digital skills. Although many users can perform basic tasks, more advanced skills, such as editing multimedia, remixing content, and making meaningful adaptations, are limited. While the use of AI for creative purposes is popular, most users are unfamiliar with leveraging intelligent media to enhance their output.

Furthermore, copyright awareness poses a significant challenge. Many users lack an understanding of proper attribution, the legal use of others' materials, and the implications of AI-generated content. As a result, they may inadvertently violate intellectual property regulations or overlook the legal and ethical considerations associated with AI-assisted creations. This gap not only increases the risk of unintentional copyright infringement but also raises broader ethical concerns regarding the ownership and accountability of creative outputs.

Ethical and inclusive representation in content creation is also lacking. Although some users demonstrate an awareness of fairness and respect when portraying others, many do not fully grasp the social and cultural implications of their creative work. Inadequate attention to these principles can perpetuate stereotypes, marginalize underrepresented groups, and contribute to the spread of misinformation.

3.8 Level of Strategic Media Use Skills

Findings

Strategic media use skills are the most advanced set of skills described in this book. These skills build upon other content-related skills; they follow information skills, for example when information searched for is combined, compared, and applied to make optimal decisions. They build on communication skills, for instance, when individuals consult online contacts to reach a well-informed choice. They extend beyond content creation skills, for example when online creations are strategically used to achieve goals in publicity. Strategic media use skills largely determine the overall impact of internet and intelligent media use, allowing individuals to extract the greatest benefit (Fig. 3.7).

Fig. 3.7 Sufficient mastery of strategic media use skill components, % of adult population

The first step in achieving an optimal decision is goal orientation. This refers to an individual's awareness of the opportunities offered by the internet and intelligent media, which then informs the clear definition of a goal. The performance tests on internet skills revealed that many people struggle with goal orientation. Most participants did not carefully consider their desired outcomes or failed to establish a clear goal before starting an online task. Often, they started without a specific plan for what needed to be achieved or how it should be accomplished. Furthermore, maintaining a consistent focus on the assignment's final goal during task completion was challenging. Users were easily distracted by irrelevant online stimuli, which diverted their attention from the task at hand. In some cases, participants did not know how to begin the strategic media use assignments, an unsurprising outcome given the difficulties many people experience with information skills. In the survey, only one statement directly addressed this step, specifically in the context of smart devices: 64 percent of the respondents report that they know how to set realistic goals they want to achieve with these devices.

The second step involves taking appropriate actions to achieve the desired goal. The survey contained a statement measuring whether users know how to leverage AI to maximize their internet use, and just over 40 percent of respondents report positively. Performance tests revealed that over one-third of the participants used online decision-making platforms to support tasks such as choosing a political party or selecting an insurance or healthcare provider. While these platforms have the potential to facilitate informed decisions, users often relied on them uncritically, following the site's guidance without questioning the underlying assumptions or evaluating the content. Many participants failed to recognize whether commercial or persuasive intentions were embedded in the design of the website. Optimal digital decision-making requires the comparison and integration of multiple sources of information. However, a quarter of the participants relied on a single source, ignoring additional resources necessary for a well-considered decision. For example, choosing a political party based on multiple policy standpoints ideally requires visiting official party websites and systematically comparing the party's positions across issues. Interestingly, our tests showed that older users were less likely to restrict themselves to a single site. Finally, over 70 percent of the participants struggled to work in a structured manner. Many tended to surf the internet randomly rather than systematically gathering, comparing, and integrating information piece by piece. Owing to the absence of a methodical approach, they were unable to fully utilize the available digital resources or make well-informed strategic decisions. Performance tests related to activity trackers and smart homes underscore the difficulties users encounter at this stage of strategic media use. For example, participants using activity trackers often struggled to interpret and effectively act on the data they collected. Similarly, creating rules to automate actions in smart home environments proved to be complex. Users frequently faced challenges in selecting the appropriate triggers to initiate specific automations, which often resulted in the underutilization of the system's full capabilities.

The third step of the decision-making process involves selecting the correct option to achieve the desired goal. In the survey, 61 percent of the respondents claim that they generally make better decisions because of online information. Additionally, 58 percent of the respondents indicate that they improved their decisions by seeking advice or input from others online. However, the potential of AI remains largely untapped, with 62 percent reporting that they do not know how to leverage AI to make better decisions. The performance tests presented an even more concerning picture. Even when participants successfully collected relevant information online, many struggled to combine, compare, and evaluate these pieces to make optimal decisions. Over 40 percent of participants made decisions that were ultimately misguided, highlighting that the challenge lies not only in information access but also in the skills to use it effectively. The performance tests related to activity trackers and smart homes were even more troublesome. In both contexts, participants struggled to identify and extract actionable insights from the collected data. Users were generally unable to leverage data and functionalities for meaningful, goal-oriented use. In the case of activity trackers, participants found it difficult to define specific goals that could help them become more active and determine how and when to work toward these goals. Similar challenges emerged in the smart home environment. Users struggled to select actions that aligned with their goals and to determine appropriate triggers for initiating these actions.

Conclusions

Strategic media use skills represent the most advanced set of digital skills, building on information, communication, and content creation skills. They enable users to combine, compare, and apply information, leverage digital tools, and use online creations to achieve specific goals, ultimately determining the overall effectiveness and impact of digital media. Despite their importance, the findings reveal substantial difficulties in users' strategic media use skills. Goal orientation, the skills to define clear objectives and maintain focus, is often weak. Many users begin tasks without a specific plan or clear outcome, become distracted by irrelevant online content, or struggle to maintain their attention. Similarly, taking appropriate actions to achieve goals is challenging for them. While some users leverage decision-making platforms and AI, many rely uncritically on single sources or fail to evaluate information systematically, undermining informed decision-making processes. Performance tests highlight difficulties in structured information gathering, comparison, and integration, as well as in interpreting data from activity trackers and smart home devices. This contradicts the argument that, with the introduction of intelligent media, digital inequality would be primarily a matter of access again, since the autonomous character would automate decision-making and, thus, strategic use. Selecting an appropriate option to achieve the desired outcome is also problematic. Even when users collect relevant information, many struggle to combine, analyze, and apply it effectively. They often fail to translate available data into actionable decisions, resulting in suboptimal outcomes.

3.9 Differences across the Population

Findings

To gain insight into how levels of digital skills vary across the population, we grouped the digital skills statements presented in the previous figures into the seven categories of digital skills, as conceptualized in Chap. 2.[1] Subsequently, regression analyses were conducted to identify the key determinants of the digital skill levels. The independent variables included gender, age, education, income, employment status (work), traditional

[1] Grouping was based on theoretical reasoning rather than statistical techniques. We assessed whether the grouped items demonstrated acceptable reliability (Cronbach's alpha) to ensure internal consistency: Strategic media choice skills $\alpha = 0.70$; operational skills $\alpha = 0.90$; formal skills $\alpha = 0.70$; information skills $\alpha = 0.86$; communication skills $\alpha = 0.77$; content creation skills $\alpha = 0.89$; strategic media use skills $\alpha = 0.85$.

literacy, and social capital.[2] The factors that emerged as statistically significant in the analyses are presented in figures that display the average percentage of respondents who achieved a sufficient level of digital skills.

Figure 3.8 illustrates that strategic media choice skills decline with age. The proportion of individuals with sufficient levels differs by 26 percent between the youngest and oldest groups. These skills also increase with higher levels of education and income, with substantial gaps between the lowest and highest educational and income groups. Furthermore, individuals with below-average traditional literacy are somewhat less likely to demonstrate sufficient strategic media choice skill levels than those with above-average literacy. Finally, employed individuals are more likely to possess sufficient levels than unemployed individuals.

Regarding operational skills, Fig. 3.9 shows that more males than females report possessing a sufficient level. The difference between age groups is substantial: while as many as 92 percent of the youngest group report having a sufficient level, only 50 percent of the oldest group do. In terms of education, individuals with higher educational attainment clearly stand out, while the proportion of respondents with lower education who report having sufficient skills is notably low at 52 percent. The level of these skills also rises with income, following a pattern similar to that observed for education. Respondents with above-average literacy outperform those with below-average literacy. Finally, a higher proportion of employed than unemployed individuals report sufficient operational skills.

As shown in Fig. 3.10, age, education, traditional literacy, and income are significant contributors to formal skills. The share of respondents who self-report a sufficient level of these skills declines with age but rises

[2] Gender: dichotomous variable (male/female). Age: calculated by subtracting the respondent's birth year from the survey year. Education: categorized into three levels based on the highest degree obtained: low (primary), medium (secondary), and high (college/university). Income: assessed by asking for the annual household income over the past 12 months, with twelve response options recoded into three categories: low (<€30,000), medium (€30,000–70,000), and high (>€70,000). Employment status: based on main occupation, with employment used as the predictor. Social capital: measured with the Sherbourne and Stewart (1991) scale of support availability, responses ranging from 1 (never) to 5 (always) (e.g., having someone to trust), 18 items combined into a single scale (α = 0.97; M = 3.75; SD = 1.07), categorized into two levels: below- and above-average social capital. Traditional literacy: measured with the scale of De Greef et al. (2015) (e.g., I have difficulties reading and understanding information from my municipality), responses ranging from 1 (*strongly agree*) to 4 (*strongly disagree*) (α = 0.94), categorized into two levels: below- and above-average traditional literacy.

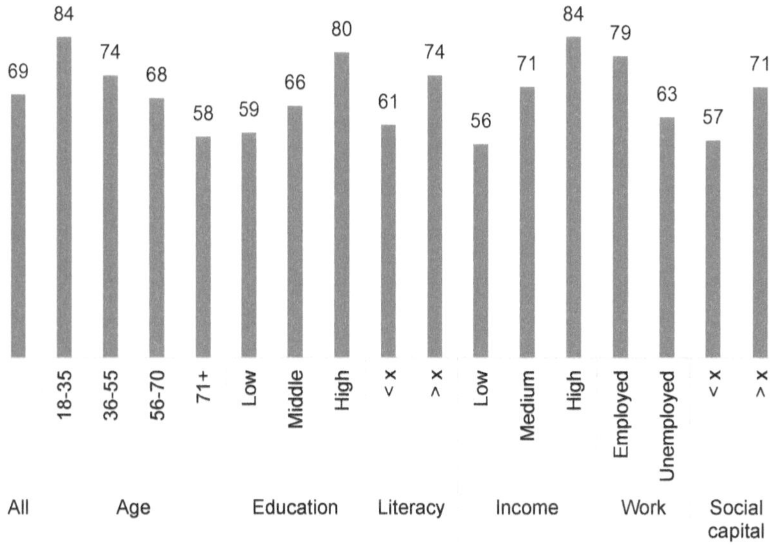

Fig. 3.8 Differences in sufficient mastery of strategic media choice skills, %

with increasing education and income. Notably, a 23 percent difference is observed between individuals with below-average and above-average literacy.

Substantial differences emerge across age and educational attainment regarding information skills. As shown in Fig. 3.11, the gap between respondents aged 18–35 and those over 70 in self-reported sufficient levels of these skills is 46 percent. There is a 40 percent difference between respondents with lower and higher levels of education. Traditional literacy also plays a significant role: individuals with above-average literacy report sufficient information skills 10 percent more often than those with below-average literacy do. Employment status further contributes to disparities, with employed respondents demonstrating sufficient skills 39 percent more frequently than their unemployed counterparts.

For communication skills, the percentage of respondents reporting a sufficient level decrease with age, although the decline is less pronounced than for information skills. See Fig. 3.12. Still, the difference between the youngest and oldest age groups amounts to 33 percent. Traditional literacy again emerges as a significant predictor: among individuals with

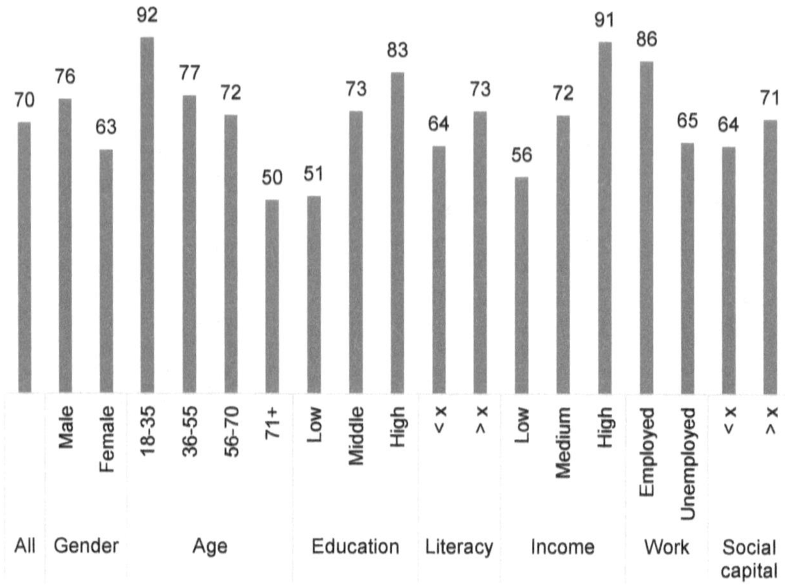

Fig. 3.9 Differences in sufficient mastery of operational skills, %

below-average reading and writing proficiency, 65 percent report having sufficient communication skills, compared to 78 percent among those with above-average literacy. Employment status also shows a notable effect, with an 18 percent gap between employed and unemployed respondents. Furthermore, social capital is positively associated with communication skills, with a 14 percent difference between respondents with below- and above-average social capital.

Regarding content creation skills, substantial differences are observed across gender, age, educational attainment, and employment status. As shown in Fig. 3.13, men report sufficient levels of these skills 8 percent more often than women. A strong decline with age is evident: while 55 percent of respondents in the youngest age group report sufficient competence, only 16 percent of those in the oldest group report so. Educational attainment also plays a significant role, with a 20 percent gap between respondents with lower and higher education levels. Employed respondents report sufficient content creation skills 23 percent more frequently than their unemployed counterparts.

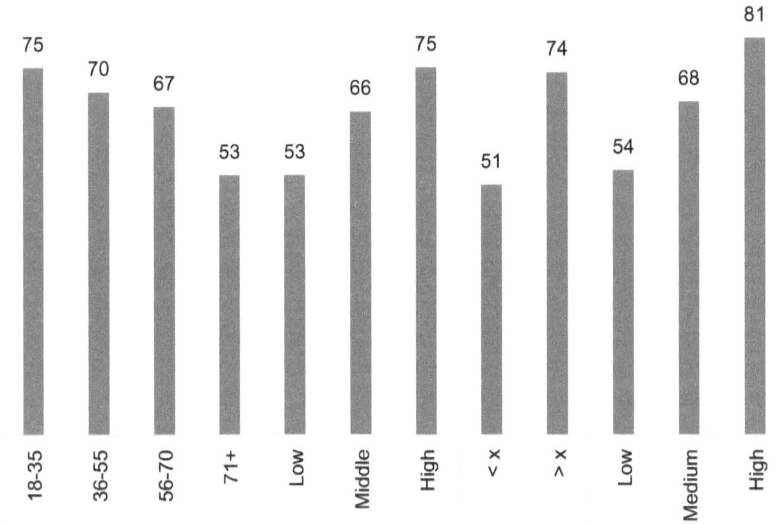

Fig. 3.10 Differences in sufficient mastery of formal skills, %

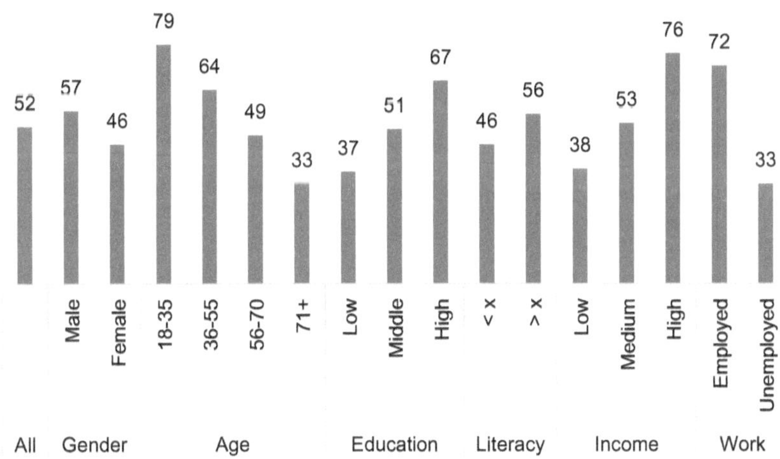

Fig. 3.11 Differences in sufficient mastery of information skills, %

Finally, Fig. 3.14 presents the differences across groups in terms of strategic media use skills. A relatively small gender gap is observed, with 8 percent more males than females reporting higher levels of these skills. Age again shows a strong variation, with 79 percent of the youngest group reporting sufficient levels compared with only 25 percent in the oldest group. Education is also an important factor: 61 percent of higher-educated respondents report sufficient levels, compared to 33 percent among those with lower education. Traditional literacy again emerges as a significant predictor: 38 percent of respondents with below-average literacy report sufficient strategic media use skills, compared to 58 percent among those with above-average literacy. The proportion of respondents with sufficient skills also rises with income, showing a 36 percent difference between the lowest and highest-income groups. Employment status further contributes to the variation, with employed individuals scoring 27 percent higher than unemployed respondents.

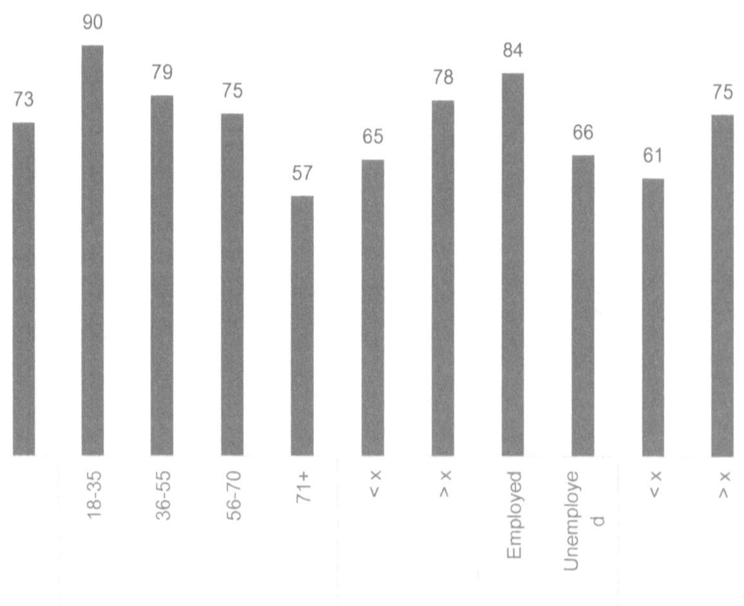

Fig. 3.12 Differences in sufficient mastery of communication skills, %

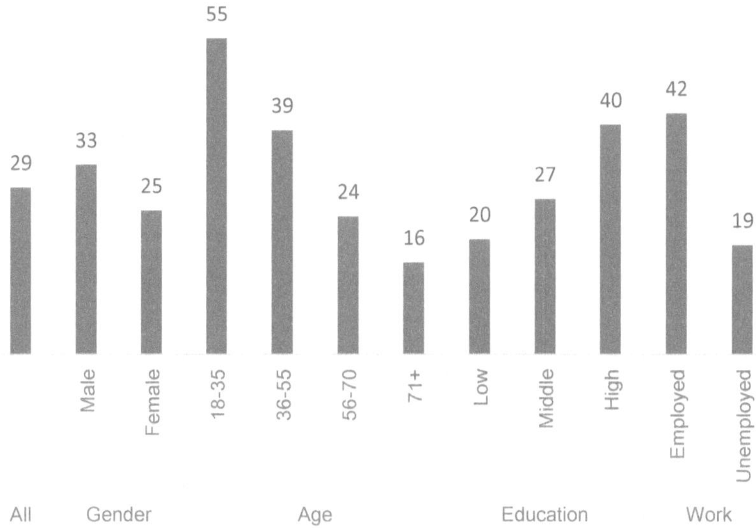

Fig. 3.13 Differences in sufficient mastery of content creation skills, %

Conclusions

The levels of digital skills are unevenly distributed across the population and vary according to several background characteristics. Men reported slightly higher levels of operational, content creation, and strategic media skills. However, these differences were observed primarily in self-assessments, and men are known to rate their digital skills higher than women. Notably, gender disparities in digital skills were much larger two decades ago. One contributing factor to the narrowing gender gap is the increasing parity in higher education attainment between men and women in developed countries. As education is a strong predictor of digital skills, this trend is reflected in diminishing gender differences.

With respect to age, younger individuals tend to outperform older adults. Respondents aged 18–35 displayed the highest proportion of sufficient digital skills across all seven domains, whereas those aged over 70 demonstrated comparatively low skill levels. The 56–70 age group also showed substantial room for improvement. Nevertheless, this does not imply that younger groups do not require support. Labels such as *digital natives* or *net generation* reinforce the misconception that all young people are inherently proficient in digital media use. Performance tests

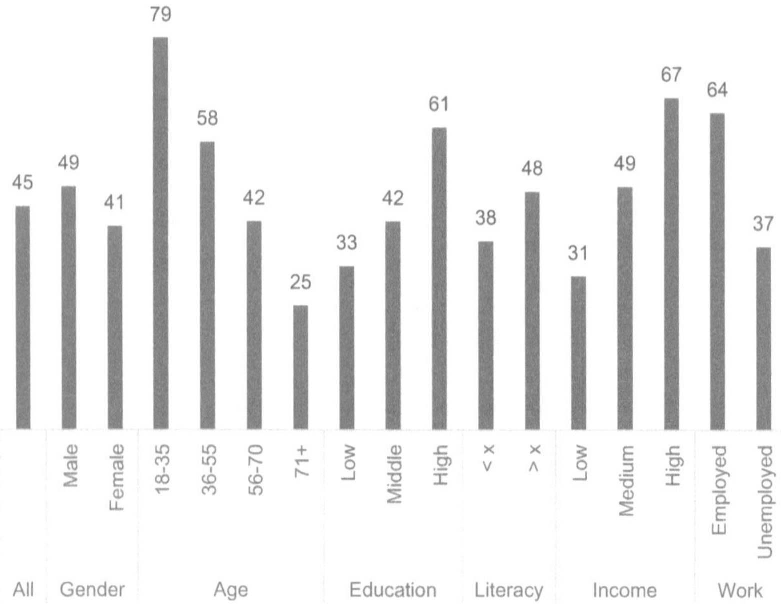

Fig. 3.14 Differences in sufficient mastery of strategic media use skills, %

among young people reveal a highly uneven distribution of digital skills. Moreover, previous research has shown that when older adults possess sufficient medium-related digital skills, they can outperform younger users in information and strategic media use skills (Van Deursen et al., 2011).

The findings further indicate that digital skill levels increase with educational attainment. This pattern exacerbates the already vulnerable position of lower-educated individuals who face heightened risks of exclusion in a society where digital skills are essential for participation. Many individuals in this group work in occupations that offer limited opportunities to develop digital skills, whereas higher levels of digital skills are increasingly recognized and rewarded in the labor market. This dynamic provides additional advantages to those with higher education, thereby reinforcing existing social and economic inequalities (Falck et al., 2016). A similar pattern is evident for traditional literacy. It is important to note that the survey sample did not contain responses from individuals with low literacy, as they are unable to complete questionnaires. Consequently, the observed differences between those with below-average and above-average literacy are likely underestimated, and the true disparities in the population are larger. Given the strong relationship between digital skills and traditional literacy, improving digital skills should not be addressed in isolation (Van Deursen & Van Dijk, 2016).

As with education, considerable differences are also observed across income groups. The gaps between the lowest- and highest-income respondents were particularly pronounced for operational and strategic media use skills. Furthermore, employed individuals reported higher digital skill levels than unemployed respondents across nearly all skills, with the largest disparities found in information, content creation, and strategic media use. These findings highlight the workplace as a key environment for developing digital skills and underscore the risk of compounding disadvantages for unemployed individuals over time.

Finally, individuals with stronger social networks reported better communication skills, suggesting that social resources play an important role in supporting media use. Robust social networks provide more opportunities for online collaboration, participation in forums, and content sharing. Moreover, being part of a digitally active community may encourage individuals to adopt new platforms and experiment with emerging features.

3.10 Conclusions

The findings of this chapter reveal several areas of digital skills that require attention. From a medium-related skill perspective, *strategic media choice skills* are crucial in today's diverse media landscape but remain underdeveloped. Many users rely on habitual or convenience-based decisions rather than conscious, ethical, and goal-oriented media and platform choices. The growing influence of AI complicates these decisions, underscoring the need for responsible AI use, including reflections on transparency, privacy, and bias awareness. *Operational skills* are generally well developed for everyday tasks, such as managing browsers and smart devices, yet users often face challenges with more complex operations, pointing to a need for targeted guidance, training, and intuitive design. The levels of *formal skills* also leave much room for improvement as a substantial number of users become disoriented toward complex platforms or misinterpret design cues. Enhancing their understanding of navigation patterns and design conventions, supported by more intuitive interfaces, can strengthen confidence and autonomy.

From a content-related skill perspective, *information skills* emerge as a major weakness. Many users struggle to define search goals, formulate effective queries, and critically evaluate information, often relying uncritically on top-ranked results or AI-generated outputs. Strengthening information skills empowers people to distinguish between facts, opinions, and misinformation and to understand algorithmic bias. *Communication skills* are generally adequate for routine exchanges, but weaker when it comes to adapting tone, managing online identity, applying netiquette, and addressing privacy concerns. Enhancing the strategic, evaluative, and socially aware dimensions of communication is crucial for enabling safer, more effective, and socially responsible engagement in online communities. *Content creation skills* remain among the least developed. Users often demonstrate limited awareness of copyright issues (particularly regarding AI-generated content) and ethical content use. Targeted education and training are needed to cultivate responsible and socially aware content creators. Finally, *strategic media use skills* remain highly underdeveloped as many users lack goal orientation, planning, and critical decision-making when engaging with internet and intelligent media. Strengthening these skills is essential for fostering goal-directed and meaningful participation.

The findings highlight considerable room for improvement across all digital skills. Combined with the demonstrated impact of digital skills discussed in the following chapter, this underscores the need for comprehensive digital inclusion policies. At present, only a relatively small and highly skilled group appears to fully understand how internet and intelligent media function. Several of the more advanced digital skills receive limited policy and educational attention. This is partly due to insufficient knowledge about how different user groups best acquire these skills and partly because designers do not always, whether consciously or unconsciously, develop inclusive user experiences. Particular attention is needed to address digital skills within the context intelligent media. The findings reveal that autonomous operations do not diminish the importance of digital skills; rather, they amplify it. As AI and IoT become more complex and integrated into everyday life, certain skills—such as understanding algorithmic decision-making, managing data privacy, and exercising informed control over automated systems—are becoming both more critical and more challenging to master.

The observations raise the question of whether acquiring advanced digital skills is feasible for everyone. The findings show that digital skills are unevenly distributed across the population and vary according to multiple background characteristics. Since digital inequalities will not disappear on their own, and digital media are essential for addressing complex tasks across all areas of life, it is crucial to identify which groups lack which skills to enable more effective and targeted interventions. For example, the role of traditional literacy—reading, writing, and interpreting textual and numerical information—remains essential for evaluating the reliability of sources, recognizing misinformation, and understanding the motives behind how texts are presented. Initiatives aimed at improving digital skills should include programs that strengthen reading, writing, and text comprehension. Such findings point to a need for targeted, context-sensitive initiatives that apply to broader digital skills in general internet use—where there is currently limited knowledge about why many programs fail to achieve their goals—and intelligent media such as AI and IoT. Effective interventions should begin by mapping the challenges faced by diverse groups and identifying the approaches that work best. Without targeted support, digital inequalities are likely to intensify, reinforcing the already strong position of the digital elite. This group continues to expand its advantage, including in developing skills for human-AI collaboration, while vulnerable populations fall further behind as media evolve and societal expectations rise.

References

De Boer, P. S., Van Deursen, A. J. A. M., & Van Rompay, T. J. (2020). Internet-of-things skills among the general population: Task-based performance test using activity trackers. *JMIR Human Factors, 7*(4), e22532.

De Boer, P. S., Van Deursen, A. J. A. M., & Van Rompay, T. J. (2023). Health on the move—Can we keep up? Activity tracker performance test to measure data and strategic skills. *International Journal of Human–Computer Interaction, 39*(17), 3377–3387.

De Greef, M., Segers, M., Nijhuis, J., Lam, J. F., van Groenestijn, M., Van Hoek, F., ... & Tubbing, M. (2015). The development and validation of testing materials for literacy, numeracy and digital skills in a Dutch context. *International Review of Education, 61*(5), 655–671.

De Boer, P. S., Van Deursen, A. J. A. M., & Van Rompay, T. J. (2024). The lights are on, but no one's home: A performance test to measure digital skills to use IoT home automation. *New Media & Society, 26*(9), 5259–5290.

Falck, O., Wiederhold, S., & Heimisch, A. (2016). Returns to ICT Skills (OECD Education Working Papers No. 134).

Helsper, E. J., Schneider, L. S., Van Deursen, A. J. A. M., & Van Laar, E. (2020). *The youth Digital Skills Indicator: Report on the conceptualisation and development of the ySKILLS digital skills measure*. ySKILLS.

Palczyńska, M., & Rynko, M. (2021). ICT skills measurement in social surveys: Can we trust self-reports? *Quality & Quantity, 55*(3), 917–943.

Statistics Netherlands. (2023). *Digital proficiency continues to rise*. https://www.cbs.nl/en-gb/news/2023/45/digital-proficiency-continues-to-rise

Statistics Netherlands. (2024). *Internettoegang en internetactiviteiten; persoonskenmerken*. Retrieved from https://www.cbs.nl/nl-nl/cijfers/detail/84888NED

Sherbourne, C. D., & Stewart, A. L. (1991). The MOS social support survey. *Social Science & Medicine, 32*(6), 705–714.

Van Deursen, A. J. A. M. (2012). Internet skill-related problems in accessing online health information. *International Journal of Medical Informatics, 81*(1), 61–72.

Van Deursen, A. J. A. M., De Boer, P. S., & Van Rompay, T. J. (2025). Smart devices require skilled users: Home automation performance tests among the Dutch population. *International Journal of Human–Computer Interaction, 41*(2), 1688–1699.

Van Deursen, A. J. A. M., & Helsper, E. J. (2020). *Digitale vaardigheden: Een onderzoeks- en beleidsagenda*. Centrum voor Digitale Inclusie, Universiteit Twente.

Van Deursen, A. J. A. M., Helsper, E. J., & Eynon, R. (2016). Development and validation of the Internet Skills Scale (ISS). *Information, Communication & Society, 19*(6), 804–823.

Van Deursen, A. J. A. M., & Van Diepen, S. (2013). Information and strategic Internet skills of secondary students: A performance test. *Computers & Education, 63*, 218–226.

Van Deursen, A. J. A. M., & Van Dijk, J. A. G. M. (2009). Using the Internet: Skill related problems in users' online behavior. *Interacting with Computers, 21*(5–6), 393–402.

Van Deursen, A. J. A. M., & Van Dijk, J. A. G. M. (2011a). Internet skills and the digital divide. *New Media & Society, 13*(6), 893–911.

Van Deursen, A. J. A. M., & van Dijk, J. A. G. M. (2011b). Internet skills performance tests: Are people ready for eHealth? *Journal of Medical Internet Research, 13*(2), e1581.

Van Deursen, A. J. A. M., & Van Dijk, J. A. G. M. (2016). Modeling traditional literacy, Internet skills and Internet usage: An empirical study. *Interacting with Computers, 28*(1), 13–26.

Van Deursen, A. J. A. M., Van Dijk, J. A. G. M., & Peters, O. (2011). Rethinking Internet skills: The contribution of gender, age, education, Internet experience, and hours online to medium-and content-related Internet skills. *Poetics, 39*(2), 125–144.

Van Deursen, A. J. A. M., Görzig, A., Van Delzen, M., Perik, H., & Stegeman, A.G. (2014). Primary school children's internet skills: A report on performance tests of operational, formal, information, and strategic internet skills. *International Journal of Communication, 8*, 13643–13656.

Van Deursen, A. J. A. M., Van Laar, E., Helsper, E. J., & Schneider, L. S. (2023). *The youth Digital Skills Performance Test Results: Report on the results of real-life information navigation and processing, communication and interaction, and content creation and production skills tasks*. ySKILLS.

Van Laar, E., Van Deursen, A. J. A. M., Helsper, E. J., & Schneider, L. S. (2025). Developing performance tests to measure digital skills: Lessons learned from a cross-national perspective. *Media and Communication, 13*, 8988.

CHAPTER 4

Impact of Digital Skills

4.1 Introduction: The Social Context of Digital Skills

Discussions of digital skills are often framed in terms of formal training and education. Attention is typically directed toward the design of courses, training programs, and curricula, the identification of necessary skills, and the selection of target groups along with suitable didactic approaches to meet specific educational needs. Rather than focusing narrowly on educational solutions, this book seeks to develop a broader social understanding of the background and consequences of digital skills. Drawing on perspectives from the social sciences and sociology, it examines not only how digital skills are acquired, but also why disparities in these skills persist and what social consequences they entail. Addressing the lack of digital skills observed in the previous chapter requires solutions that extend beyond education, engaging with the structural, cultural, and societal factors that shape digital inequality.

To address the consequences of unequal digital skills, we turn to a theoretical framework designed to explain variations in both access to digital technologies and the skills required to use them: Resources and Appropriation Theory (Van Dijk, 2005, 2020a). As illustrated in Fig. 1.1, effective and meaningful usage of internet and connected intelligent media depends on motivation, material access, and digital skills. Figure 4.1 further demonstrates that this appropriation process is shaped by both social and technological context. The *social context* encompasses personal and positional inequalities among users. As discussed

A. van Deursen and J. van Dijk, *Digital Skills*, Digital Education and Learning, https://doi.org/10.1057/978-1-349-96162-7_4

in the previous chapter, disparities in digital skills are associated with several factors, including age, educational background, traditional literacy, health, employment status, and school enrollment—relationships that are examined in greater detail in Chap. 6. These personal characteristics and social positions determine the resources available to individuals, which represent the most critical intermediary factor, summarized in Box 4.1. These resources directly influence motivation, access, digital skills, and usage of digital media. Resources do not operate in isolation; rather, they interact in ways that either amplify or constrain a person's engagement with internet and intelligent media. For example, young people's comparatively advanced operational and formal digital skills may stem from their temporal resources (ample free time to explore media and platforms), social resources (peer networks that facilitate knowledge exchange, active participation, and skill sharing), cultural resources (the personal enjoyment and social recognition associated with digital skills), and mental resources (cognitive development shaped by growing up in a digital media landscape). However, this is less evident among young people in developing countries, who might lack the material resources necessary to access and learn digital media. Consequently, their opportunities to acquire and refine digital skills are severely constrained, regardless of motivation.

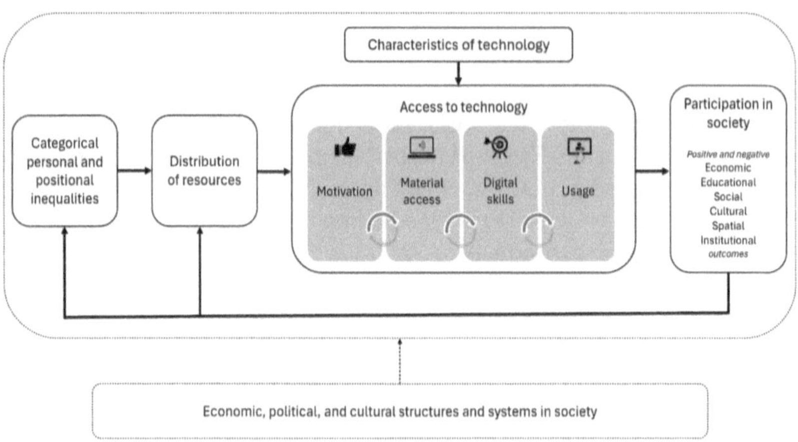

Fig. 4.1 A causal model of resources and appropriation theory (after Van Dijk, 2005)

Box 4.1 Overview of Resources People Have

- *Temporal* resources: Time to engage meaningfully with digital media. Without sufficient time, individuals may struggle to gain experience, deepen their understanding, or make full use of the opportunities.
- *Material* resources: Tangible assets and financial means that enable access to digital media.
- *Mental* resources: The cognitive capabilities needed to use digital media effectively. This covers general intelligence, problem-solving skills, and the capacity to learn using digital media, as well as specific technical know-how.
- *Social* resources: The support and assistance available through one's social network or surrounding environment.
- *Cultural* resources: The knowledge, values, and symbolic capital that influence how and why digital media are used. This includes a personal appreciation for digital media (enjoyment, curiosity) as well as the social prestige or recognition gained from using certain media or platforms.

The appropriation process in terms of motivation, material access, skills, and usage is also affected by the *technological context* of digital media. Technological characteristics not only influence how individuals engage with technology but also how digital skills are developed and sustained. Chapter 5 examines how designers can integrate considerations of digital skills into the development process and how design choices affect users' adoption of technology, the speed at which they acquire skills, and the depth of their engagement. An intuitive medium or platform that demands minimal prior knowledge is more likely to encourage experimentation and sustained use. Smart devices exemplify this by combining mobility with simplified and personalized interfaces that allow users to interact through touchscreens, voice commands, or apps. These characteristics make them accessible at first glance, lowering the immediate threshold for engagement. Moreover, many smart devices operate with autonomous or semi-autonomous features, such as automatic software updates, adjusting settings, filtering content, and providing personalized recommendations. Such automation might suggest that digital skills have become less critical, since smart devices increasingly work in the background and make certain decisions for users (Van Deursen & Mossberger, 2018). Paradoxically, without the skills to operate smart devices, retrieve, manage, and interpret collected data, and use them strategically, the potential benefits are difficult to achieve. In this sense, the ease of initial use does not necessarily translate into depth of effective use, and those lacking digital skills risk becoming passive consumers rather than active and critical participants.

Figure 4.1 shows that the primary consequence of the differential appropriation of digital media is unequal participation across various societal domains. This idea forms the core argument of this chapter and has gained increasing scholarly attention through the concept of the *third-level digital divide*, which highlights disparities in the actual outcomes individuals achieve from their internet use (Wei et al., 2011; Van Deursen & Helsper, 2015). Engagement with specific types of content, activities, and services in the media landscape can lead to both positive and negative outcomes. These outcomes either enhance or diminish a person's temporal, material, mental, social, or cultural resources. As these resources shape how individuals interact with digital media, social inequalities are associated with digital inequalities: existing social inequalities influence what outcomes are achieved from internet and intelligent media, which, in turn, reinforce the original social disparities. Those who lag in motivation, access, digital skills, or actual usage are less likely to fully benefit from the opportunities provided by the internet and intelligent media. This can directly, consciously or unconsciously, affect their daily lives. Over time, these disadvantages tend to accumulate, creating a self-reinforcing cycle in which digital exclusion exacerbates existing social inequalities (Van Dijk, 2005, 2020a). The degree of participation feeds back into personal and positional inequalities, either by building new resources or depleting them.

Recognizing that inequalities throughout the appropriation process of digital media, including disparities in digital skills, perpetuate and intensify broader social inequalities, highlights that digital skills are not an end goal in themselves. Rather, they are a crucial means to achieve a broader objective: promoting an individual's well-being and meaningful participation in society. Digital skills encompass engaging with a wide spectrum of media, whether traditional, digital, and converged, in ways that are both autonomous and responsible. Importantly, this does not always mean increased use; it can also involve making informed choices to avoid or bypass media that may be harmful, distracting, or irrelevant (Van Deursen & Helsper, 2021). Among the factors involved in the appropriation process, digital skills are pivotal. They are essential for translating access and usage into meaningful outcomes, whether in education, employment, social connections, or civic engagement. Research suggests that the level of digital skills often outweighs the mere availability of resources in achieving positive outcomes (Van Deursen & Helsper, 2018). Thus, digital skills serve as the key to unlocking the potential of a smart society, where technology integration is not only widespread but also effective and empowering for all individuals. Without adequate skills, even the best digital media and platforms remain underutilized or misused, limiting their potential benefits.

The following section explores in greater detail the various domains of participation influenced by digital skills and how they shape opportunities and inequalities across society. Before addressing these domains, it is important to note that the process of appropriation is affected by broader political, economic, and cultural systems and structures (Van Deursen & Helsper, 2021). These not only influence the form and nature of the media landscape but also play a decisive role in enabling or constraining the resources that individuals can access and mobilize in their interactions with internet and connected intelligent media. For instance, government policies and regulations impact the availability and quality of internet infrastructure. Decisions regarding broadband rollout, net neutrality, data privacy, and digital skills programs can either expand or restrict internet access for different segments of the population. Similarly, economic systems and market dynamics shape the affordability and availability of devices, software, and digital services. The pricing of smartphones, tablets, and internet subscriptions is influenced by factors such as competition, subsidies, taxation, and global supply chains. Cultural norms and values profoundly influence media platforms, formats, and content embraced or marginalized within society. Attitudes toward privacy, trust in technology, language preferences, and social practices determine the popularity and legitimacy of certain digital spaces. Together, these forces shape not only the media landscape but also the distribution of resources that individuals rely on to engage effectively with digital media. Understanding this broader context is important for addressing digital inequalities and designing interventions that promote equitable access and meaningful participation.

4.2 What Is At Stake: Digital Skills as Enablers of Participation

In a smart society, digital media use is deeply woven into almost every aspect of daily life, shaping how individuals communicate, learn, work, and engage with others. Consequently, participation in key areas of life increasingly depends on one's skills to utilize digital media effectively. Without sufficient digital skills, individuals risk social exclusion, which limits their access to essential information, services, and opportunities, many of which are now available primarily through digital platforms. Moreover, as the digital and physical worlds become increasingly interconnected, new forms of collaboration, social interaction, and innovation have emerged. This growing interdependence makes digital skills even more critical; those who fall behind risk becoming progressively more marginalized. In this section, we explore the domains of participation in which digital skills play a crucial role and examine how these skills impact individuals' opportunities and inclusion in society. We examine participation in economic, educational, political, social, cultural, spatial, and institutional domains (Van Dijk, 2005).

Economic Participation

Economic participation can be understood broadly as how people take part in the economy through various forms of work, production, consumption, and finances. In today's job market, every job seeker understands that digital skills are essential for finding and securing employment. Most job listings are posted online, and applications are increasingly submitted through digital portals. Digital skills empower jobseekers to efficiently search for relevant positions, upload resumes, complete application forms, and communicate professionally with potential employers via email or messaging platforms. Beyond the application process, digital skills enable candidates to thoroughly research companies and industries, allowing them to prepare effectively for interviews. Additionally, creating and maintaining a professional online presence, such as a professional social networking profile or personal portfolio, has become a key factor in standing out to recruiters and expanding one's professional network.

Employers increasingly require proof of digital skills during hiring processes, frequently requesting certifications or other evidence. Today, most jobs require familiarity with various applications, including communication platforms, project management applications, and data analysis software. Mastering these applications is essential for maintaining productivity and meeting the expectations of the workplace. As AI becomes increasingly embedded in organizational processes, workers are also expected to develop skills in effectively interacting with AI-driven tools, such as decision-support systems, automation software, and generative AI applications. Effective human–AI collaboration maintains worker decision-making autonomy while utilizing AI as a resource for performance enhancement (rather than as a substitute for human labor). The growing prevalence of telecommuting and virtual collaboration further highlights the importance of digital skills, as workers must use video conferencing tools, cloud-based services, and collaborative platforms to perform their duties effectively in remote or hybrid settings.

The economic advantages of digital skills are multifaceted. Higher earnings potential and better job opportunities often arise from increased productivity associated with skilled internet use and improved access to information. For organizations that rely on skilled employees to achieve high productivity and profitability, AI adoption has become a strategic necessity (Hughes et al., 2026). Digital skills facilitate faster and more efficient communication, provide greater access to continuous learning opportunities, and lead to higher job satisfaction and stronger commitment to one's role (DiMaggio & Bonikowski, 2008). Individuals with strong communication skills are better able to leverage their social networks and use their relationships to gain information about job openings and career advancement. Moreover, demonstrating digital skills during interactions with employers signals candidates' qualifications and adaptability, which are highly valued in the modern workforce (Rahmat et al., 2022).

Economic participation extends beyond obtaining and performing a job. It also involves active engagement in the broader market economy as both consumer and producer. This participation increasingly depends on digital skills that enable individuals to interact effectively with online markets and digital platforms. Engaging in buying and selling activities online requires the skills to make informed purchasing decisions, compare prices across platforms, evaluate the credibility of sellers, and conduct secure online transactions. Using price comparison engines or customer review systems directly influences the quality and safety of these interactions. Moreover, successful participation in digital marketplaces demands communication, negotiation, and strategic decision-making. These are particularly important in more dynamic environments like online auctions, where participants must interpret real-time information, anticipate others' behavior, and respond rapidly to shifting market conditions.

Financial participation in the digital economy increasingly depends on individuals' digital skills to use mobile banking, digital wallets, and online payment platforms. These require not only basic digital skills but also skills to locate, interpret, and apply online financial information and procedures. These skills enable individuals to check balances, transfer funds, pay bills, and save or invest using digital (mobile) media and platforms. Moreover, digital skills provide access to digital financial markets, including online stock trading, investment platforms, and cryptocurrency exchanges. Participation in these markets demands a combination of operational and formal skills to navigate trading interfaces safely, protect sensitive personal and financial data, and implement secure online practices, as well as information and strategic media use skills to interpret market data, evaluate risks, and make informed investment decisions.

Educational Participation

Educational participation refers to the extent to which individuals engage in formal education—specifically, whether they enroll in, attend, and complete different levels of schooling such as primary, secondary, and tertiary education. It is a key indicator of social and economic development, as high levels of participation are generally associated with greater literacy, improved employment outcomes, reduced poverty, and stronger civic engagement. In developed countries, the use of the internet is firmly embedded in curricula across all levels of education. This integration takes several forms. In some education systems, digital media are introduced as dedicated subjects such as *Informatics*, *Data literacy*, or *Media* Literacy. In others, they are treated as a cross-curricular theme, integrated across multiple subjects (e.g., mathematics, languages, science, and the arts) rather than taught in isolation. A further approach embeds these media directly in teaching practice: rather than being the subject of instruction, digital media and platforms are used as everyday teaching resources, including online learning environments. Moreover, the integration of digital media extends to teacher education and professional development, where training programs prepare educators to effectively incorporate digital media into their classrooms. Although the degree of embedding varies widely by country and school system, in practice, attending school in developed contexts has become almost synonymous with acquiring at least basic digital skill levels.

Intelligent media are further transforming the educational landscape. AI applications such as adaptive learning platforms, automated tutoring systems, and AI-driven content creation have introduced many possibilities for personalized education. They enable to analyze learner data in real time to adjust the pace, content, and complexity of instruction, thereby providing tailored learning experiences that address individual strengths and challenges. Immediate, automated feedback mechanisms also enhance learner engagement and autonomy, allowing students to monitor their own progress and make informed adjustments to their learning strategies. In addition, cloud-based collaboration platforms, virtual classrooms, and real-time translation systems have expanded the boundaries of traditional education by enabling interaction and cooperation among learners across different geographical backgrounds. Such innovations underscore the growing importance of advanced digital skills. Learners and educators alike must possess the skills to critically evaluate AI-generated information, understand algorithmic bias, and manage digital interactions ethically and safely. Skills in data privacy, cybersecurity awareness, and the strategic use of intelligent learning tools are becoming increasingly important.

In primary education, many children gain early exposure to digital media at home, often before they enter school. Once in school, this familiarity is expanded through structured instruction, with an emphasis on using digital media for educational purposes rather than entertainment. As will be discussed in Chap. 6, primary and secondary education tends to concentrate on the development of operational, formal and, to some extent, informational skills. These skills have become prerequisites for full participation in education at every stage, from initial schooling to adulthood. Completing formal education without these skills is virtually impossible. Advanced information skills, along with strategic media choice, communication, content creation, and strategic media use skills, are equally critical. The role of education extends beyond academic achievement and serves as preparation for sustainable societal engagement. These skills are increasingly essential for obtaining opportunities related to online courses, professional development programs, and digital certification pathways. However, these skills are often not embedded in mainstream instruction. When they are taught, they are often narrowly applied to curriculum-driven tasks, such as completing assignments or preparing for exams, rather than being integrated into broader, lifelong learning strategies. Communication skills for digital interaction and content creation are mainly addressed in isolated media-education classes.

Political Participation

Political participation encompasses the ways in which citizens engage with political life and influence public decision-making. It spans a spectrum from formal and institutionalized forms of engagement such as voting, joining political parties, or participating in public consultations, to informal and expressive activities, including forming opinions, engaging in political discussions, or supporting social causes outside established structures. Traditionally, these forms have been classified into dimensions such as conventional and unconventional, electoral and non-electoral, and individual and collective participation. Digital media and platforms have given rise to a new dimension, namely online participation or teledemocracy. The internet grants people broad access to political information, express opinions, and coordinate collective action. Through forums, blogs, social media platforms, and news aggregators, individuals can follow political developments in real time, engage in debate, and mobilize around causes with unprecedented speed and reach. These spaces support not only information dissemination but also active engagement, blurring the traditional boundaries between political actors and audiences. Intelligent media further extend these possibilities. Online voting guides, digital petitions, and referenda platforms facilitate participation in electoral processes, while AI-powered chatbots and recommendation systems deliver tailored political information or assist users with voter registration. Cloud-based collaboration and real-time translation systems further open participation to multilingual and cross-cultural publics, supporting the collective and global dimensions of political life.

However, these innovations come with challenges. The spread of misinformation and algorithmic bias threatens the quality and integrity of public discourse. Think of *filter bubbles* when recommendation systems show content aligned with prior preferences. As a result, individuals are less exposed to diverse perspectives, leading to fragmented and increasingly polarized public debates. Moreover, the mere availability of digital media does not ensure their effective or equitable use. Persistent inequalities in motivational access, material access, and digital skills limit participation for many citizens, particularly those with lower levels of education or socioeconomic status. Engaging meaningfully in online political discussions and digital decision-making processes requires a combination of information, communication, content creation, and strategic media use skills, which as we have seen in the prior chapter, remain unevenly distributed. Thus, while internet and intelligent media can democratize participation and enhance civic empowerment, they also risk reinforcing existing inequalities if digital skills are not widely cultivated.

Social Participation

Social participation refers to the various ways in which people engage with activities, networks, and interactions within their communities or society at large. It encompasses an individual's involvement in and connection to networks that provide access to knowledge, resources, and social support. Social participation spans a spectrum of relationships—from strong ties, such as family members and close friends, who provide emotional intimacy and direct support, to weak ties, such as acquaintances, colleagues, or interest-based connections, who offer valuable information, opportunities, or instrumental assistance. These networks often emerge through shared activities, common interests, cultural or religious affiliations, and familial or other relational bonds, and they are frequently situated within the private or semi-private sphere of life. Beyond personal benefits, such networks can facilitate social integration, trust-building, and the circulation of resources.

The advent of the internet and intelligent media has expanded the scope of social participation by facilitating communication, sustaining relationships, and fostering a broader sense of community. Social networking sites, online communication platforms, and AI-powered platforms serve as important instruments for maintaining and expanding social networks, complementing and reinforcing offline interactions. AI-driven recommendation systems, virtual assistants, and adaptive social platforms, can personalize content, suggest relevant social connections, and highlight opportunities for social engagement, making online social participation more targeted and efficient. By enabling frequent, tailored interaction, intelligent media can further enhance self-esteem, strengthen perceived social support, and promote overall well-being, especially among younger users who are highly socially active online (Best et al., 2014). Beyond personal interactions, intelligent media also expand opportunities for collective and community-oriented activities. Crowdfunding and crowdsourcing platforms increasingly use AI algorithms to optimize visibility, connect like-minded contributors, and improve coordination for local initiatives such as community gardens, cultural events, or neighborhood improvement projects. They empower individuals to participate more effectively in social projects, civic initiatives, and collaborative problem-solving, overcoming traditional barriers of geography, time, and resources. Moreover, intelligent media facilitate cross-cultural and intergenerational engagement, enabling users to access broader communities.

The positive effects of online social networking (mediated by intelligent media) do not exist for all individuals in the same way or to the same extent. Although these platforms have gained widespread popularity across various demographic groups, their usage remains the highest among younger people and those with higher education levels (Gottfried, 2024). Successful interactions depend on clear and empathetic exchanges and involve skills such as initiating contact and maintaining dialogue. Strong communication skills are essential for forming and sustaining relationships. Equally important are the skills to manage one's self-presentation: individuals must craft their profiles using text, images, and other visual cues in ways that attract new contacts, maintain existing connections, and encourage meaningful engagement. These dynamics are particularly evident in online dating, where users must navigate a wide pool of potential partners. This process demands not only strong information skills, such as selecting and evaluating suitable candidates, but also skills to create appealing profiles and filter out unwanted attention. Finally, effective social participation extends beyond individual interactions to collective engagement. Actively joining and contributing to online or offline associations illustrates a higher-order form of strategic media use, highlighting how digital skills shape opportunities for personal connections and broader social participation.

Cultural Participation

Cultural participation refers to the ways in which individuals engage with, experience, and contribute to cultural life, including arts, heritage, media, and creative activities. It encompasses both consumption and production of culture, such as attending concerts, visiting museums, reading literature, participating in traditional rituals, creating art, or engaging with digital media content. Cultural participation is closely tied to identity formation and the experience of belonging (Helsper, 2012).

Through engagement with cultural practices, individuals explore personal and collective identities, connect with communities, and negotiate social values and norms. It allows people to express themselves, experience shared meanings, and build social cohesion, fostering a sense of membership within groups or society at large. Cultural participation can occur across formal and informal settings, from structured programs like music or art classes to informal spaces such as fan communities or collaborative creative initiatives.

Cultural participation encompasses not only traditional activities, such as playing games, listening to and sharing music, watching videos, or pursuing hobbies, but also new forms of creative and collaborative engagement enabled by digital media. Internet and intelligent media increasingly facilitate cultural participation by providing wider access to cultural content, opportunities for creative production, and interactive spaces for intercultural exchange, while simultaneously shaping how people experience, share, and interpret culture. For instance, streaming platforms dominate music and video consumption, offering personalized recommendations powered by AI algorithms that tailor content to individual preferences, thereby influencing cultural tastes and engagement patterns. Social media and collaborative platforms support the collective practice of hobbies, the sharing and trading of cultural objects such as images, stories, digital art, and non-fungible tokens (NFTs), and the emergence of new digital marketplaces and forms of creative ownership. These platforms enable real-time interactions between content creators and audiences, blurring the traditional boundaries between consumption and production and fostering participatory and co-creative cultural experiences. Moreover, tourism has emerged as a major sphere of cultural (and economic) participation, as planning and booking holidays have become a global phenomenon. Advanced digital tools such as AI-powered travel assistants, dynamic pricing algorithms, integrated review systems, and virtual tour experiences help individuals make more informed and personalized travel decisions, enhancing their engagement with cultural heritage and global experiences.

While much cultural content is preprogrammed and designed for mass consumption, a minimum level of operational and formal skills is essential for meaningful engagement. Users must be able to navigate diverse platforms, manage multiple streams of information, and make informed decisions about which content to access and how to interact with it. Information, communication, and strategic media use skills are critical for curating experiences across music, video, gaming, social media, and other cultural domains. Beyond passive consumption, contributing to user-generated content requires content creation skills that enable individuals to actively produce, share, and shape culture in their everyday lives. Smartphone apps, content creation software, social media platforms, and generative AI platforms facilitate this process, lowering technical barriers and enhancing creative expression. Engagement in these digital cultural practices not only provides personal satisfaction but also allows creators to participate in meaningful projects, build communities around their work, and, in some cases, generate economic value. In this way, the intersection of digital skills and intelligent media transforms cultural participation from a largely consumptive activity into an interactive, co-creative process, empowering individuals to both experience and actively contribute to the cultural landscape.

Spatial Participation

Spatial participation refers to the ways in which individuals engage with and move through various geographical locations in their daily lives, whether for work, leisure, education, or social activity. In a smart society, internet and intelligent media are increasingly intertwined with spatial participation, extending the concept beyond physical presence. They coordinate movements, optimize travel, and integrate schedules across multiple contexts, enabling individuals to navigate both personal and social spaces. Calendars and scheduling applications, for example, synchronize across devices and employ AI-driven suggestions that automatically adjust appointments based on traffic, travel time, or last-minute changes. Navigation platforms provide real-time route optimization, whereas location-based reminder systems ensure that tasks are linked to specific locations. Advancements in mobile connectivity have further expanded spatial participation beyond traditional travel planning. Mobile ticketing and digital passes for public transportation, ride-sharing applications, and micro-mobility services allow individuals to move through urban areas with greater efficiency and flexibility. At longer distances, integrated travel platforms combine multiple modes of transportation, offering a single interface for booking trains, buses, and flights. Moreover, wearable devices, such as smartwatches, provide hands-free, on-the-go assistance, making movement fluid and context-aware. By combining AI-driven insights, real-time data, and seamless connectivity, intelligent media not only enhance personal mobility and convenience but also foster participation across diverse spatial environments. Digital skills are required to integrate these media into daily routines and provide individuals with more opportunities to be effective and efficient, both in leisure activities and in professional contexts. However, persistent inequalities remain. People from lower socioeconomic backgrounds often lead more locally bound lives, with work that is location-specific and predominantly manual, whereas individuals in higher socioeconomic positions tend to have intellectual or managerial roles with greater spatial mobility, both physically and virtually (Van Dijk, 2020b).

Institutional Participation

Institutional participation refers to people's involvement in formal organizations, structures, or systems that make up civic life. It encompasses engagement with public, governmental, and health services. Access to public and governmental services, such as healthcare, social welfare programs, unemployment benefits, and tax rebates, often represents a crucial means of sustaining life. Internet and intelligent media have transformed the landscape of government and public participation. Online platforms enable individuals to access information, submit forms, and interact with public services more efficiently. AI-powered chatbots, recommendation systems, and personalized interfaces are used to guide citizens through complex administrative processes. In many countries, public institutions increasingly operate under the assumption that these platforms and tools can reach the entire population. Some anticipate phasing out traditional channels of service provision. This assumption is highly optimistic and unrealistic. As we have seen in the previous chapter, a substantial portion of the population lacks the skills to engage effectively with online public services. Difficulties in locating necessary information, completing online forms, and conducting online transactions are still widespread. Individuals who are unable to perform these online tasks face a distinct disadvantage: they are less likely to access public, social, or financial benefits, and even when they do, the process tends to be slower and less transparent. Those who rely solely on physical service desks or telephone support are increasingly marginalized and receive less timely and comprehensive assistance.

Healthcare is the most critical domain, as participation is rarely voluntary and can be a matter of life and death. The use of online health services has expanded rapidly, with applications ranging from general health information portals to telemedicine platforms. Uses include searching for medical information, participating in online peer support groups, or engaging in virtual consultations. The advantages are significant: immediate, comprehensive, and convenient access to medical guidance, anonymity in sensitive cases, and the ability to seek second opinions or validate professional advice through multiple sources. New technological developments are expanding these potential benefits. Telehealth and telemonitoring systems allow patients to consult doctors, share diagnostic data, and receive treatment guidance without leaving home. AI-driven symptom checkers and diagnostic assistants can provide preliminary assessments, triage recommendations, and personalized treatment recommendations. Wearable health devices, such as smartwatches and medical-grade sensors, enable continuous health monitoring and the feeding of real-time data to healthcare providers. The potential benefits include earlier diagnosis and detection of anomalies, more personalized care, reduced hospital visits, and better patient engagement. Unfortunately, people with the most frequent health problems and the highest mortality rates, that is, people with low education and older adults, have the least access to and skills in using these opportunities. Digital skills are especially important in the health field because medical information is complex, specialized, and difficult to find. This is true for both online and offline health media, but digital applications do not simplify this matter. These applications can increase the difficulty of retrieving the required information. Many health websites and platforms tend to present available information in technical and specialist terms to a population that is unfamiliar with them. Additionally, the skills to assess the reliability of AI recommendations, especially given recent concerns regarding algorithmic bias and accuracy, requires critical thinking. A mixture of medium- and content-related digital skills is required for effective online health participation.

4.3 Lacking Digital Skills: Such a Big Deal?

From the overview in the previous section, we can conclude that the stakes of insufficient digital skills are higher than before. As services increasingly migrate online, those unable to participate effectively risk not only reduced inclusion but also tangible harm to their health and well-being. The skills to use digital services are becoming a decisive factor in determining social inclusion, economic opportunities, and life expectancy. However, despite debates about the importance of technological advancements, some observers downplay the problem of digital inequality, presenting four main arguments. First, they argue that traditional media and offline channels remain available for the most practical purposes and forms of participation in society. Second, they argue that the social inequalities observed in digital media skills and usage are not unprecedented. Throughout history, disparities in access to and mastery of media have become increasingly common. Literate, educated, and influential individuals have consistently been the first to adopt and most effectively utilize new media developments, such as the printing press, radio, and television. Third, they argue that individuals lacking digital skills often have someone nearby, family members, friends, neighbors, or colleagues, who can assist them or even carry out a digital task entirely on their behalf. Fourth, they argue that intelligent media limit the need for digital skills because these function autonomously and in the background. Each of these four arguments warrants careful scrutiny.

Argument 1: Traditional Media Remain Available for Many Societal Functions

The first argument is becoming increasingly weaker. While many public and private organizations employ multichannel strategies combining service desks, telephones, printed forms, email, and websites, the share of digital media is steadily growing. In high-access countries, businesses and government agencies are increasingly shifting to online-only services, often closing traditional service desks and call centers (and when phone numbers still exist, locating them can require a detective-like search through complex websites). Essential activities, such as submitting tax returns, applying for jobs, booking travel, accessing healthcare consultations, or even purchasing event tickets, are increasingly conducted online, sometimes without any offline alternatives. Recent developments have further accelerated this trend. Mobile-first service design is often the norm, with many organizations optimizing their services exclusively for smartphones and tablets, sometimes at the expense of desktops or in-person services. Relatively inexpensive AI-powered chatbots handle a substantial portion of customer service interactions, seemingly reducing the need for human-operated call centers. Furthermore, digital identity systems enable online authentication for banking, taxation, voting, and other essential services, further embedding the expectation of digital participation. Cashless payments and app-based ticketing platforms are also becoming dominant, rendering physical payments and ticket counters obsolete in some sectors.

Obligatory online access and use are not the only reasons why the continued availability of traditional media is an increasingly weak argument. A more compelling reason is that digital media provide a range of opportunities that traditional media cannot match. These technologies were created for practical purposes—speed, precision, personalization, and interactivity—capabilities that their analog predecessors cannot replicate. For example, price comparison platforms not only enable faster and more accurate evaluation of products than physically visiting multiple shops, but also integrate AI-driven recommendation engines that personalize results based on purchase history, location, and even predicted needs. Similarly, searching for a particular illness through a reliable digital health platform provides more focused, updated, and targeted information than a printed brochure or a medical encyclopedia. AI-powered symptom checkers, virtual health assistants, and telemedicine platforms go further, offering personalized risk assessments, instant appointment booking, and real-time translation for cross-border consultations. Also communication and networking have undergone significant transformations. Maintaining and expanding one's social network is now facilitated not only by static social media sites but also by integrated messaging with video calls, group collaboration tools, and event scheduling, all of which are available in real time. Algorithms continuously update users regarding important life events, news, and shared interests, creating a more dynamic and informed network than can be sustained through occasional phone calls or face-to-face meetings. For individuals with limited access or insufficient skills, these developments represent missed opportunities, opportunities that are not merely novel conveniences but, in many cases, more efficient, informative, and socially connected alternatives to traditional media. The rapid proliferation of smart mobile applications, cloud-based platforms, and voice-activated digital assistants ensures that the advantages of digital participation continue to grow, making non-participation an increasingly significant disadvantage.

Argument 2: Inequalities of Media Literacy and Knowledge Are Age-Old, at least Since the Invention of Reading and Writing

The second argument for downplaying digital inequality is that (1) traditional and digital media skills are fundamentally similar and (2) they affect the same social groups in a similar way: people with lower levels of educational attainment, people living in poverty, older adults, and people with disabilities. Both claims are only partially correct.

Regarding the first claim, a first look at the traditional and digital media skills listed in Boxes 1.1 and 1.2 reveals considerable similarity and overlap. However, this claim tends to downplay the differences between traditional and digital media skills. Concerning traditional media skills, inequalities in literacy, knowledge, and mental activity are emphasized. Digital media require additional skills from the user. In addition to these (and other) mental skills, they require active interaction with interfaces, managing transactions, creating content, and engaging in two-way communication. The internet's multi-functionality requires critical content-related skills. Internet and intelligent media offer platforms for various types of communication and engagement in all domains of human life. They are used at work, school, home, and during transit. The range of skills required to fully use these platforms is broad; inequalities in their use amplify all other existing inequalities. The societal impact of the inequality of digital skills is much larger than that of traditional media skills and can be demonstrated in the observation of a *usage gap* comparable to the *knowledge gap* suggested in the 1970s concerning traditional mass media (Van Dijk & Hacker, 2003). Tichenor et al. (1970) claimed that when the infusion of mass media information into a social system increases, segments of the population with higher socioeconomic statuses tend to acquire this information at a faster rate than the lower-status segments. In short, people with higher education and status would learn more from television, radio, newspapers, and other mass media than people with lower education and status. While the knowledge gap refers to the differential derivation of knowledge from mass media, the usage gap is a broader thesis that potentially reaches further and is more relevant to society. It refers to differential uses and activities in all spheres of daily life, not just the perception and cognition of mass media. The usage gap thesis claims that people with better social positions and higher education use significantly more serious internet applications that aid them in their work, careers, business, and studies, whereas people with lesser positions and lower education use more applications for entertainment, simple communication, and shopping. Behind the concept of a usage gap, a clear normative account emerges. The assumption is that several online activities are more beneficial or advantageous than others. Some activities offer users more opportunities and resources to advance people's careers, work, education, and societal position than other activities that are mainly consumptive or entertaining. The background of this usage gap lies in a combination of technological, social, cultural, and personal characteristics. Technological characteristics include the complexity, expensiveness, and multi-functionality of internet media, which invite different uses (Van Dijk, 2005). Personal characteristics are varied motivations for using internet and other digital media. They range from information-seeking, education, and career development to online shopping, gaming, and other forms of online entertainment. Social characteristics include the occupied positions. Individuals with high-level jobs or courses of study are stimulated to use more serious applications, whereas those with low-level jobs or who are unemployed are less motivated to use these serious applications. Parents of school-aged children are motivated to engage with the educational programs that their children practice in their homework. Cultural backgrounds are the differentiation and individualization of (post)modern society, leading to an increasing number of diverging interests. However, differences in digital skills are another cause of the usage gap. A lack of content-related skills prevents internet users from engaging in complex and serious applications.

The second claim is that traditional and digital media inequalities affect social categories in the same way. However, this claim is only partially correct. Educational background seems to be equally related to differences in traditional and digital media skills. However, the complexity of internet and intelligent media creates an added barrier that appears to be greater for the less educated than for the highly educated population. For example, using AI-based tax-filing systems, navigating blockchain-based identity verification, or applying for jobs through algorithm-driven recruitment platforms requires technical and strategic knowledge that is absent in traditional media. In terms of gender, there is probably little difference between the skills of males and females in using traditional and digital media in developed countries, where women's emancipation occurred in the twentieth century. However, in less developed countries, often with cultures of male domination, digital media erect an extra barrier. When digital media are scarce, they are reserved for males (Antonio & Tuffley, 2014). Age disparities are especially pronounced; younger individuals adapt quickly to innovations such as app-based banking and generative AI tools, while many older adults struggle with even basic interface navigation that requires merely formal skills. The opposite is true for traditional skills, as with advancing age, people can increase their traditional literacy as long as their vision and mental ability allow.

Argument 3: Individuals with Limited Digital Skills Get Assistance from People Close to Them

The third argument of those trying to downplay the importance of digital skill insufficiencies is that people often receive assistance from those around them. Family members, friends, neighbors, or acquaintances with digital skills are presumed to be available to almost everyone. While social networks are important for acquiring digital skills, this argument is flawed. It echoes the outdated nineteenth-century belief that a low literate father could rely on his literate son to read letters on his behalf, thus eliminating the need to learn reading himself. In a smart society, every individual, regardless of age, requires a basic level of digital skills to function independently in society. This is not merely a matter of convenience; it is a prerequisite for accessing education, employment, healthcare, and civic services. Reflecting this reality, many countries now incorporate digital skills into compulsory education, while adult education targets older citizens and others who missed earlier opportunities to develop these skills.

Beyond this normative point lies a deeper structural issue: those with lower digital skills are more likely to have fewer people in their vicinity with sufficient digital skills than those who already possess adequate skill levels. Sociological research shows that individuals living in low-income neighborhoods or belonging to lower social strata tend to have smaller and less resourceful networks (Tilly, 1998). This applies equally to digital skills (Boerkamp et al., 2024; Courtois & Verdegem, 2016; Helsper & Van Deursen, 2017). In such settings, skilled assistance may be unavailable, unreliable, or delayed, leading to time loss and missed opportunities to access digital resources. Moreover, relying on others compromises privacy and autonomy, particularly when dealing with sensitive matters such as medical records, financial transactions, or legal applications.

Argument 4: Intelligent Media Lower the Need for Digital Skills

Some argue that AI makes tasks so easy that digital skills become less important. Conversational tools reduce the need for advanced search techniques, Boolean operators, and database expertise to find information. It can summarize or synthesize content without requiring mastery of complex search tools, and it streamlines content creation by writing, summarizing, translating, or formatting without the user needing to know a software program's detailed features or conventions; desired outputs can simply be requested in plain language. In spreadsheets, users are no longer required to memorize every formula command if AI platforms can generate them upon request. Basic coding can also be outsourced because these tools can write scripts, troubleshoot syntax, and explain errors. Generative image and video tools are increasingly able to replace specialized technical tasks—traditionally requiring formal training in design, photography, or video editing—with simple language prompts and automated processing. The shift toward smart systems and connected applications reflects similar trends. Driven by AI, they are increasingly capable of purposefully observing situations, autonomously making decisions, and carrying out actions behind the scenes once the initial configurations are set. For utopian thinkers, this is the reason to predict that everyone will automatically benefit.

However, these developments demand renewed attention to digital skills (Van Deursen & Mossberger, 2018). For instance, in the case of generative AI, users still need to know what to ask (and why they are asking it) and how to judge whether the answer is relevant or accurate. The skills to verify sources, cross-check facts, and detect bias are essential. While AI can generate ideas, selecting which ideas are worth pursuing, and shaping them appropriately, requires human judgment. In this sense, AI does not eliminate the need for digital skills; rather, it shifts them further from technical know-how to critical thinking and strategic media use.

In the case of connected intelligent media, developments might lower the barrier for certain tasks, especially by reducing the emphasis on operational and formal skills owing to the increasing invisibility and autonomy of smart devices. Such skills are still important, for example, when installing and configuring these devices or avoiding vendor lock-ins by connecting products from different manufacturers (Van der Zeeuw et al., 2024). Notably, the ubiquity of smart devices has led to an enormous increase in the amount of data collected. Devices, sensors, interactions, and other digital sources generate large, complex, longitudinal, and/or distributed datasets, often referred to as big data. That these data are complex and often ambiguous, and that many human actions are now replaced by automatic, behind-the-scenes judgments and decisions, does not suggest less skills. The autonomous collection and processing of data can have unexpected or unintended consequences. Moreover, a smart system is not simply a set of interconnected devices; it also includes organizations and stakeholders with different and sometimes conflicting objectives. Companies may use the collected data to improve their products, hospitals and doctors may use it for research, and insurers to determine premium levels. For users, it is often unclear which personal data are being collected, who has access to them, and what the implications are (Van Deursen & Mossberger, 2018). Because of greater data volumes, reduced user control, higher ambiguity, and increased risks, there is more emphasis on information, communication, and strategic media use skills to understand the uses and consequences of AI-driven smart systems. To realize the benefits of AI and smart devices, users need the skills to control and automate these systems, retrieve and understand the collected data, and make informed decisions. In the previous chapter, we saw that many users struggle to make sound decisions based on this data or to evaluate decisions made automatically by the system. This explains why the use of smart devices does not always lead to sustainable behaviors. For example, smart thermostat users often fail to configure automatic adjustments to energy consumption patterns. A lack of digital skills can even increase energy use through misconfigured preheating schedules or by running smart home devices that consume power.

4.4 Unequal Digital Skills as Indicator of Broader Social Inequality

Building on the preceding discussions, it becomes evident that the shift from traditional to digital media skills, and from internet-based to intelligent media skills, involves substantial changes rather than remaining the same. However, similar types of social and information inequalities appear in the skills required for traditional, internet, and intelligent media. The main difference is the use of media in particular social practices. This creates several additional barriers for those who experience problems using digital media and provides new opportunities for those who can skillfully use them. For example, operational, formal, communication, and content creation skills are important obstacles for older adults; however, information and strategic media use skills that they learned in traditional media might prevail when the obstacle of insufficient operational and formal skills is removed. For people with low education, operational and formal skills often create additional barriers. Removing these barriers does not automatically provide information, communication, content creation, or strategic media use skills. For people with disabilities and those with low literacy, the difficulty and novelty of internet and intelligent media are an additional handicap, although they may also provide solutions. In Chap. 6, we discuss barriers and opportunities for these users.

The Resources and Appropriation Theory shown in Fig. 4.1 argues that access to digital media is determined by both the characteristics of digital media and existing personal and positional inequalities that lead to the possession of different resources. These inequalities and the resources that they produce are a reflection of existing social and information inequality. The theory posits that the differences in access that they produce tend to reinforce the inequalities of participation in society and that this effect feeds back on greater inequalities between persons, positions, and resources. For example, when people have jobs that include daily work with digital media, they are more likely to develop digital skills than those without such a job. These skills will increase their career opportunities (economic participation), new personal characteristics ("technical intelligence"), and new resources (higher wages, more time spent on digital media, experience with intelligent media, or more online social contacts). Workers in industries adopting AI, such as marketing professionals using AI analytics or engineers working with machine learning platforms, gain new skills that improve employability and earning potential. In contrast, workers in sectors with limited digital media integration may see their skill sets stagnate. Similarly, individuals using online collaboration platforms are more adept at navigating remote and hybrid work environments, whereas those without such experience risk being excluded from emerging job opportunities. In healthcare, patients who actively use telemedicine services, wearable health devices, or patient platforms not only gain better health outcomes but may also develop valuable skills for navigating other digital services. Even in civic life, citizens who engage with online government platforms gain knowledge that can be transferred to other areas of digital participation. In all these cases, the use of digital media amplifies existing advantages.

Network theory accounts for these reinforcement effects. Van Dijk (2020b) outlines several *laws of the web*, including the law of trend amplification. Networks are relational structures that tend to amplify existing social and structural trends. Digital skills strengthen one's relative position in a network, for instance, in the labor market when applying for a better job online. They help those in a better social position and those with socially higher-qualified personal characteristics more than those with worse positions and qualifications. For example, professionals with advanced digital skills can leverage professional networking platforms to build influential connections, access exclusive job postings, and showcase digital portfolios, which are often unavailable to those with less digital skills. Similarly, entrepreneurs who master e-commerce tools and digital marketing can expand their businesses globally through online platforms, whereas those lacking such skills remain confined to local or traditional markets. In the educational sphere, students with strong digital skills benefit from online learning networks, discussion forums, and collaborative platforms that enhance their academic performance and peer connections. Conversely, students with limited digital skills miss out on these networking benefits, further widening educational inequality. In short, digital skills strengthen a person's relative position in a network. They help those in a better social position and those with socially higher-qualified personal characteristics more than those with worse positions and qualifications.

At first sight, it seems that improving people's digital skills will always help the advantaged more than the disadvantaged, increasing relative inequality between people. Unfortunately, this is true, but only for two important qualifications. These qualifications inspire a feasible and realistic policy for skills improvement, which will be the core subject of next chapters in this book.

1. The first qualification is that improvements in digital skills have a bottom line and an upper limit. The bottom line is the command of digital skills to such an extent that one can gain access to and use digital media required to function in a smart society. The minimum condition for this purpose is an adequate level of strategic media choice, operational, and formal skills. In this way, one obtains the key and is able to unlock a smart society. Subsequently, content-related skills are required to fully leverage the possibilities of such a society. Typically, these reflect the level of education that has been previously achieved. The upper limit occurs when the most advanced users no longer seek further training or guidance because they have

already mastered these skills. The difference between these upper and lower limits offers a space for skill improvement that motivates those in greatest need to participate in educational solutions.

2. The second qualification is that those in the worst social positions and with the lowest personal qualifications can be placed in better positions and supported in their personal development. The "law" of trend amplification is not a natural law but a social "law" that is subject to change. The social and personal conditions of people who must increase their digital skills can be improved through economic, social, and cultural policies. Thus, narrowly defined digital skills improvement only partially works. For example, it may be more effective to provide an unemployed individual with a job involving digital tasks such as remote data entry, content moderation, or basic tech support rather than offering a standalone computer course. Similarly, in low-income or rural areas, establishing community internet hubs or digital kiosks with ongoing access to devices, high-speed internet, and support, such as those using solar-powered connectivity in parts of Sub-Saharan Africa or India, can be far more impactful than a one-time digital skills workshop. Additionally, programs that combine digital skills training with social support, such as mentorship or peer learning groups, may be promising for improving sustained digital engagement. Ultimately, the material, social, and personal conditions that enable digital skill development are more crucial than training alone.

The main conclusion is that improving digital skills can help reduce social and information inequality despite the reinforcing effects that tend to widen gaps. Chapters 5 and 6 focus on the two most important and popular solutions to digital skills inequality. The first solution is to improve interface design of digital media. Enhancing accessibility, usability, and comprehensibility can prevent many digital skill problems from arising. For example, the use of more intuitive devices, such as tablets instead of desktop PCs, reduces operational and formal skill requirements. Similarly, clearer, more user-friendly content supports users with employing information and communication skills. When prevention through better design fails, the second solution is to repair the problem by providing education and support. This includes formal and informal education across primary, adult, workplace, and community settings, offering targeted courses and training to help people effectively use digital media. However, improved interfaces and digital skills training alone are insufficient, and broader conditions must be addressed. In the concluding chapter, we discuss a range of policy measures aimed at governments, businesses, citizens, and organizations to improve the social, economic, and cultural conditions that enable the use of digital media by all.

4.5 Conclusions: Digital Skills as Gateway to Participation

This chapter discussed the social roots and far-reaching consequences of digital skills inequality. Drawing on the Resources and Appropriation Theory, we argued that disparities in individuals' temporal, material, mental, social, and cultural resources shape the extent to which they can access and effectively appropriate digital media, including the development of digital skills. This highlights the need for research and interventions promoting digital skills to account for the diverse resources available to different groups. Digital skills are a gateway to full participation and without them, individuals face barriers to opportunities that many take for granted: holding and advancing in a job, earning a higher salary, accessing better healthcare, building social networks, engaging politically, securing cultural events, and receiving government benefits. Furthermore, digital skills act as multipliers, as the participation opportunities they enable reinforce and expand the resources people possess, creating a powerful feedback loop of inequality. This loop places vulnerable groups at a heightened risk of exclusion.

Despite the increasing importance of digital skills, public debates on social inequality rarely address the role of digital media. Instead, they focus on the potential to create opportunities and drive change for everyone. Meanwhile, national policies often prioritize preparing people for employment in the tech industry while society urgently needs to strengthen digital skills for everyday use. Equally concerning are claims that digital skills inequality is overstated—arguments suggesting that traditional media still meet most needs, that media inequalities are not new, that those lacking digital skills can rely on help from others, or that intelligent media reduce the need for such skills. We reject these views. Traditional media are becoming increasingly inferior to digital media in a growing number of societal practices. Despite some similarities with traditional media skills, digital skills differ because they require mastery of relatively complex operations, interfaces, and applications. Moreover, individuals with limited digital skills often have less access to assistance from others. We also argued that AI developments demand renewed attention to digital skills.

Both traditional and digital media skills reflect broader patterns of social inequality. As seen in the previous chapter, groups facing disadvantages in material wealth, social networks, education, and culture are the same groups with fewer digital resources and skills. The only possible exception may be older adults, who often lag in media-related skills, but this might be temporary as younger generations age. Importantly, digital media do not simply reflect inequality, they amplify it. As digital media and platforms are powerful enablers of work, education, politics, and social life, those who master them strengthen their social, economic, and cultural status. In a smart society, high levels of digital skills are not just personal assets; they are also critical for maintaining and expanding one's position in an increasingly interconnected world.

References

Antonio, A., & Tuffley, D. (2014). The gender digital divide in developing countries. *Future Internet, 6*(4), 673–687.

Best, P., Manktelow, R., & Taylor, B. (2014). Online communication, social media and adolescent wellbeing: A systematic narrative review. *Children and Youth Services Review, 41*, 27–36.

Boerkamp, L. G., Van Deursen, A. J. A. M., Van Laar, E., Van der Zeeuw, A., & Van der Graaf, S. (2024). Exploring barriers to and outcomes of internet appropriation among households living in poverty: A systematic literature review. *SAGE Open, 14*(1).

Courtois, C., & Verdegem, P. (2016). With a little help from my friends: An analysis of the role of social support in digital inequalities. *New Media & Society, 18*(8), 1508–1527.

DiMaggio, P., & Bonikowski, B. (2008). Make money surfing the web? The impact of Internet use on the earnings of US workers. *American Sociological Review, 73*(2), 227–250.

Gottfried, J. (2024). *Americans' Social Media Use: YouTube and Facebook are by far the most used online platforms among U.S. adults; TikTok's user base has grown since 2021.* Pew Research Center.

Helsper, E. J. (2012). A corresponding fields model for the links between social and digital exclusion. *Communication Theory, 22*(4), 403–426.

Helsper, E. J., & Van Deursen, A. J. A. M. (2017). Do the rich get digitally richer? Quantity and quality of support for digital engagement. *Information, Communication & Society, 20*(5), 700–714.

Hughes, L., Davies, F., Li, K., Gunaratnege, S. M., Malik, T., & Dwivedi, Y. K. (2026). Beyond the hype: Organizational adoption of Generative AI through the lens of the TOE framework—A mixed-methods perspective. *International Journal of Information Management, 86*, 102982.

Rahmat, A. M., Mohd, I. H., Omar, M. K., Kamalludeen, R., Zahari, W. M. Z. W., Azmy, N., & Adnan, A. (2022). Integrating socio-digital skills in the Industry 4.0 era for graduates' employability: An employers' perspective. *Journal of Positive School Psychology, 6*(3), 8493–8507.

Tichenor, P. J., Donohue, G. A., & Olien, C. N. (1970). Mass media flow and differential growth of knowledge. *Public Opinion Quarterly, 34*, 159–170.

Tilly, C. (1998). *Durable inequality*. University of California Press.

Van der Zeeuw, A., Van Deursen, A. J. A. M., & Jansen, G. (2024). The orchestrated digital inequalities of the IoT: How vendor lock-in hinders and playfulness creates IoT benefits in every life. *New Media & Society, 26*(10), 5658–5676.

Van Deursen, A. J. A. M., & Helsper, E. J. (2015). The third-level digital divide: Who benefits most from being online? In L. Robinson, S. R. Cotten, J. Schulz, A. Williams, & T. M. Hale (Eds.), *Communication and information technologies annual: Digital distinctions & inequalities* (pp. 29–52). Emerald Group Publishing.

Van Deursen, A. J. A. M., & Helsper, E. J. (2018). Collateral benefits of Internet use: Explaining the diverse outcomes of engaging with the Internet. *New Media & Society, 20*(7), 2333–2351.

Van Deursen, A. J. A. M., & Helsper, E. J. (2021). *Mediawijsheid: Conceptualisering en belang in een gemedieerde samenleving. Lacunes in bestaand onderzoek en beleid*. Universiteit Twente.

Van Deursen, A. J. A. M., & Mossberger, K. (2018). Any thing for anyone? A new digital divide in Internet-of-Things skills. *Policy & Internet, 10*(2), 122–140.

Van Dijk, J. A. G. M. (2005). *The deepening divide: Inequality in the information society*. Sage.

Van Dijk, J. A. G. M. (2020a). *The digital divide*. Polity Press.

Van Dijk, J. A. G. M. (2020b). *The network society*. Sage.

Van Dijk, J., & Hacker, K. (2003). The digital divide as a complex and dynamic phenomenon. *The Information Society, 19*(4), 315–326.

Wei, K. K., Teo, H. H., Chan, H. C., & Tan, B. C. (2011). Conceptualizing and testing a social cognitive model of the digital divide. *Information Systems Research, 22*(1), 170–187.

CHAPTER 5

Enhancing Interfaces and Content

5.1 Introduction: The Role of Designers

In the preceding chapters, we highlighted differences in the levels of seven digital skills across various societal groups and emphasized that these skills are no longer optional; they are essential for meaningful participation in economic, educational, political, social, cultural, spatial, and institutional life. This underscores the urgent need for policies that actively address digital skills, with particular attention paid to groups at the highest risk of being left behind. However, the policy challenge is complex and requires both technological solutions, such as more accessible and user-friendly interface designs, and provision of educational opportunities. The next chapter discusses educational solutions. This chapter highlights recommendations for designers, whose role in addressing digital skill inequalities is often underestimated. Frequently, the responsibility for acquiring skills is placed solely on users, while the influence of design is overlooked. However, poorly designed or inaccessible systems can even hinder skilled users and further exacerbate the challenges faced by those with limited digital skills. Although the precise relationship between interface design and digital skill level is not yet fully understood, our tests suggest that individuals with limited skills encounter disproportionately large obstacles. This chapter builds on the distinction between medium- and content-related skills and explores ways to improve both interface design and the provision of online content. First, it examines how thoughtful

A. van Deursen and J. van Dijk, *Digital Skills*, Digital Education and Learning, https://doi.org/10.1057/978-1-349-96162-7_5

design can reduce operational and formal skill barriers and provide practical guidance for designers. Second, it addresses how designers can ensure that content is clear, accessible, and tailored to the intended audience. Special attention is paid to the development of transparent and explainable AI systems to help users understand and trust automated processes.

5.2 Medium-Related Skill Design Improvements

Designers must recognize that a considerable share of the population—including older adults, individuals with limited education, those with low literacy, users without digital support, and people with minimal internet experience—lack sufficient strategic media choice, operational, and formal skills. Prioritizing aesthetic appeal or advanced features over accessibility risks ignoring the unique challenges that these groups face. Many online services, particularly in government, healthcare, and education, assume a baseline level of digital skills that is not possessed by all users. Consequently, essential information and services remain inaccessible to those who need them the most. Seniors, in particular, benefit from applications and services designed with lower levels of operational and formal skills. Once they acquire these skills, they often outperform younger users in terms of information and strategic media use skills (see Chap. 3).

Accessibility Principles for the Web

Several frameworks and guidelines are available to help designers improve interfaces.[1] The World Wide Web Consortium (W3C) offers internationally recognized standards for making online platforms accessible to diverse users, including older adults, individuals with disabilities, and those with limited operational and formal skills. Their Web Content Accessibility Guidelines (WCAG) provide detailed recommendations based on four core principles: content must be perceivable (information can be detected through sight, hearing, or touch), operable (users can navigate and

[1] The European Accessibility Act (EAA) has transformed accessibility from a voluntary design choice into a legal and regulatory obligation for businesses operating within the European Union. By establishing common accessibility requirements for products and services—such as websites, mobile applications, e-books, banking services, and e-commerce platforms—the Act ensures that accessibility is embedded throughout the design and development process. In doing so, the EAA aligns market practices with the broader principles of universal design and digital inclusion, promoting equal access to digital media.

interact through various input methods), understandable (content and interfaces are clear and predictable), and robust (compatible with current and future assistive technologies). Despite the existence of recognized standards, evidence from our task-based performance tests, as discussed in Chap. 3, shows that many websites, including official government and health-related sites, seem to fail to meet these standards. To support users with limited operational and formal skills, interface designers can use the following steps as points of departure.

- *Simplify navigation and interaction*. Interfaces should aim to reduce unnecessary complexity by limiting the number of steps required to complete tasks and avoiding deeply nested menus that can overwhelm users with limited digital skills. Establishing a clear visual hierarchy supported by consistent layouts helps users quickly identify what is most important on a page. Predictable behavior of interactive elements further builds confidence, ensuring that users know what to expect when they click or tap. Navigation components, such as menus, search bars, and back buttons, should remain in consistent locations across all pages so that users can rely on familiarity rather than relearning with each interaction. Simultaneously, interactive elements should be reinforced with uniform visual cues, such as icons, colors, and button styles, making it obvious what can be clicked or tapped. To support orientation, progress indicators can show where users are in a process and how to move forward, while feedback mechanisms, such as highlighting selected menu items, provide reassurance that their actions have been recognized. Finally, practical design choices make the experience more approachable: large, clearly labeled buttons are easier to identify, related functions grouped together reduce cognitive load, and a consistent menu structure across the site prevents confusion.
- *Provide guided and contextual support*. Step-by-step instructions, tooltips, walkthroughs, and interactive tutorials provide users with the confidence to complete their tasks successfully. These forms of support are especially valuable for complex processes, such as filling out government forms, applying for social benefits, navigating healthcare portals, managing online banking, completing job applications, and using digital tax services. Rather than relying on static instructions, support should be adapted to the user's actions in real

time. Highlighting relevant menu options, providing examples, and explaining unfamiliar terms ensure that users understand how to proceed. For instance, a healthcare portal could display tooltips that explain medical terminology, suggest common responses when users complete a symptom form, and offer contextual prompts to remind users of the required documents.

- *Provide clear feedback and error prevention mechanisms.* Users should receive immediate confirmation of successful actions, such as "Your application has been submitted" or "Payment completed." Errors should be readily identifiable, and users should be able to rectify them with minimal effort. Explanations ought to be presented in plain language, devoid of technical jargon, and accompanied by clear, actionable guidance on how to resolve the issue. Undo options or confirmation dialogs for critical actions can help prevent mistakes. For example, a senior citizen submitting an online tax form should be reassured through step-by-step confirmation that each section is complete, reducing the frustration of lost or incorrect submissions. Similarly, a user booking an appointment on a healthcare portal could receive instant feedback confirming the chosen date and location, along with clear guidance on how to modify or cancel the appointment if needed to prevent scheduling errors.
- *Use personalization and adaptive interfaces.* By analyzing interaction patterns, novice users can be shown a simplified interface, whereas advanced features remain available to more experienced users. Similarly, multimodal support—such as combining text with icons, audio instructions, or video demonstrations—can make interfaces more accessible to those with limited operational and formal skills, language barriers, or disabilities such as visual impairments. For example, a public transportation app might provide step-by-step directions with visual maps for first-time riders, whereas experienced commuters can access full-route planning and real-time traffic analytics.
- *Consider progressive disclosure.* Unlike personalization, which adapts the interface to a user's experience level or preferences, progressive disclosure focuses on the sequencing and timing of feature exposure to reduce cognitive load (Carroll & Carrithers, 1984). This allows individuals to gradually build confidence and skills without feeling overwhelmed. For example, a mobile banking app might first teach users how to check balances and make simple transfers, introducing

more complex features such as bill payments, budgeting tools, or investments only after users are comfortable with the core functions. Similarly, an online learning platform can start with simple video lessons and quizzes, progressively introducing collaborative tools, interactive simulations, or advanced analytics once learners become familiar with the essential components.

In addition to following design guidelines like those outlined above, designers should adopt User-Centered Design (UCD) principles (Norman & Draper, 1986). UCD emphasizes designing interfaces around the needs, skills, and limitations of real users rather than expecting users to adapt to the technology. Gould and Lewis (1985) identified three central principles that define UCD.

- The first is an *early focus on users and tasks*, which requires designers to understand who the intended users are, what tasks they need to complete, and the context in which they operate. As seen in Chap. 3, users are not a homogeneous group—differences in age, education, internet experience, social support, or cognitive or physical abilities all affect digital skill levels and thus how they interact with digital interfaces. For example, older adults or people with lower education, or users with limited digital skills may approach technology with very different expectations and challenges compared to younger or highly skilled users. By considering these differences early in the design process, designers can make informed decisions regarding the layout, navigation, and interaction patterns. This proactive approach ensures that interfaces are built on a realistic understanding of user diversity rather than on assumptions or generalized design practices. It also allows designers to anticipate potential barriers, such as confusion caused by excessive options or unclear instructions, and to create solutions that accommodate a wide range of skills and expectations.
- The second principle is *empirical measurement*. This principle emphasizes testing designs with real users to observe how they interact with the interface, rather than relying on assumptions or theoretical models. For users with limited operational and formal skills, empirical testing can reveal which functions they do not understand or where they become confused or disoriented. By observing interactions firsthand, designers gain concrete insights into how

well an interface supports users' goals and where improvements are needed. Collecting feedback from representative groups helps to reveal barriers that might otherwise remain invisible. This feedback can guide adjustments to the layout, navigation, labeling, and interactive elements, thereby ensuring that the interface is intuitive and accessible.

- The third principle is *iterative design*. This approach involves repeated refinement of interfaces based on user feedback and observed performance. UCD treats usability as an ongoing process of improvement, where each cycle of testing, feedback, and revision brings the system closer to meeting real user needs. For users with limited operational and formal skills, this is especially important because their struggles often highlight overlooked design flaws, such as overly complex navigation, ambiguous icons, or insufficient feedback when errors occur. By incorporating these insights into successive design cycles, designers can gradually simplify workflows, clarify instructions, and enhance interactive elements, thereby rendering the interface more intuitive and accessible.

Together, the three principles form a cohesive approach: understanding users and tasks grounds design in real-world needs, empirical measurement reveals where the design succeeds or fails, and iterative refinement ensures continuous improvement, producing interfaces that are both accessible and empowering for all users. These principles help shift the design mindset away from flashy features toward practical usability. Human-centered design (HCD) takes this approach a step further by emphasizing human interests and values rather than a goal-directed focus on solving predefined design problems (Gill, 1991). A human-centered approach frames the design challenge through the perspectives of participants within their specific social and organizational contexts, rather than treating it as an abstract, context-free information-processing issue (Lehaney et al., 1999). HCD goes beyond usability and task efficiency to encompass the ethical, social, and emotional dimensions of design. The following recommendations derive from HCD principles and highlight areas that traditional UCD often overlooks:

- *Co-create with communities*. Engage users and stakeholders as partners throughout the design process, not merely as test subjects.

Co-design workshops with community members ensure the final solution aligns with local culture and needs.

- *Address emotional and psychological needs.* Design should foster positive emotions such as trust, comfort, and empowerment, rather than focusing mainly on usability. For example, a healthcare interface might use reassuring language and tone to reduce patient anxiety and build confidence.
- *Include non-users and indirect* stakeholders. Consider the needs of individuals who are indirectly affected by a product, not only those who interact with it directly. For example, a public transport application should consider accessibility needs of caregivers, elderly passengers, and people without smartphones.
- *Respect human values and diversity.* Design should be sensitive to cultural differences, values, and local contexts. Elements such as color choices, metaphors, and interaction styles should be adapted to local meanings and accessibility norms.
- *Consider broader human and societal impact.* Designers should evaluate how their solutions affect individuals, communities, and the environment, not just end users. For example, an online delivery service should consider the working conditions of freelancers alongside customer convenience.
- *Incorporate ethical reflection.* Designers should anticipate ethical implications, including privacy, fairness, and inclusivity, and integrate safeguards into design decisions. For example, a social networking platform should be designed to give users clear control over what personal information is shared publicly, thereby preventing unintentional disclosure of sensitive data.
- *Promote sustainability and long-term thinking.* Design for durability, adaptability, and responsible use of resources. Encourage digital products that promote mindful usage and avoid manipulative design that drive overconsumption.

Smartphones, Tablets, and Smart Devices

Special attention is required when designing applications for smartphones, tablets, and smart devices with small screens, variable computing power, and context-dependent usage. Users often interact with these devices while multitasking during daily activities, commuting, or standing in crowded public spaces, creating challenges that differ from those encountered on desktops or laptops. These usage contexts can increase both cognitive load and physical strain, making careful and thoughtful interface design especially important to ensure usability and positive user experience. On the positive side, the intuitive, touch-based nature of smartphones, tablets, and similar devices allows many users to quickly learn basic operations, such as swiping, tapping, or zooming. At the same time, however, their reduced functionality, smaller screens, and sometimes inconsistent interface designs can make more complex or creative tasks, such as editing documents, completing detailed forms, or producing content, challenging. From this perspective, some researchers have highlighted the concept of a "mobile underclass," in which individuals, often from disadvantaged backgrounds, rely solely on smartphones for internet access (Napoli & Obar, 2014). This underscores the importance of mobile-specific design principles that recognize the advantages and limitations of these devices, ensuring that interfaces are accessible, efficient, and empowering for all users.

Designers can draw on established frameworks to guide mobile interface design. For example, W3C's *Mobile Web Best Practices* aim to make web content usable across all ages, abilities, education levels, and devices. These guidelines explicitly prioritize accessibility over aesthetics or branding and recommend strategies such as minimizing navigation depth, providing clear labels, ensuring readable text, supporting keyboard navigation, and offering offline access. Apple's *Human Interface Guidelines* (HIG) emphasize aesthetic coherence, platform consistency, and intuitive gestures. HIG focuses on creating visually appealing interfaces that feel natural across devices. For users with limited operational and formal skills, this can translate into predictable behaviors—for example, swiping to go back or tapping clearly labeled icons. The HIG also emphasizes guidance through onboarding tutorials, contextual tooltips, and clear feedback on actions. However, aesthetic focus sometimes leads to minimalistic designs that may hide options behind gestures or menus that novices might overlook. Google's *Material* Design *Guidelines* (MDG) prioritize consistency across devices, responsive layouts, and touch-friendly interactions. The MDG's specifications for button size, spacing, typography, and hierarchy ensure that interactive elements are accessible to users with limited dexterity. The focus on clear visual hierarchy and intuitive navigation reduces cognitive load, while progressive disclosure ensures that advanced features appear only after basic functions are learned, helping build confidence among novice users.

While each framework offers distinct strengths, integrating their principles is most likely to yield effective outcomes for users with limited digital skills. In essence, this emphasizes the following:

- *Prioritize touch-friendly interactions.* Interactive elements such as buttons, links, and menus must be large enough to tap accurately, with sufficient spacing to prevent accidental selections. This is particularly important when users interact with their fingers rather than with a precise cursor. Small or closely packed touch targets can frustrate users, particularly those with limited dexterity, older adults, or individuals using assistive devices. For example, MDG suggests touch targets of at least 48 × 48 pixels for Android apps, supporting accurate navigation and reducing errors on smaller screens. Beyond size, the spacing between elements, visual cues such as highlighting or color changes on touch, and consistent placement of interactive components contribute to a more accessible and user-friendly experience.
- *Simplify navigation and reduce hierarchy depth.* Mobile interfaces must prioritize simplicity because deeply nested menus and complex structures that work on larger desktop or laptop screens often overwhelm users on smaller devices. Using flat navigation structures, clearly labeled menus, and persistent navigation bars help users orient themselves quickly and complete tasks efficiently. For example, a banking app can display essential functions, such as account overview, transfers, and payments, prominently on the home screen, whereas less frequently used features are grouped in secondary menus that remain easy to access. Similarly, a messaging platform might consolidate core actions such as chats, contacts, and calls into a single persistent menu at the bottom of the screen, ensuring that users can navigate without confusion. The idea is to keep the primary tasks immediately visible, reduce the number of steps required to reach them, and minimize the cognitive load for users with limited formal skills or less familiarity with digital interfaces.
- *Aim for clarity and brevity.* Each screen should focus on essential information, avoid overwhelming text, and minimize scrolling. Clear headings, short sentences, and visual cues help guide attention, whereas touch-friendly buttons and icons make actions easier

to complete. Progressive disclosure, in which advanced options or secondary details are hidden until needed, prevents clutter and supports gradual learning. For instance, a healthcare booking system may initially display only appointment scheduling, with options for viewing medical records, managing prescriptions, or requesting follow-up reminders revealed progressively.

- *Apply immediate confirmation.* Users benefit from instant feedback that reassures them that their actions have been successfully completed. On small screens and touch interactions, this can be achieved in several ways: haptic feedback (a subtle vibration when a button is tapped signals that the input has been registered), auditory cues (a short sound, such as a "ding" when a message is sent or a transaction is completed, provides an additional layer of confirmation), or visual confirmation (small indicators such as checkmarks show that an action has succeeded without taking up excessive screen space). Such immediate confirmations reduce uncertainty, prevent repeated or mistaken inputs, and build user confidence, particularly for sensitive tasks.
- *Provide contextual and adaptive guidance.* When screen space is limited, interfaces must deliver real-time, context-sensitive assistance without overcrowding the display. Tooltips, onboarding tutorials, and pop-up hints can be adapted to a user's behavior and offer guidance when and where it is needed. This approach prevents errors and allows users to focus on completing tasks without being overwhelmed by all available options at once. For example, a social media platform might highlight key functions, such as posting messages, adding contacts, or sharing media during a first-time walkthrough, whereas more advanced features remain hidden until the user is familiar with the basics.
- *Be consistent across applications and devices.* On mobile and smart devices, consistency in gestures, layouts, and visual cues helps users transfer knowledge from one application to another, thereby reducing the learning curve and minimizing errors. Familiar patterns allow users to interact confidently without the need to relearn basic interactions on each new interface. For example, swipe gestures to delete or archive messages are common across many mobile email and messaging applications, enabling users to apply the same action consistently. Similarly, bottom navigation bars with three to five

icons appear in multiple apps, helping users quickly locate primary functions like home, search, notifications, or settings.

Connected Intelligent Media

While the core design principles outlined earlier remain foundational, challenges in connected intelligent media demand additional focus on transparency, trust and explainability, guidance, user autonomy, consistency, and feedback and error prevention. Many AI and IoT applications adapt invisibly, which can confuse users with limited operational or formal skills when the system behavior diverges from their expectations. Automated prompts, alerts, and performance indicators may appear opaque, leaving users uncertain about how to respond. To address these challenges and improve trust, designers should consider the following:

- *Ensure transparency*. Clearly explain what the system is doing, using visible status indicators and plain language notifications. IoT devices should indicate when they are active, collect data, or transmit information. For instance, a smart speaker can display a light signal when voice recording is active. Users should be alerted when automation overrides their previous settings.
- *Increase explainability*. While transparency shows users what the system is doing and its current status, explainability clarify why the system behaves as it does and how its decisions are made. This is particularly important for AI-driven recommendations and autonomous IoT actions, which can otherwise feel unpredictable or opaque. Designers should provide mechanisms that communicate the reasoning behind system outputs—for example, answering questions like "Why am I seeing this?" Explainable AI techniques, such as simple models, natural-language explanations, and visual indicators, can support this (see also the next section). Additionally, interfaces can incorporate visual cues or dashboards that summarize decision logic in a digestible, user-friendly manner, helping users understand and act confidently on system recommendations.
- *Provide guidance*. Guidance is needed to help users navigate complex, adaptive AI- and IoT-driven systems, where behaviors can change dynamically and outputs may not be immediately intuitive. Effective guidance includes step-by-step instructions and explicit

options, particularly for critical and unfamiliar tasks. Complex operations should be divided into clear sequential steps. For example, a smart home setup app might guide a user through connecting a thermostat, linking it to energy-saving schedules, and testing automated routines. Progressive disclosure can be employed, presenting only the options needed at each stage and revealing advanced features as users gain confidence in the system (Springer & Whittaker, 2019). This helps users to complete tasks safely and confidently.

- *Support user autonomy*. User autonomy ensures that individuals maintain control over AI- and IoT-driven systems, even when these systems operate independently or provide automated recommendations. Because users often have unique preferences, specific contextual needs, or safety concerns that automated systems may not fully anticipate, they must be equipped with the skills to intervene when necessary. Without these skills, users may feel disempowered, frustrated, or compelled to rely on the system without question. User autonomy is therefore essential for exercising strategic media use skills. To support autonomy, systems should allow users to adjust settings, override automated actions, and personalize their behaviors. For example, a smart lighting app can allow users to set brightness levels, choose color schemes, or create automated schedules while keeping default AI suggestions optional. Similarly, a smart thermostat may automatically lower the temperature to save energy; however, users must be able to manually override it when desired. It is also important to clearly indicate which functions are automated and which can be controlled manually to help users make informed decisions about when to rely on AI and when to intervene.
- *Maintain consistency*. Holding uniform gestures, layouts, visual cues, and interaction patterns helps users transfer knowledge from one medium and platform to another, thereby reducing their cognitive load and minimizing errors. Interfaces should behave predictably across media and platforms. For example, controlling smart lights or thermostats should follow the same navigation structure, terminology, and interaction flow, whether using a mobile app or a wall-mounted control panel. Visual and interaction consistency are equally important. Using the same icons, colors, and layouts for the system status, notifications, or alerts helps users quickly recognize patterns and reduces their learning curves. For instance, a warning icon on a smart security camera should have the same meaning as

that on a mobile application or dashboard. Automated AI behaviors, such as recommendations and energy-saving routines, should follow predictable patterns. Sudden or inconsistent changes can confuse users, particularly when multiple devices interact.

- *Establish feedback and error prevention*: Without timely feedback and clear error prevention mechanisms, users may feel uncertain and make mistakes in autonomous or semi-autonomous systems. Effective feedback ensures that users understand the outcomes of their actions, can easily correct mistakes, and maintain confidence. Interfaces should provide immediate feedback through visual, auditory, or haptic signals. For example, a smart lock can emit a sound and display a light indicator when it is successfully locked, reassuring the user that the action has been completed. When errors occur, the explanations should be clear and actionable. For instance, a health-monitoring app could clarify why a measurement failed: "Heart rate sensor disconnected—please place your finger on the sensor and retry." Users should also be able to undo or modify their actions with minimal effort. In a smart home system, if an incorrect lighting schedule is set, users should be able to adjust or cancel it quickly without navigating through multiple menus.

5.3 Content-Related Skill Design Improvements

Content-related challenges on the internet and connected intelligent media largely depends on an individual's level of information, communication, content creation, and strategic media use skills. From each of these skill perspectives, we discuss how designers can address potential difficulties.

Information Skill Perspective

Chapter 3 revealed that the level of information skills is relatively low among the general population. Many participants struggled in the search process and spent more time on search tasks than the difficulty of the assignments warranted. The problems encountered were compounded by developers' insufficient consideration of users with lower information skill levels. Enhancing the provision of online content is particularly beneficial for users with lower-to-intermediate educational backgrounds. To identify potential improvements, we refer to the information-searching process described in Chap. 2. Examining each stage of this process reveals valuable opportunities for refining the functionality of search systems and online information services.

- The first step in the information-seeking process is *problem definition*. This stage involves clarifying the required information. The performance tests revealed that many difficulties in online information searching stemmed from problems that were vague, fragmented, or poorly articulated. When users are unsure of what they are looking for or cannot clearly express their goals, the resulting searches are often inefficient, incomplete, or overwhelming. Designers can play a pivotal role in facilitating this step by embedding features that help users to structure and refine their information needs. Structured prompts, for example, can guide users in specifying the type of information they seek, such as factual data, instructions, comparisons, or conceptual explanations. These prompts act as scaffolds, helping users organize their thoughts and articulate their queries more clearly.

  Specialized portals, particularly in sensitive or complex domains such as health, education, and government services, can further facilitate problem definition by offering predefined categories, templates, or example queries. These tools provide users with a clear starting point for their inquiries, reducing uncertainty and helping them navigate unfamiliar landscapes. For example, a government portal might present categories such as "tax filings," "benefit applications," or "permit requests," enabling users to select the relevant area before entering their detailed questions.

  AI can enhance problem definition by transforming vague or incomplete intentions into precise and actionable queries. AI-powered chatbots, for example, can engage users in clarifying dialogues and ask questions such as whether a user is searching for causes, symptoms, or treatments, thereby narrowing the scope of the search. AI can also suggest alternative phrasings to improve search relevance or predict user intent based on context and prior behavior.
- The next stage from which designers can draw valuable insights is the user's *selection of a source* when searching for information. At this stage, users decide where to begin their search, often relying on platforms or portals with which they are most familiar. People tend to adapt their information-seeking strategies to the tools and

entry points they know, using these as primary starting points, even if these are not the most efficient sources. Designers can benefit from monitoring how users first arrive at their websites and develop entry points to better support user needs.

Some users seem to gravitate toward general online portals when seeking specific information. Although such portals are often designed to organize vast amounts of digital content, they can complicate the search process. Broad content scopes and complex navigation structures can overwhelm users, making it difficult to locate relevant materials. Performance test results confirm this, showing that excessive information and poorly structured menus often hinder users' ability to find what they need to complete their tasks. At a minimum, portals should clearly communicate their purposes, identify the organization behind them, and set realistic expectations for their users. Providing concise overviews of available resources or "start here" guides can further orient users and reduce their initial confusion.

AI can play an important role in supporting source selection. For instance, AI-powered predictive entry points can anticipate a user's preferred starting page based on historical behavior, search patterns, or contextual factors, efficiently guiding them toward the most relevant sources. Conversational AI and virtual assistants can provide real-time guidance. They can recommend whether to start by browsing categories, performing targeted searches, or using guided wizards. AI can also provide context-aware recommendations by dynamically adjusting guidance based on the patterns of similar users. For example, if multiple users with similar profiles frequently begin a search in a particular section or follow certain navigation paths, AI can proactively suggest these routes.

- The third step in the information-seeking process involves the *formulation of search queries*, which proved to be challenging for many participants. Users often struggle to create queries that accurately capture the information they seek, thereby highlighting the need for tools and features to assist in the query formulation process. Modern search engines provide several mechanisms to support users. For instance, they suggest queries as users begin typing in the search bar, offering autocomplete recommendations that can guide users toward more precise or commonly searched terms. Similarly, spelling correction tools automatically adjust misspelled words, and prompts such as "Did you mean…?" appear when the query is overly broad or ambiguous. However, AI-driven support can also introduce new challenges. Users may take suggestions at face value without checking whether the recommended queries align with their actual information needs. Autocorrect features can sometimes override the user's intended search term, especially in specialized domains, causing confusion or directing the user away from niche information. Moreover, AI recommendations are often shaped by popularity or historical trends, which may bias the results toward common queries and neglect less frequent but equally valid user needs.

More advanced AI tools can significantly enhance how users formulate and refine their queries. Among these, *Natural Language Processing (NLP)* models represent a powerful class of AI systems that employ machine learning and deep learning techniques to recognize and analyze patterns in human language. These models are designed to understand, interpret, and generate both written and spoken language, enabling computers to process text in a way that mirrors human comprehension. By interpreting incomplete, ambiguous, or poorly structured queries, NLP models can generate contextually relevant suggestions, alternative search terms, or even entire reformulated queries that better align with users' intentions and information needs. Additionally, conversational AI chatbots can interact in real time, asking clarifying questions such as, "Are you looking for instructions, examples, or explanations?" or "Do you mean a local permit or a national application?" This helps users refine vague queries and prevents frustration. Predictive search systems can anticipate the next steps by presenting related queries, options, or categories before the user explicitly requests them. For example, a user searching for "symptoms" on a healthcare portal might see predictive suggestions like "common cold," "flu," or "COVID-19," each accompanied by a short description and a link to structured guidance. To maximize the benefits of AI, designers should develop transparent and adaptable query assistance tools. Suggestions should be presented as guidance rather than authoritative answers, and users should be able to accept, modify, or reject them easily. In this way, AI can facilitate more effective search query formulation, helping users articulate their needs clearly while preserving critical thinking and control over the search process.

- The step of *selecting relevant information or suitable search results* is heavily influenced by the quantity and quality of online content. The sheer quantity of online content presents challenges as the mere presence of information does not guarantee its relevance or reliability. Users are frequently confronted with excessive amounts of information, a phenomenon commonly referred to as *information overload*, which can lead to confusion, frustration, and feelings of being overwhelmed. Public service platforms, such as government or health portals, often aim to provide as many services as possible, but this breadth can come at the expense of usability and focus. When content is abundant but poorly prioritized, users may struggle to identify what is truly relevant, undermining the platform's effectiveness. Public initiatives would benefit from prioritizing content according to the actual needs and interests of different population segments to ensure that key information is immediately accessible.

  In IoT environments, information overload arises from different angles. Devices continuously collect and process large volumes of data from multiple sources, and poorly presented information can overwhelm users, increase their cognitive load, and reduce system effectiveness. Effective data presentation should focus on displaying only the most relevant information in a clear, intuitive, and actionable format. Highlighting information that is immediately pertinent to the user's tasks or decisions is essential, and data should be represented using easy-to-understand graphics, such as charts, progress bars, icons, or dashboards. Additionally, AI can support users by summarizing complex outputs from smart devices into digestible, actionable insights. For example, a health-monitoring application might consolidate multiple biometric readings into a single actionable alert rather than displaying raw data streams, while providing contextual historical trends or comparisons to inform decision-making.

  In addition to concerns about quantity, there are problems with quality when selecting relevant information. Many search results do not provide the precise information that users require. Often, users believe they have found a satisfactory answer, whereas an outside observer might conclude that better or more accurate resources exist if the user had examined additional results pages. This tendency to accept the first seemingly plausible answer reflects the common phenomenon of premature satisfaction, in which users underestimate the difficulty of identifying high-quality information in search engines. Another challenge lies in users' limited ability to differentiate between commercial and non-commercial content. This lack of discernment can lead to biased or incomplete understanding. Search engines should clearly label sponsored results and provide guidance to help users critically evaluate sources. Chapter 3 highlighted that individuals with lower levels of educational attainment are particularly disadvantaged. As educational attainment is closely linked to reading, writing, and understanding texts, challenges in these areas can hinder the selection of relevant content across various online services and applications. This disadvantage is even more pronounced for those with low literacy, as partial or non-literacy effectively excludes individuals from accessing online information. The next chapter addresses the digital skill challenges faced by low-literate users in greater detail and provides recommendations for educational interventions. Several institutions focus on improving the clarity and accessibility of online content, particularly textual material. For example, the Plain Language Action and Information Network (PLAIN) is a cross-agency initiative of federal employees dedicated to promoting clear communication in government writing. The resources and best practices offered by such initiatives should not be overlooked by web developers or communication professionals, particularly those working for official institutions, whose content is often overly complex for the target audience. The language used by officials frequently differs from that employed by general internet users, creating a barrier to comprehension. Several readability metrics are available to estimate text difficulty and guide improvements.

AI can play a supporting role in the selection of information. AI-powered ranking algorithms can prioritize results that are more likely to be relevant, reliable, and contextually appropriate based on the user's query. AI can also personalize search results by learning from past behaviors to surface content that better matches a user's needs. However, AI also presents challenges. In many cases, AI does more than prioritize results and provides direct answers to the user's query, which can discourage people from exploring the broader list of results. Reliance on ranking algorithms and AI summarization tools can exacerbate the tendency to accept the first answer encountered without critical evaluation. Furthermore, algorithms are often opaque, and users may not understand why certain results are prioritized, which can reinforce biases or limit exposure to diverse perspectives. Personalized AI rankings may create *filter bubbles*, where users are only shown content aligned with prior searches, potentially narrowing their understanding of the topic.

- The final step in the search process involves the ***evaluation of information***, which according to our task-based performance tests, is rarely performed by users. Many users seem to operate under the assumption that the content found online is inherently true, which poses a significant risk of misinformation. This highlights the critical need for mechanisms that help users effectively assess the reliability and quality of online information. One approach is to use quality hallmarks or certification marks on official websites. These marks can signal that the content has been reviewed and validated and meets the established standards of accuracy and trustworthiness. Several domain-specific marks exist; however, their effectiveness is questionable, as not all users recognize them. Additionally, some organizations issue proprietary quality marks to encourage engagement with their services, which can create confusion or skepticism.

AI can play an important role in the evaluation process. AI can assist by automatically assessing the credibility of content and analyzing factors such as the authority of the source, citation quality, and consistency with established knowledge. NLP models can flag content that is misleading, outdated, or inconsistent, thereby helping users distinguish reliable information from questionable sources. However, AI also introduces potential challenges. Users may overrely on AI-generated evaluations without critically engaging with the content, potentially reinforcing blind trust in algorithms. In addition, AI systems are trained on existing datasets, which may carry biases or inaccuracies, meaning that the evaluation itself is not infallible. Therefore, transparency and interpretability are essential; AI-driven quality assessments should clearly indicate the criteria used to determine trustworthiness and allow users to explore the underlying rationale. This is the central aim of ***explainable AI (XAI)***: to make the decision-making processes of AI systems understandable to humans (Dwivedi et al., 2023). Most advanced AI models, such as deep neural networks, operate as "black boxes." Although they can generate highly accurate predictions, their internal reasoning is difficult to understand. XAI seeks to open this black box and clarify how conclusions are reached. Transparency involves demonstrating how an AI system processes data to make decisions. For instance, a navigation app should not merely suggest a route but also explain that a certain route is faster because of lighter traffic. Interpretability refers to making AI predictions understandable to humans. In healthcare, for example, an AI system might not simply label a patient as high-risk for heart disease but also indicate that age, blood pressure, and cholesterol levels are decisive factors. When decisions are explained in this way, users are more likely to develop trust. Accountability is equally important, as it enables the identification of errors, biases, and risks in AI models. In the financial sector, if a loan application is denied, an explainable system can provide a clear justification, such as a low credit score or a high debt-to-income ratio, rather than leaving the decision opaque.

Improving Content from a Communication Skill Perspective

In this section, we provide general suggestions on how to improve online content based on the definition of communication skills provided in Chap. 2.

- The definition begins with *managing online contacts*. As discussed in Chap. 3, many people struggle to manage their contacts effectively. For example, on social networking sites, users often group all contacts under a single undifferentiated label, making it difficult to tailor messages or effectively control privacy. Applications that allow users to add or remove contacts from lists could further support users by offering features to categorize or segment contacts according to their relationships, roles, or contexts. Encouraging and supporting users to manage their online contacts more deliberately can help them make more selective and appropriate decisions regarding who should receive specific information. Clearer options for setting messages as intended for public versus private audiences are essential, as poorly understood settings can lead to unintended disclosure. A useful analogy is to imagine all contacts on a social network platform gathered in a single large room: partners, parents, great aunts, nephews, ex-partners, college friends, work colleagues, and friends of friends are all randomly seated. Without careful management, users may forget the diversity of their audience, leading to messages that are inappropriate, misinterpreted, or potentially harmful. AI-driven suggestions can help users automatically categorize contacts based on interaction patterns, communication frequency, or contextual metadata, such as workplace or family connections. AI can also assist in visualizing the composition of a user's network, highlighting clusters or subgroups to make audience diversity more salient.

- The definition of communication skills continues with *encoding, decoding, and exchanging* messages. In online discussions, communication is often direct, abrupt, or even impolite. Users frequently lack awareness of who is receiving their messages and how their communication might be interpreted, which can lead to misunderstandings, conflict, and unintended offense. In certain contexts, such as public discussion forums, employing moderators can help manage interactions. Moderators do not restrict freedom of speech but ensure that discussions adhere to the general norms of politeness and constructive dialogue. They can provide clear guidelines or rules, often referred to as *netiquette*, which outline the expected standards of behavior. Users can be informed of these rules before engaging, helping them to understand the social context and expectations of the online space. From our test results, we concluded that despite the availability of netiquette guidelines, many users neglect these recommendations and post messages, photos, or videos without fully considering their appropriateness for the intended audience. AI can assist moderators by identifying posts that may violate guidelines or require attention, allowing human moderators to focus on more nuanced judgments. Practical recommendations for improving online communication include encouraging users to reflect on whether a message is suitable for the audience, verifying that the content accurately reflects their intended meaning, and reviewing grammatical correctness. NLP models can provide real-time feedback on tone and clarity, alerting users if a message may be perceived as rude, aggressive, or ambiguous. Grammar and spelling checks can be automated, and AI-driven suggestions can help users rephrase messages to convey their intended meaning better. AI can also detect content that may be inappropriate for public sharing and recommend alternative ways to express the message privately or diplomatically.

- The skills to *attract attention* are often challenging for the general internet user. Capturing and maintaining attention online requires creativity and knowledge of effective strategies for visibility and engagement. Many marketing agencies specialize in this area and offer services to increase traffic to websites, blogs, and social media profiles. However, ordinary users often lack the skills to attract audiences. From a skills perspective, attracting attention involves understanding the audience's behavior and effectively using metadata, such as tags, titles, and descriptions. Users must also be able to analyze which types of content resonate with different audiences and adapt their strategies accordingly. Supporting users in developing these skills can help them engage more effectively with their intended audience. AI can play a crucial role in this process. Platforms can leverage AI-driven recommendation systems to suggest optimal tags, titles, or thumbnails that increase the likelihood of user engagement. AI can analyze trends, user interactions, and engagement metrics to provide tailored guidance, showing which types of content are most likely to attract attention in specific contexts. For example, AI can recommend adjustments to the format, timing, or visual elements of a video or post to maximize visibility. Additionally, AI can support users by highlighting underutilized opportunities for targeting audiences, identifying gaps in content coverage, or predicting which topics are likely to go viral. However, algorithmic guidance is also shaped by existing trends and biases, which may reinforce popular content patterns and make it harder for new or unconventional voices to gain visibility. From a design and user support perspective, platforms can enhance communication skills by attracting attention through examples of successful content, tutorials on tagging and metadata usage, and AI-driven insights into audience engagement. Combining educational guidance with AI assistance allows users to develop both the practical skills needed to reach a larger audience and critical awareness to use AI recommendations thoughtfully. This integrated approach empowers users to optimize their visibility while maintaining authenticity and quality in their online communication.
- Designers should take greater responsibility in supporting users in the communication skills required to create an *online profile*. Profile creation is a form of self-presentation that requires users to make thoughtful decisions regarding what information to disclose, how

to frame their identity, and how to protect their privacy. Many social networking sites implicitly encourage users to reveal as much personal information as possible without adequately highlighting potential risks or providing guidance on responsible disclosure. From a skills perspective, creating an effective and safe profile requires awareness of privacy implications, audience considerations, and the long-term consequences of sharing personal information. Users should be prompted to consider who can access their posts and what risks they might incur by publicizing certain information. Designers could integrate features that encourage reflection before publishing, such as prompts asking users to review the visibility of sensitive data or to question what could be lost if their profile is widely accessible. Although online dating platforms often implement more explicit privacy guidance, most social networking sites provide limited support in this area, leaving many users vulnerable to unintentional exposure. Implemented AI can analyze profile content in real time, flagging potentially sensitive information and providing recommendations for safer sharing practices. AI-driven suggestions can help users categorize information according to their privacy levels, identify content that may be risky to make public, and offer guidance on audience segmentation. For instance, AI can prompt users to restrict access to personal contact information or recommend profile elements that should be visible only to trusted connections.

- To engage with *serious games and simulations*, users require skills in collaboration. In collaborative environments, designers should incorporate features that encourage exploration and experimentation, provide clear objectives, and allow flexibility in how tasks are approached. Collaboration can be further supported through structured communication channels, shared objectives, and tools for monitoring team progress, which help participants coordinate effectively. Tutorials, scaffolding, and guided practices can be implemented to support users. Alternative learning paths, adjustable difficulty levels, and solo practice modes ensure accessibility and may reduce frustration.
- A final recommendation emerges from the observation that people might compensate for deficiencies in one skill by leveraging another (Van Deursen et al., 2014). For instance, individuals who lack information skills may use communication skills to request assistance

from others online to obtain the knowledge required. Designers can anticipate such situations and create environments that facilitate skill compensation. Ideally, users are enabled to ask and answer questions, drawing on the expertise of the community. Moreover, users participate in content regulation by voting on the quality of answers, marking interesting questions, and reporting inappropriate or abusive behaviors. Such participatory features enable individuals with limited information (or communication) skills to benefit from the collective knowledge and judgment of a community.

Improving Content from a Content Creation Skill Perspective

Content can take many forms, ranging from written text, such as articles, blog posts, and reviews, to visual and auditory media, such as photographs, videos, and music. Education plays a crucial role in teaching people how to design and create content that accurately and effectively communicates information to the intended audience. However, developers can encourage individuals to produce higher-quality content in several ways. Numerous guidelines exist to support creators by offering recommendations to those with little prior experience. A wide variety of tools are available that enable individuals to produce almost any type of content, from websites, weblogs, and bulletin boards to e-cards, tutorials, music clips, and full-length films. Many of these tools provide practical recommendations during the design process. However, their primary focus has traditionally been on lowering technical barriers, making it easier for non-experts to publish their work. While this democratization of content creation is important, it does not automatically guarantee textual clarity, coherence, or effective communication. The quality of the content determines whether it resonates with the intended audience and sustains their interests. From a developer's perspective, the challenge is therefore not only to simplify the technical aspects of creation but also to support users in producing content that is purposeful, clear, and audience centered. This can be achieved by embedding mechanisms into creation tools that prompt users to reflect on the effectiveness of their messages. For instance, systems might ask creators to verify whether their work addresses the needs and interests of the intended audience or suggest that they seek feedback from their peers before publishing.

Developments in AI have added a new dimension to this process. AI-powered writing assistants can analyze drafts in real time, offering feedback on clarity, tone, coherence, and potential bias. They suggest improvements in wording, provide alternative structures, or adapt content to different reading levels and cultural contexts. In the visual and multimedia domains, AI can help optimize image quality, recommend video-editing improvements, or even generate entirely new creative elements, such as background music or graphics. This raises additional responsibilities for AI tool developers. Their role extends beyond creating technically sophisticated systems; they must also ensure that these tools foster fairness, inclusivity, transparency, and empowerment. Several considerations are particularly important.

- *Transparency and explainability.* AI recommendations should not be opaque instructions. Designers need to develop platforms that make their reasoning visible, allowing users to understand why a certain edit, recommendation, or adjustment is proposed. For example, a writing assistant might not only flag a sentence as unclear but also explain that phrasing is ambiguous for readers with limited knowledge of the domain. Similarly, an AI video editor might recommend trimming a segment, but should also clarify that the suggested cut removes redundant material or improves pacing to keep viewers engaged. By making these rationales explicit, creators not only see what the tool suggests, but also why the suggestion matters.
- *Responsibility.* In all forms of AI- design improvements discussed in the previous sections, the user remains responsible for accepting and applying the results provided. This responsibility is an integral part of exercising strategic media use skills. Accordingly, designers and service providers must clearly communicate to users that they remain accountable for the content, explain how results are generated, and highlight any limitations in the underlying data, for example, by leveraging XAI techniques, as previously discussed.
- *Fairness and bias mitigation.* Because AI systems learn from large datasets, they inevitably reproduce the biases present in the training data. Developers must proactively test for and reduce such biases, ensuring that their recommendations do not unintentionally marginalize certain groups, reinforce stereotypes, or prioritize dominant cultural perspectives at the expense of diversity. Achieving fairness requires careful attention to both the data and the algorithms

used to process them. For example, an AI writing assistant trained primarily on texts from a particular cultural or linguistic background may produce suggestions that favor idioms, examples, or stylistic norms familiar to that group, potentially marginalizing users from other regions or linguistic traditions. Developers can address this by training models on more diverse datasets and incorporating mechanisms to detect culturally insensitive or exclusionary language use. Bias can be even more apparent in visual AI. Historically, image recognition systems have struggled to accurately identify people of certain skin tones or age groups, resulting in misclassifications or omissions. AI-powered photo and video-editing tools require fairness-aware algorithms that ensure features such as facial recognition, lighting adjustments, or automated tagging work reliably for all users, regardless of ethnicity, gender, or age.

- *Support for reflective practices.* Designers can embed prompts that ask creators to consider their target audience, the purpose of their message, or whether the tone aligns with their intended impact. In doing so, AI systems have moved from being passive assistants to active partners in the creative process. For example, a writing assistant could suggest that a user reviews whether the tone of a blog post is appropriate for a certain audience or ask whether key concepts are clearly explained for readers with limited background knowledge. Then, the tool does not simply correct grammar or style but encourages the creator to think critically about clarity, relevance, and accessibility. Similarly, video-editing AI might recommend trimming certain clips but also prompt the creator to consider whether the pacing maintains audience engagement or whether the sequence effectively conveys the intended emotional impact.
- *Adaptability to different users.* As we have seen in Chap. 3, there is much room for improvement when it comes to content creation skills, and the levels vary widely. Most are novices who need step-by-step guidance, whereas others are highly skilled and require advanced customizable features to support their complex projects. Designers should develop AI systems that can adapt to this range of expertise and provide feedback and assistance that are appropriately scaled to each user's digital skill level. For example, a beginner using a writing assistant might benefit from basic suggestions such as grammar corrections, sentence clarity improvements, and simple style tips. In contrast, an intermediate user may require feedback on tone,

audience engagement, or logical flow, whereas an expert may seek highly nuanced suggestions such as alternative rhetorical strategies or advanced stylistic recommendations. A novice video editor might receive step-by-step guidance for adding transitions, captions, or audio overlays, whereas a professional editor could access advanced features, such as color grading, motion tracking, or automated scene composition. By recognizing varying levels of digital skills, AI can adjust explanations, prompts, and interface complexities accordingly. Moreover, adaptability encourages sustained engagement and learning. Users can gradually progress from basic guidance to more complex features as their content creation skills improve, fostering long-term development rather than creating a one-size-fits-all experience.

- *Feedback and collaborative development.* Designers can integrate mechanisms that allow content creators to critique, refine, and customize AI-generated suggestions, thereby establishing a dynamic feedback loop. This approach ensures that the system improves its accuracy, relevance, and usefulness over time, while also fostering stronger user engagement and trust. By participating in this iterative process, users become co-shapers of the tool, actively influencing its functioning and development. For example, a user might disagree with a suggested edit or tone adjustment. By providing feedback, users can train the system to align better with their personal style or audience expectations. Over time, AI learns from these corrections, producing recommendations that are increasingly tailored to individual creators' preferences. Beyond individual customization, feedback and co-evolution can improve the system for an entire user base. Designers can analyze aggregated user input to identify common issues, biases, or gaps in functionality, thereby enabling iterative improvements that benefit all users. For instance, a writing AI application might detect that multiple users are rejecting certain grammar recommendations because they are contextually inappropriate, prompting developers to adjust the underlying algorithms. This co-evolutionary process also strengthens users' trust. When users see that their input influences the system and improves its future performance, they are more likely to actively engage and rely on its suggestions. It transforms the user-AI relationship from a one-way interaction into a collaborative partnership, where both human judgment and machine intelligence contribute to content quality, creativity, and ethical standards.

- *Ethical design principles.* Designers must embed ethical safeguards into generative AI tools from the outset to ensure responsible and trustworthy content creation. These include respecting intellectual property rights, protecting user privacy, and discouraging the generation of manipulative or misleading content. Ethical design goes beyond technical compliance; it requires anticipating the social, cultural, and psychological impact of AI outputs on users and audiences. For instance, AI content generation applications should avoid producing plagiarized material or suggesting copyrighted work without proper attribution. In multimedia applications, AI-driven image, video, or music generators should incorporate safeguards that prevent the unauthorized use of protected content, ensuring that creators and original authors are respected. Privacy is another crucial consideration in this regard. AI systems often collect and analyze user data to improve their recommendations or feedback. Developers must implement strong data-protection measures, minimize unnecessary data collection, and provide users with transparency and control over how their data is used. For example, writing or video tools could allow users to opt out of data sharing for model training or anonymize contributions before analysis. Ethical AI also discourages manipulative or misleading outputs. Recommendation systems, generative models, and persuasive content tools should not amplify sensationalized, false, or harmful information for the sake of engagement or efficiency. Developers can address this by integrating fact-checking mechanisms, content-quality scoring, and warnings for potentially misleading suggestions.

Improving Content from a Strategic Media Use Skill Perspective

Access to the internet and connected intelligent media does not automatically translate into equal benefits for all users. As demonstrated in previous chapters, gaining positive outcomes requires a high level of strategic media use skills. As explained in Chap. 2, an important aspect of these skills is decision-making. While relatively simple decisions, such as comparing prices or choosing a product, can be supported by online decision-support tools, assistance for more complex, multifaceted decisions remains relatively scarce. The empirical evidence presented in Chap. 3 shows that most internet users and users of smart devices struggle with the various stages of decision-making. The first stage, problem orientation, is particularly challenging. Overcrowded webpages, rapidly changing multimedia content, and irrelevant notifications create an overwhelming environment that makes it difficult for users to focus on effectively identifying and framing their problems. The second stage, taking appropriate actions, such as consulting relevant sources and synthesizing information, is equally demanding because of the sheer number of potential choices and actions. Most users rely on a single source and make decisions based on incomplete information. Although users may feel confident about their choices, their decisions often lack the comprehensive perspective necessary for achieving optimal results. Consequently, integrating and evaluating a complete set of relevant information before making a choice remains rare.

Developers can play a key role in supporting those with lower strategic media use skills. *Decision support systems (DSS)* support decision-making by automating certain steps and reducing distractions. They are increasingly available for everyday personal choices—such as selecting mobile phone subscriptions, identifying affordable internet providers, choosing holiday packages, or finding banks with the highest interest rates—offering structured guidance for organizing thoughts, evaluating alternatives, and maintaining focus. By streamlining complex tasks, DSS can, to some extent, compensate for the lack of strategic media use skills, allowing users to make more informed choices. For example, price comparison platforms, healthcare provider selectors, and voting guides enable users to compare multiple options quickly and efficiently. However, many DSS are influenced by commercial interest. For instance, a smartphone recommendation tool may prioritize options from certain providers, whereas independent platforms may rely on user engagement metrics to justify their existence. To mitigate such biases, quality certifications or hallmarks can be used to indicate the reliability and independence of these systems, allowing users to differentiate between impartial guidance and potentially commercially skewed advice.

The development of AI has expanded the capabilities of DSS. An AI-powered DSS can analyze vast amounts of data, identify relevant patterns, and provide personalized recommendations tailored to individual needs. For example, AI can suggest optimal healthcare providers based on treatment outcomes, patient reviews, and location, or predict financial options suited to a user's risk profile and long-term goals. Machine learning algorithms can also help users synthesize multiple information sources, highlight conflicting viewpoints, and visualize potential outcomes, thereby making complex strategic decisions more manageable. Moreover, social networking platforms introduce a new dimension of collective intelligence to decision-making. Modern DSS increasingly incorporate user-group data and peer-generated insights, allowing individual users to learn from the choices and evaluations of others. For instance, such a system shows which mortgage options other users with similar financial profiles selected, the criteria they considered important, and the perceived benefits of these options. This collective approach helps users identify patterns, weigh trade-offs, and contextualize decisions in real-world experiences. Importantly, designers should develop systems that give users control over their decision-making processes. Users can select which stakeholders to consult, such as political advisors, financial consultants, or medical experts, and determine how and when to interact with these sources. AI can facilitate this interaction by recommending relevant stakeholders, summarizing their feedback, and integrating these insights into the decision-making workflow. In doing so, DSS move beyond automation, becoming interactive and adaptive tools that support reflective, informed, and context-sensitive decision-making. Despite these advances, designers must remain vigilant. Users should be informed of the limitations of DSS and cautioned against blind reliance on automated recommendations. The systems must be transparent about data sources, algorithmic reasoning, and potential biases. Furthermore, DSS should be designed to accommodate varying levels of user expertise, ensuring that novices are guided effectively without overwhelming more experienced users. Ethical considerations, including privacy, fairness, and avoidance of manipulative content, remain a priority. To maximize the effectiveness of DSS, many of the principles discussed in the prior sections apply:

- *Transparency and explainability.* DSS should clearly communicate how recommendations are generated, including data sources, algorithmic reasoning, and potential limitations. For example, a healthcare DSS may explain why certain providers are recommended based on patient outcomes, experience, and location.
- *Ethical safeguards.* Developers must ensure that recommendations do not favor certain groups, commercial interests, or dominant

perspectives at the expense of others. Independent quality certifications or hallmarks can indicate an unbiased and reliable DSS. Furthermore, developers should prioritize privacy, security, and ethical standards. DSS should avoid manipulative or misleading content, respect intellectual property, and ensure that recommendations serve users' best interests.

- *Support for reflective decision-making*. DSS should prompt users to consider their goals, target audiences, and priorities, moving beyond automated suggestions to foster critical thinking. For example, a financial DSS could encourage users to evaluate both the short- and long-term implications of their investment decisions.
- *Adaptability to diverse users.* DSS must accommodate users with varying digital skill levels. Layered guidance ensures engagement with diverse populations.
- *Interactive feedback and co-creation.* DSS should allow users to provide feedback, refine AI suggestions, and adapt systems to their preferences. This iterative process not only improves system accuracy but also strengthens user trust and agency.
- *Integration of collective intelligence.* By incorporating insights from peer networks or expert communities, DSS can help users benefit from group knowledge while maintaining individual autonomy over their final decisions.
- *User empowerment and control.* Users should be able to select which stakeholders, experts, or data sources influence the DSS and determine how and when to integrate these insights into their decision-making process.

5.4 Conclusions

Poorly designed interfaces can hinder users from developing and effectively applying digital skills, reinforcing cycles of exclusion between inaccessible systems and low digital skills. Unfortunately, many platforms seem to operate under the assumption that all users possess sufficient skill levels. This chapter proposes improvements based on both medium- and content-related digital skill perspectives.

From a medium-related skill perspective, this chapter emphasizes the need for designers to develop interfaces that are not only visually appealing but fundamentally accessible, intuitive, and user-friendly. Many digital media and platforms seem to prioritize aesthetics over usability, overlooking users who struggle with operational and formal skills. Given that many services assume a high level of digital skills, this trend is particularly concerning. To mitigate these barriers, designers should follow established frameworks such as the WCAG, which encourage simplified navigation, clear feedback mechanisms, step-by-step guidance, personalization options, and the gradual disclosure of advanced features. User- and Human-Centered Design are highlighted as critical approaches in this context. By engaging real users early on, conducting diverse and iterative testing, and refining interfaces based on empirical insights, these approaches challenge designers to reassess assumptions about how people interact with technology. This becomes especially important in the context of smart devices. Although their intuitive interfaces may lower entry barriers, they can also limit more complex, productive uses and reinforce consumptive behavior. As AI and IoT become more pervasive, traditional usability principles must be expanded to address the challenges of transparency, trust, guidance, user autonomy, consistency, and feedback. Intelligent systems frequently adapt in ways that are invisible to users, leading to confusion when system behavior shifts unexpectedly. Therefore, designers must clearly communicate what the system is doing and why, provide actionable guidance, enable users to override automated decisions, maintain consistent interaction patterns, and deliver timely and meaningful feedback while preventing errors.

From a content-related skills perspective, enhancing user interaction with online content requires addressing four digital skill domains: information, communication, content creation, and strategic media use. In terms of information skills, many users face difficulties at various stages of the information-seeking process. Designers can support them by implementing clearer navigation structures, guided prompts, AI-assisted query formulation, transparent ranking mechanisms, and features that help reduce information overload. Regarding communication skills, platforms should promote safer and more intentional interactions by enabling contact grouping, fostering netiquette, offering AI-based feedback on tone and clarity, and encouraging responsible profile management. Although all kinds of tools have lowered the threshold for content creation, challenges related to clarity, inclusivity, and relevance remain. Embedding AI-driven feedback can help users improve coherence, fairness, and alignment with audience needs, thereby producing higher-quality and more meaningful content. Finally, from the perspective of strategic media use skills, many users struggle to make informed decisions in complex digital environments. Decision Support Systems, particularly when supported by AI, can assist users in evaluating options and structuring decisions, as long as they remain transparent, unbiased, adaptive, user-controlled, and supportive of reflective and ethical engagement.

References

Carroll, J. M., & Carrithers, C. (1984). Training wheels in a user interface. *Communications of the ACM, 27*(8), 800–806.

Dwivedi, R., Dave, D., Naik, H., Singhal, S., Omer, R., Patel, P., et al. (2023). Explainable AI (XAI): Core ideas, techniques, and solutions. *ACM Computing Surveys, 55*(9), 1–33.

Gill, K. S. (1991). Summary of human-centred systems research in Europe, Part 1. *Systemist, the Journal of the UK Systems Society, 13*(1), 7–27.

Gould, J. D., & Lewis, C. (1985). Designing for usability: key principles and what designers think. *Communications of the ACM, 28*(3), 300–311.

Lehaney, B., Clarke, S., Kimberlee, V., & Spencer-Matthews, S. (1999). The human side of information development: A case of an intervention at a British visitor attraction. *Journal of End User Computing, 11*(4), 33–39.

Napoli, P. M., & Obar, J. A. (2014). The emerging mobile Internet underclass: A critique of mobile Internet access. *The Information Society, 30*(5), 323–334.

Norman, D. A., & Draper, S. W. (1986). *User centered system design; new perspectives on human-computer interaction*. L. Erlbaum Associates Inc.

Springer, A., & Whittaker, S. (2019, March). Progressive disclosure: Empirically motivated approaches to designing effective transparency. In *Proceedings of the 24th international conference on intelligent user interfaces* (pp. 107–120).

Van Deursen, A. J. A. M., Courtois, C., & Van Dijk, J. A. G. M. (2014). Internet skills, sources of support, and benefiting from Internet use. *International journal of human-computer interaction, 30*(4), 278–290.

CHAPTER 6

Fostering the Learning of Digital Skills

6.1 Introduction: Pathways of Learning

The second approach to addressing digital skill insufficiencies focuses on user learning. Interestingly, formal (adult) education accounts for only a small fraction of how most people acquire digital skills. Informal learning remains the dominant pathway, characterized as a self-directed, incidental, and often socially supported form of learning that takes place outside formal educational contexts (Lucas & Moreira, 2009). It includes hands-on experimentation, consulting manuals, exploring online resources, and seeking help from peers, friends, and family. These approaches are natural, flexible, convenient, and often motivating. Their significance has grown steadily in recent years, likely due to the increasing user-friendliness of digital media and platforms, which reinforces the belief that individuals can teach themselves simply through use. However, as demonstrated in Chap. 3, this confidence can be misleading: merely engaging with a medium or platform does not necessarily translate into comprehensive digital skills. Moreover, informal learning can be laborious and inefficient, and once ineffective routines are adopted, individuals tend to persist with them. As a result, users often master only a narrow subset of available functions, leaving a wide range of potentially beneficial applications unexplored. A further challenge arises when users mistake a few basic operations for genuine digital skills. In reality, their skills may fall far short

A. van Deursen and J. van Dijk, *Digital Skills*, Digital Education and Learning, https://doi.org/10.1057/978-1-349-96162-7_6

of the broader spectrum required for effective participation in a smart society, namely, the seven digital skills discussed in this book.

This chapter argues that formal education and structured training remain indispensable components of digital skill development. Schools, in particular, have both a unique opportunity and a clear responsibility to prepare children and adolescents for living and working in a smart society. While young people often engage intensively with digital media, this exposure does not automatically translate into the skills required for purposeful participation. Although they typically possess basic operational and formal skills due to early and frequent digital exposure, they often lack more advanced content-related digital skills. For adults, the situation is even more complex. Relatively little research has examined the current landscape of adult digital skills provision (Eynon, 2021). Special attention should be directed toward adults who lacked structured opportunities to acquire digital skills during their formal schooling. This includes individuals aged 50 and above, workers in occupations historically insulated from digital media, and groups facing structural barriers, such as people with disabilities, migrants, those experiencing non-literacy or low literacy, and older adults. For these populations, accessible adult education programs and community-based initiatives are essential.

To better understand how digital skills can be effectively developed, this chapter begins by examining *informal learning* throughout the life course. For children and adolescents, informal learning often takes place outside school through self-directed exploration at home and support from parents, siblings, or peers. This occurs largely in the context of entertainment, gaming, and social networking, with only a smaller proportion connected to school-related tasks. For adults, informal learning similarly plays a substantial role. Colleagues frequently provide support in workplace settings, while older adults may rely on younger family members for support. After exploring informal learning, the chapter turns to *formal education*, where digital skills are integrated into school curricula, vocational training programs, and structured instructional environments. Next, we examine *workplace learning*, encompassing employer-sponsored training, professional development programs, and learning embedded in daily work practices. Finally, the chapter addresses *lifelong learning opportunities* outside of formal employment, including community-based resources such as public libraries, community centers, and internet cafés, as well as distance education or specialized training institutions. These avenues are essential for reaching groups who may not have access to structured training at school or at work, and they provide flexible ways for individuals to update or expand their digital skills.

6.2 Learning by Doing and Learning from Others

In this section, we examine two forms of informal learning. The first is learning by doing or self-study, and the second is seeking assistance from people in one's immediate social environment. These two methods remain the most common ways in which individuals acquire the skills to use digital media.

Learning by Doing

It is hardly surprising that learning by doing plays a prominent role in overcoming digital skill deficiencies. This age-old form of experiential learning, described by Bruner (1961) as an *enactive mode of experience*, is rooted in direct interaction with one's environment. Unlike the more passive *iconic* and *symbolic* modes, which involve learning through images and language, the enactive mode is grounded in exploration, manipulation, and action (Bruner & Olsen, 1973). This is also referred to as *discovery learning*, in contrast to learning through direct instruction. In the context of digital skills, learning by doing offers several advantages. First, it is intrinsically rewarding (Schank & Cleary, 1995). Success through trial and error motivates learners to continue exploring and deepens their engagement with internet and intelligent media. Second, the design of contemporary media encourages discovery learning. User-friendly interfaces, intuitive icons, and responsive navigation structures encourage people to start experimenting immediately instead of turning to a manual or help function, which many perceive as a last resort. This design evolution contrasts sharply with earlier decades. In the 1980s, personal computers were so complex that manuals and courses were considered indispensable, whereas today, users can switch on a smart device and begin experimenting with gestures, icons, and menus almost instinctively. Third, learning by doing strengthens memory retention. Skills discovered through one's own actions are more likely to be remembered than those introduced through rote instruction (Bruner, 1961). The active involvement of learners reinforces both understanding and recall.

Despite its advantages, learning by doing has several drawbacks. The process may be frustrating and failure to identify the right steps may lead to discouragement and abandonment of the medium or platform. Furthermore, learning by doing is limited in the absence of essential knowledge. Many applications require a fundamental conceptual understanding before their functions can be explored meaningfully. Even for those with a basic understanding, keeping up can become challenging as media and platforms continue to advance. Similarly, learners may succeed in executing a task but fail to grasp the underlying principles or problem-solving rules (Mayer, 2004). Consequently, they may forget the procedure over time and may be unable to replicate it. Learning by doing imposes a high demand on working memory, which hampers the transfer of knowledge into long-term memory (Kirschner et al., 2006). Learning by doing is also opportunistic and narrow in scope. Once a solution is found, even if it is inefficient or suboptimal, users are likely to adopt it permanently, neglecting alternative and more effective methods.

We recommend educational policymakers, curriculum designers, school administrators, instructional coaches, and researchers to:

- *Promote blended* learning *approaches* that integrate learning by doing with structured guidance, peer support, and formal training. While learning by doing fosters motivation and engagement, it is most effective when supported by scaffolding that helps learners overcome frustration, inefficiency, and cognitive overload. This combination retains the experiential strengths of discovery learning while ensuring a deeper understanding and long-term knowledge retention. For instance, learners might independently explore online sources to create reports or infographics, while instructors offer credibility checklists, facilitate peer discussions to refine interpretations, and provide short workshops on data visualization. Similarly, learners could draft articles or social media posts on their own, supported by structured style guides, peer feedback, and brief lessons on audience engagement.
- *Leverage AI to enhance this blended learning approach.* AI can detect when learners are struggling and offer just-in-time hints, prompts, or explanations to prevent discouragement and abandonment. In addition, AI can generate feedback loops, identify when users rely on inefficient or suboptimal strategies, and suggest more effective alternatives.

Getting Help from People Around You

The second natural way to acquire digital skills is to seek help from others. People often develop digital skills within specific social contexts, assisted by individuals with whom they share relationships. The relevant social context depends on an individual's current stage of life. In developed societies, home is the primary context for young children, whereas the workplace becomes central after school. In countries with high household internet connectivity and widespread internet use at work, home and workplace environments may play a more prominent role than schools and training centers in shaping digital skills. In contrast, in developing countries, schools and community facilities such as access centers, internet cafés, and mobile phone networks play a relatively important role (Van Dijk, 2020), although computer and laptop use is often bypassed in the Global South, with populations adopting smartphones directly (Arora, 2019).

Getting help from others to learn digital skills progresses through the development of all stages of life. In developed countries, young children primarily learn digital skills at home, either independently or with parental guidance. While research suggests that children often do not discuss their internet use with older generations (Kalmus et al., 2015), online platforms increasingly provide parental controls that allow children to be gradually exposed to different layers of the internet. As children grow, siblings, friends, and neighbors increasingly contribute to learning. Even at school age, the home remains an important site for practice, leisure, and informal skill development. While schools may provide instruction and teacher-led guidance, children continue to refine their skills and receive support from their peers at home.

For adults, the home context is an important source of assistance when performing digital skills. In the survey discussed in Chap. 3, 62 percent of Dutch adults confirmed that there was someone at home who could help them with their internet use. Recent findings (Hammer et al., 2025) furthermore show that informal digital support is widespread: 59 percent of adults in the Netherlands assist someone with online issues—33 percent do so occasionally and 26 percent on a regular basis. This help is primarily rooted in family relationships. Four out of five helpers (80%) support a family member, most commonly their parents (54 percent). Moreover, three-quarters (75 percent) believe that the person they help would be unable to manage important digital tasks without their assistance. This underscores the critical role that informal helpers play in the everyday digital lives of people who struggle with online tasks. Beyond the family, people also provide support to friends (15 percent), neighbors (13 percent), and colleagues (7 percent), indicating that informal digital help extends into broader social networks, though to a lesser extent.

Besides the home context, the workplace is an important environment in which adults can acquire digital skills. Colleagues are often the primary source of learning, followed by helpdesks. A nationally representative survey of the Dutch labor force examined the primary sources of digital skills learning at work (Van Deursen & Van Dijk, 2014). Consistent with the findings on informal learning, most respondents cited co-workers as their main source of support (38 percent), followed by self-directed learning through the internet and books (19 percent) and assistance from people outside the workplace (15 percent). Increasingly, AI functions as a powerful supplemental tool for digital skills development at work, particularly for hands-on learning, practice, and efficiency, but it is likely to work best when combined with human guidance and formal training as it does not inherently teach underlying principles, critical thinking, or context-specific judgment.

For older generations who did not acquire digital skills during their schooling or early careers, home support and formal training (courses and instructional materials) are essential. In these cases, individuals may learn from their spouses, children, grandchildren, neighbors, or extended family members. This type of support not only helps older adults to engage in everyday digital tasks such as online banking, communication, or information retrieval, but also builds confidence and reduces anxiety when interacting with digital media.

Learning from people within one's social circle offers several advantages. Assistance from family members, friends, or colleagues is typically immediate, familiar, and tailored to the learner's specific needs. Helpers usually understand the learner's context and communicate in a shared language, making the interaction more relatable and less intimidating for the learner. Moreover, this type of support is likely to be faster and more practical than consulting helpdesks, manuals, or instructors. This aligns closely with learning by doing, which occurs naturally when individuals encounter obstacles while performing a task and seek quick, situation-specific guidance. However, learning from people we know also has limitations. There is no guarantee that the support provided is accurate or effective. Helpers are rarely trained educators, and their explanations may be incomplete, overly simplified, or based on personal "shortcuts" rather than on a sound understanding of the underlying principles. For instance, younger individuals may struggle to teach older family members because they lack insight into their perspectives or because they proceed too quickly through explanations (Gallistl et al., 2020). The reverse can also occur, with older adults finding it difficult to guide younger learners due to differences in familiarity with new media or teaching approaches. Access to informal support is also uneven; those who most need digital skill development are often least likely to receive such assistance (Helsper & Van Deursen, 2017). Children and adults from low-income or less-educated households typically have fewer knowledgeable people to turn to, while individuals from wealthier or more educated families can rely on broader support networks that include parents, siblings, or friends with higher levels of digital literacy. Furthermore, among the adults who provide support, about one in four (22 percent) report sometimes feeling *overburdened*, and one in five (19 percent) say they occasionally feel *uncomfortable* with the help request—for example, when the issue involves very personal or sensitive information (Hammer et al., 2025). It is important to note that, beyond uneven access to support, the digital media landscape and digital media repertoires of children and adults from low-income or less-educated households often differ from those of higher social classes. These differences are reflected not only in the devices and platforms they use, but also in the types of skills and practices they develop. Informal support is shaped by this context, as guidance is typically provided in response to specific requests for help rather than through proactive instruction, which can limit opportunities to explore, experiment, and develop broader digital skills.

The evolving media landscape also introduces new forms of assistance. AI applications such as chatbots, virtual tutors, or intelligent assistants, can act as digital proxies for human support. They provide real-time feedback, troubleshoot problems, and suggest optimal methods for completing tasks. By offering personalized, on-demand guidance, AI can make digital learning more accessible and immediate, particularly for those who lack access to skilled human helpers. However, this development is not without risks. Overreliance on AI may limit opportunities for collaborative learning, critical reflection, and in-depth engagement with digital media, particularly when users' social environments (family, peers, or educators) lack experience with AI applications. Effective digital skill development requires a balanced approach: learning not only through trial and error or social interaction but also through the thoughtful integration of intelligent systems. The challenge for learners and educators is to cultivate the skills needed to collaborate productively with both human and artificial sources of knowledge.

We recommend educational policymakers, curriculum designers, school administrators, instructional coaches, and researchers to:

- *Strengthen home-based digital learning support* for children by encouraging parental involvement and fostering sibling and peer collaboration.
- *Expand workplace-based digital learning opportunities* by supporting peer-to-peer knowledge exchange, mentoring, and accessible organizational help desks.
- *Provide targeted training for older generations*, combining family-based support with formal learning opportunities, such as community courses and instructional resources.
- *Integrate AI assistants* into digital learning ecosystems as complementary support tools, offering personalized, real-time help for troubleshooting and skill building.

6.3 Acquiring Digital Skills Through Formal Education

Terms such as *digital generation* or *digital natives* create the misleading impression that pupils and students naturally possess digital skills (Livingstone et al., 2011). This assumption usually stems from their apparent ease, speed, and familiarity in using digital media. Consequently, some teachers, especially those from older generations, may underestimate their role in cultivating students' digital skills. Moreover, teachers sometimes adopt a narrow view of what digital skills entail, focusing primarily on operational and formal skills, such as installing applications or navigating online platforms. This overlooks the more complex content-related dimensions of digital skills that involve critical thinking, ethical judgment, and responsible participation. Consequently, students often find that the digital environment at school differs sharply from their everyday experiences, which are increasingly shaped by social media, online communities, and interactive games. This disconnect can make school-based digital learning feel restrictive, outdated, or detached from the dynamic digital practices that define students' daily lives (Buckingham, 2012). Schools are increasingly addressing this challenge by encouraging students to use the internet for a variety of purposes, including completing homework, conducting research, preparing and delivering presentations, collaborating on group projects, participating in discussion forums, using learning management systems, creating digital portfolios, accessing educational videos and tutorials, analyzing data with online tools, and communicating with classmates. However, these practices are not consistently embedded in curricula, and it is questionable whether teachers feel confident enough to teach them. In member countries of the Organization for Economic Co-operation and Development, only about 65 percent of teachers report having the technical and pedagogical skills needed to effectively integrate digital devices into their teaching (OECD, 2018). Just 60% of teachers received training in digital technologies in the previous year. Furthermore, many pre-service teacher education graduates in the US do not feel adequately prepared to use technology in teaching (Office of Educational Technology, 2017). In several EU countries, less than half of teachers had been exposed to digital technologies during their initial teacher education (European Commission, 2019). As a result, more than 60% of EU students are taught by teachers who developed their digital skills independently in their spare time. This reliance on self-directed learning underscores the need for systematic teacher training.

Although schools have the unique possibility (and responsibility) to prepare students for living and working in a smart society, the current education system requires careful updating to meet these demands. Besides the challenge of preparing students to engage critically and responsibly in the expanding media landscape, special attention should be paid to comprehending how AI works, recognizing its limitations, and applying it responsibly (recognized under the concept of *AI literacy*). Related aspects include identifying algorithmic bias, assessing the reliability and provenance of AI-generated content, and strategically employing AI for problem-solving, creativity, and knowledge construction. Classrooms can play a crucial role by providing structured guidance and reflective space required to transform intuitive trial-and-error interactions into informed and responsible practices. This requires schools to create a learning environment that allows students to experiment through hands-on experiences, collaborate and share insights with peers, and reflect on their learning processes (Webster, 2015). Moreover, learning spaces that are diverse, adaptable, multimodal, and flexible can shift the educational focus from *what* students learn to *how* they learn, fostering deeper engagement, creativity, and critical thinking in digital contexts (Cobo, 2013). A suitable approach in this context might be problem-posing education, in which the teacher acts as a facilitator rather than a lecturer, guiding the class to collaboratively explore and address a problem or challenge through dialogue (Freire & Ramos, 1972). This method fosters deep and sustainable learning outcomes, benefiting both students and teachers. When applied to digital skills, it encourages learners and instructors to engage actively with real-world digital challenges—experimenting, questioning, and reflecting—so that knowledge is constructed collaboratively rather than passively received, and skills are more likely to transfer effectively to everyday contexts.

In the following sections, we examine how the seven types of digital skills distinguished in this book can be developed within formal education and how schools can adapt to the challenges posed by rapidly evolving media, including AI.

Strategic Media Choice Skills

In everyday life, strategic media choice skills are largely shaped by immediate needs, social context, and peer influence. Children and adolescents not only select apps, websites, or social media platforms because they offer information, entertainment, or convenience, but also because their friends use them or because they are trendy. Social validation and a desire to belong strongly influence these choices. Additionally, social media algorithms track users' behaviors and amplify them, creating feedback loops that reinforce existing interests, preferences, and social networks, further shaping how (young) people encounter and engage with content. Decisions about whether to use AI-based platforms and applications are probably, in most cases, made instinctively without critical reflection on their benefits, limitations, or ethical implications. While informal learning strongly influences how individuals engage with digital media, it rarely fosters deliberate, reflective, and strategic decision-making. In contrast, formal education has the potential to develop these skills, but its contribution remains limited. Schools typically prescribe the media or platforms students should use for assignments, projects, or collaborative activities. While this guidance ensures that curricular goals are met, it is less likely to prompt students to critically evaluate why they are using a particular platform or consider whether alternatives might be more effective.

Students would benefit from being engaged in explicit reflection on their choices: Assignments should require students to explain why they select particular platforms, and schools might consider providing frameworks for evaluating them. Currently, it is questionable whether lessons incorporate critical comparisons of platforms or discussions of the implications of choosing to use AI. Furthermore, students typically have few opportunities to experiment with multiple tools, reflect on outcomes, or receive systematic feedback from their teachers. Consequently, the development of conscious and strategic approaches to digital media use remains limited. To account for strategic media choice skills in formal education, we recommend educational policymakers, school administrators, curriculum designers, teachers, and researchers to:

- *Integrate strategic media choice into curricula*, encouraging students to critically evaluate why they use specific apps, platforms, or AI tools rather than simply following trends or peer influence.
- *Introduce frameworks for evaluating* digital media *and platforms*, focusing on criteria such as purpose, efficiency, accuracy, privacy, and ethical implications.
- *Encourage reflective assignments*, requiring students to explain and justify their media choices as part of projects and coursework.
- *Provide opportunities for comparison and experimentation*, allowing students to test multiple tools, reflect on outcomes, and discuss trade-offs.
- *Embed critical discussions on AI in education* to help students understand not only how to use AI-based tools, but also *when* and *why* they should or should not be used.
- *Strengthen teachers' capacity to guide reflection*, equipping educators with resources and training to support students in developing deliberate, strategic approaches to media choice.
- *Promote feedback-rich learning environments* where students receive systematic input from teachers on the effectiveness and implications of their media and platform choices.

Operational and Formal Skills

Although experimentation with digital media fosters familiarity, developing sufficient levels of operational and formal skills requires structured guidance. Differences in family backgrounds further highlight the need for schools to play an active role. Students from households with digitally skilled parents are more likely to benefit from richer, more varied digital media use, while others receive little or no support (Zhang & Livingstone, 2019). This inequality in access to both skills and guidance makes formal education essential for ensuring that all learners have equal opportunities. This is even more pressing with the growing integration of AI and IoT into daily life and education. Smart devices in homes and classrooms, ranging from connected tablets to interactive whiteboards and wearable trackers, create new contexts for operational and formal skills. Without structured guidance, students risk developing partial, biased, or even unsafe practices. Schools must provide systematic training to ensure that all students, regardless of their background, acquire the operational and formal skills necessary to develop information, communication, content creation, and strategic media use skills. To account for operational and formal skills in education, we recommend educational policymakers, school administrators, curriculum designers, teachers, and researchers to:

- *Assess students' existing* digital skills *before introducing advanced tools* and offer remedial instruction where operational or formal skills are insufficient.
- *Embed consistent, hands-on digital practices across subjects* such as research, collaboration, presentations, data analysis, and digital portfolios.
- *Integrate AI and IoT into curricula*, teaching students how to operate, configure, and critically engage with AI-driven platforms and connected devices.
- *Move beyond the digital native assumption*, recognizing that familiarity with devices does not equate to having the skills to use them; explicit teaching of operational and formal skills is essential.
- *Strengthen teacher training in internet and* intelligent media, including both digital skills and pedagogical strategies for integrating digital media and platforms into teaching.
- *Ensure continuous professional development for educators*, including pre-service and in-service training to build confidence and effectiveness in using digital media and platforms.

Information Skills

The situation regarding information skills is markedly different from that regarding operational and formal skills. These skills are rarely acquired at home through informal practice or by trial and error. They require deliberate instruction, particularly when adapted to the context of intelligent media. When teachers and administrators equate digital skills with basic operational skills, they are likely to focus primarily on using devices or software rather than teaching how to locate, evaluate, and use information critically. Traditional instruction may emphasize information skills in the context of printed media or conventional learning materials, but these approaches do not automatically transfer to internet and intelligent media. The evidence presented in Chap. 3 shows that many students lack the necessary information skills. Students frequently take an excessive number of steps and spend considerable time completing searches, often struggling with defining effective search queries, selecting relevant results, and evaluating sources for reliability and validity. AI-powered search assistants, recommendation systems, and chatbots can support these steps, but they require students to critically assess algorithmically curated results. Without proper guidance, students may over-rely on AI suggestions, click through results without evaluating sources, or fail to distinguish between credible and unreliable content. Moreover, the integration of AI in educational contexts, such as smart classrooms and adaptive learning platforms, makes the development of information skills even more critical. Students must learn not only how to retrieve information efficiently but also how to analyze outputs from AI systems, interpret data generated by IoT devices, and make informed decisions based on complex, algorithmically filtered information. These advanced information skills cannot be developed through casual exploration alone; they require explicit instruction, guided practice in real digital environments, and ongoing support from educators who understand both traditional media and emerging digital skills. Ideally, such learning is embedded within existing curriculum areas, such as language, history, biology, or geography, so that students can apply digital skills in authentic academic contexts. This not only increases the practical relevance but also motivates subject teachers to actively use digital media. To make this possible, teachers need targeted professional development in advanced internet and intelligent media use, enabling them to integrate digital skills into their courses and design materials suited for dynamic digital learning environments. We recommend educational policymakers, school administrators, curriculum designers, teachers, and researchers to:

- *Provide explicit instruction in information skills*, including searching, evaluating, and critically using information in online and intelligent media contexts. This can be supported by employing creative approaches, such as playing serious video games in which children learn to recognize manipulation techniques and develop resilience to misinformation.
- *Bridge traditional and emerging search systems*, linking conventional information skills with digital, AI-mediated learning environments to ensure transfer and relevance.
- *Develop students' critical assessment of AI outputs*, including search engines, recommendation systems, and chatbots, to prevent overreliance on algorithmically curated results.
- *Integrate information skills into existing subjects*, such as language, history, biology, or geography, so students apply skills in authentic, motivating learning contexts (and receive hands-on experience in, for example, retrieving, analyzing, and interpreting data from AI and IoT systems).
- *Train educators in information skills related to intelligent media* so that they can effectively teach these skills and develop tailored educational materials.

Communication Skills

Formal education still provides limited attention to the communication skills outlined in Chap. 2. Essential skills, such as online networking, interpreting and creating digital messages, managing attention, constructing digital identities, and negotiating meaning, are rarely integrated into the curriculum. Although some media literacy or media education programs address concerns such as online safety, cyberbullying, and exposure to harmful content, these initiatives are often peripheral to mainstream education and depend heavily on individual teachers' interests or expertise. As a result, young people acquire most of their digital communication skills outside formal educational settings, through social media, online communities, collaborative gaming, and informal peer interactions. These skills are often learned experientially through trial and error, everyday digital interactions, and spontaneous practice. While such experiences can enhance creativity, adaptability, and problem-solving, they rarely provide the structured guidance, ethical grounding, or opportunities for reflection that schools could offer. Consequently, young people engage in increasingly complex media landscapes with limited support or understanding of the principles that underlie responsible and effective communication.

Meanwhile, the demands of a smart society increasingly call for collaboration, collective intelligence, intercultural communication, and negotiation skills, areas where formal schooling is frequently underdeveloped. The ethical and social dimensions of digital communication, such as netiquette, privacy, consent, and reputation management, are seldom taught systematically or reinforced consistently. Consequently, the current curriculum remains fragmented and insufficient in preparing students to communicate effectively, responsibly, and strategically in online and intelligent media contexts. As young people continue to demonstrate insufficient communication skills (see Chap. 3) there is a need for systemic reform. Curricula, teacher training, and educational practices need to be rethought to ensure that young people develop not only operational skills but also advanced, ethical, and strategic communication skills required in a networked society. We therefore recommend educational policymakers, school administrators, curriculum designers, teachers, and researchers to:

- *Integrate communication skills into curricula,* including online networking, encoding/decoding online messages, exchanging meaning, attention management, identity construction, and negotiation.
- *Embed ethical, social, and strategic dimensions* into education, covering topics such as netiquette, privacy, consent, and responsible self-presentation.
- *Promote collaborative and intercultural learning*, encouraging teamwork, collective intelligence, and adaptive negotiation to reflect contemporary digital environments.
- *Incorporate hands-on authentic learning experiences* such as participation in online communities, collaborative games, and multimedia projects to foster communication skills in practical contexts.

- *Strengthen teacher training in digital communication,* equipping educators with technical, pedagogical, and ethical knowledge to teach communication skills effectively.

Content Creation Skills

Content creation skills are becoming increasingly essential, yet most young people seem to acquire them independently, often through personal experimentation and social media engagement. Despite the widespread availability of tools for producing text, images, videos, audio, and multimedia content, it is questionable whether formal education offers structured instruction or guided classroom practice. While content creation tools lower technical barriers and foster creativity, they often result in amateur-level outputs, as students typically lack a deeper understanding of design principles, storytelling, and ethical considerations. Critical elements, such as narrative design, audience alignment, stylistic choices, and achieving communicative goals, are largely absent from most curricula. Consequently, users may be able to publish content, but they lack the skills to ensure that it is coherent, engaging, and purposefully crafted. The integration of intelligent media, including AI applications, adds further complexity. Without proper guidance, students may rely on AI to generate essays or create digital content without critically evaluating potential biases, inaccuracies, or limitations, highlighting the urgent need for structured education in both technical and human-centered content creation skills. Even when multimedia tools are available, educators may not be equipped to use them effectively in teaching content creation skills. Without structured guidance, students may produce content that lacks coherence, engagement, or purpose.

It is also questionable whether formal education provides sufficient instruction on the ethical and legal dimensions of content creation. Topics such as copyright, licensing, and proper attribution must be addressed in depth to equip students to navigate complex digital rights issues. Similarly, ethical considerations, including fairness, respect for others, cultural sensitivity, and avoidance of misrepresentation, need to be integrated into content creation curricula. Guidance on transparency and authenticity, including the responsible use of AI-generated content and the disclosure of edits or manipulations, seems to be largely absent. Moreover, educational systems do not consistently teach students to critically assess content for audience impact, potential misinterpretation, or societal consequences. Students need to be trained to combine creativity with strategic thinking, such as selecting appropriate formats, channels, or styles to maximize engagement and meaning. To enhance content creation skills through education, we recommend educational policymakers, school administrators, curriculum designers, teachers, and researchers to:

- *Provide systematic classroom guidance* in creating text, images, video, audio, and multimedia content and move beyond informal experimentation to structured projects with clear objectives and feedback. If teachers themselves lack expertise, adopt approaches in which they act as a facilitator rather than a lecturer, guiding the class to collaboratively explore and solve problems or challenges.
- *Emphasize design and storytelling principles.* Teach narrative design, audience alignment, stylistic choices, and methods for achieving communicative goals. Encourage students to plan and structure content purposefully rather than simply publishing.
- *Include exercises for analyzing the impact* of content on different audiences and anticipating potential misinterpretations.
- *Educate students on the use of AI tools for content generation*, highlighting potential biases, inaccuracies, and ethical concerns. This includes teaching reflective practices to balance AI assistance with human judgment, creativity, and authenticity.
- *Cover legal and ethical dimensions* and provide instruction on copyright, licensing, and proper attribution for digital content. Ethical considerations, including fairness, respect for others, and cultural sensitivity, should be integrated.
- *Equip educators with content creation instruction.* Provide teacher training on multimedia tools, AI platforms, and pedagogical strategies for content creation.

Strategic Media Use Skills

Strategic media use skills are the most advanced digital skills and require decision-making: it involves young people to plan, implement, and evaluate digital actions in a purposeful, goal-oriented way, often using multiple digital tools, online sources, and AI. They need to be critical, analytical, and reflective, capable of aligning information, communication, or content creation skills with their goals. It is questionable whether formal education sufficiently recognizes strategic media use skills. Structured, practice-oriented guidance is needed to equip young people to actively shape beneficial outcomes from their media use. Critical dimensions of strategic media use need to be addressed systematically, including understanding algorithmic recommendation systems, interpreting AI-generated outputs, balancing automated insights with personal goals, and applying reflective, goal-directed decisions. The growing integration of intelligent media—including AI-powered chatbots, recommendation algorithms, and IoT-enabled educational tools such as interactive whiteboards, smart tablets, and wearable devices—further underscores the need for structured instruction. Collaboration with intelligent systems is increasingly important, and guided experiences can help students develop both critical thinking and practical decision-making skills in these contexts. For example, students may use AI platforms to receive personalized learning recommendations or monitor fitness and health metrics via connected devices. Effective engagement requires the skills to evaluate outputs, adjust actions based on feedback, and reflect on outcomes in alignment with personal, academic, or societal goals. Embedding strategic media use within existing curriculum subjects such as history, biology, or geography provides authentic contexts for applying these skills. Students might analyze historical data using AI-powered visualization tools, evaluate environmental sensor data for a biology project, or model energy usage patterns in geography lessons. We recommend educational policymakers, school administrators, curriculum designers, teachers, and researchers to:

- *Provide structured, practice-oriented guided classroom exercises in strategic media use* where students set goals, assess outcomes, and refine strategies.
- *Teach critical engagement with AI* and offer instruction on balancing automated insights with personal objectives. Provide opportunities to interact with AI-driven learning platforms, wearable devices, and IoT-enabled tools in controlled, reflective learning scenarios.
- *Incorporate reflective activities* where students analyze the outcomes of their digital interactions and adjust strategies accordingly.

- *Strengthen ethical, legal, and societal awareness.* Teach responsible navigation of algorithmic recommendations.
- *Integrate strategic media use into curricula.* Embed skills such as goal setting, decision-making, and reflecting on outcomes across authentic contexts (e.g., history, biology, geography) to allow students to apply digital tools meaningfully.
- *Empower teachers with training and resources.* Encourage teachers to design structured activities that guide students in applying strategic media use skills in real-world contexts.

6.4 Learning Digital Skills in the Workplace

Despite rapid technological advancements, human capital remains one of an organization's most valuable assets for achieving long-term success. Employee development contributes to higher retention rates, greater innovation, and a stronger competitive advantage (Sousa & Wilks, 2018). Workplaces increasingly demand a highly skilled workforce capable of handling complex, dynamic, and collaborative tasks. Yet, much on-the-job learning occurs outside formal structures. The survey among the Dutch labor force shows that only a small proportion of employees develop digital skills through formal organizational provisions, for example, through training (11 percent) or helpdesk support (11 percent). These patterns are especially relevant in the context of AI and IoT, where many workplaces increasingly integrate smart devices and AI into routine operations. Learning to use intelligent media occurs mostly through hands-on experience combined with guidance from colleagues who have prior experience. However, despite the sharply rising demand for digital skills, particularly in response to the growing influence of AI, persistently low levels among employees underscore the need for more structured and targeted upskilling and reskilling initiatives (Morandini et al., 2023). Only a small proportion of European workers have received training in AI-related skills. Even more concerning, a significant number of employees perceive that their organizations are unlikely to offer such opportunities in the future (Cedefop, 2024). This gap persists despite growing pressures on employers, who increasingly struggle to recruit candidates equipped with the necessary digital skills. As intelligent media become integral to everyday business operations, the lack of formal training not only limits employees' professional growth but also constrains organizational innovation and competitiveness. Therefore, we recommend employers to:

- *Scale up workplace digital training programs*, with a focus on upskilling workers in manual jobs and with lower levels of formal education who face the greatest risk of digital exclusion.
- *Prioritize digital skill development for intelligent media contexts*, ensuring employees receive structured training on advanced applications such as analytics dashboards, automated workflows, and connected systems.
- *Promote blended learning* strategies, combining hands-on experience with formal instruction, so workers can move beyond trial and error and peer reliance.

The survey among the Dutch labor force furthermore shows that when employees encounter hardware or software issues that exceed their current skill level, only a minority attempt to solve these issues independently (29 percent). Most turn to institutional or social support: nearly half contact an internal helpdesk (48 percent), while another group relies on assistance from co-workers (18 percent). A small proportion (3 percent) seek support outside the workplace. Helpdesks generally provide technical assistance, such as troubleshooting hardware or software, but they rarely have the pedagogical capacity to address skill gaps. Courses or workshops, when offered, are still largely underutilized. Only 20% of employees had received computer training in the previous three years. Ironically, those who might benefit the most, senior or lower-educated workers, attended these programs least frequently. Both management and employees tend to underestimate the benefits of structured training: respondents who had not attended ICT courses estimated that they would gain 16 minutes of work time per day, while those who participated reported actual gains of 33 minutes daily (Van Deursen & Van Dijk, 2014). Overall, organizations often leave employees to manage digital skill-related challenges on their own. Only 22 percent of respondents reported learning primarily through formal training or helpdesks. Instead, most rely on informal strategies, such as learning by doing and consulting colleagues or external contacts. This indicates a lack of systematic monitoring and active skill development by employers, particularly for those who need training the most, such as lower-educated workers.

Some organizations assume that the rapid rise of AI-based support systems is expected to reduce the amount of continuous training provided to existing employees. This raises the question whether such assistance can compensate for the persistent gap left by formal organizational training, which often fails to meet employees' evolving skill-development needs. The answer is not straightforward. Some AI applications may be considered labor-saving innovations that automate tasks formerly carried out by humans, thereby reducing the perceived need for traditional training. Other AI applications, however, enhance rather than replace human labor. These systems can increase the demand for new skills, particularly those related to managing, collaborating with, or supervising intelligent media (Mühlemann, 2024). Some organizations also assume that hiring younger employees will solve skill gaps, but the survey found no evidence that younger workers lost less time due to skill deficiencies compared to older colleagues. Age mainly affects operational and formal skills, whereas skills such as effectively processing information, evaluating online content, and using digital media strategically require continuous development across all age groups. Consequently, formal training, continuous upskilling, and structured workplace support are essential to ensure employees can fully leverage the potential of digital innovations, including the increasing presence of AI and IoT that introduce new tools, interfaces, and problem-solving. We recommend employers to:

- *Strengthen organizational support systems*, moving beyond troubleshooting to include pedagogical training that helps employees build lasting digital skills.
- *Encourage proactive employer involvement*, with systematic monitoring of employees' digital skill needs instead of leaving workers to manage challenges informally.
- *Reduce underutilization of training initiatives* by raising awareness of their proven productivity benefits and incentivizing participation (particularly among senior and lower-educated employees).
- *Leverage peer learning while professionalizing support*, ensuring that co-worker assistance is complemented by structured training and reliable resources.
- *Integrate continuous upskilling into workplace culture*, recognizing that younger employees are not inherently more digitally skilled, and that digital skills require lifelong development.

6.5 Learning in Adult and Distance Education

When individuals leave school and do not engage with internet or intelligent media in their professional lives, they are often left to acquire digital skills through self-directed learning. Those who are now around 50 years old, roughly three decades after the introduction of the World Wide Web, had limited or no exposure to digital media during their schooling years. Computers and the internet were not yet fully integrated into educational curricula and digital skills were not considered a core learning topic. Fortunately, the structured learning opportunities for adult education have evolved substantially alongside the digital transformation of work and media (Rott & Schmidt-Hertha, 2024). Digitalization has expanded the boundaries of lifelong learning, making it possible for adults to pursue education anytime, anywhere, and at their own pace. Online learning platforms, virtual classrooms, and open educational resources allow learners to personalize their learning pathways, revisit content as needed, and balance education with professional and family responsibilities. Digitalization furthermore broadened the scope and content of adult education. The proliferation of digital media and platforms has expanded the range of subjects and skills that can be taught online and has changed how adult education is conceptualized, designed, and delivered (Nadrljanski et al., 2022). The learning process is no longer confined to traditional classrooms but increasingly takes place in hybrid, networked, and interactive spaces, where learners engage with content, educators, and peers across digital environments. Recent advances in AI have introduced even greater potential for personalized and adaptive adult learning. AI-driven educational platforms can analyze learner performance in real time, detect gaps in understanding, and suggest tailored materials or activities. These systems can provide immediate feedback, adaptive challenges, and context-sensitive resources, enhancing learner engagement and improving knowledge retention. Such technologies hold promises for addressing the diverse learning needs of adult populations, particularly those who benefit from individualized guidance and flexible learning trajectories.

Despite the advances, most adult learners engage in education that uses digital media as tools for learning (e.g., online platforms, video lectures, or digital collaboration), rather than education that explicitly aims to develop their understanding and mastery of digital media themselves. Moreover, adult education remains out of reach for those without reliable internet connections, up-to-date devices, or the economic or social resources needed to use online platforms effectively. In recent years, participation in adult learning has declined in more countries than it has increased, despite the expanded opportunities of adult learning, (OECD, 2025). This is paradoxical given that adult learning is seen as essential to addressing technological and economic change. Participation tends to be concentrated among employed individuals who use digital skills professionally. Several barriers contribute to low participation in adult learning initiatives. Besides suffering from a lack of basic infrastructure that includes learning centers and technological devices (Edwards-Fapohunda, 2024), common obstacles include time constraints, especially for working adults balancing employment and family responsibilities; financial costs associated with tuition or materials; and limited availability of suitable courses in local or online formats. Language barriers may hinder some learners from immigrant backgrounds while others may be affected by cultural diversity in engaging themselves into adult study programs (Edwards-Fapohunda, 2024). In addition, adults might perceive digital learning as irrelevant to their daily routines, particularly if their current occupations or lifestyles do not require extensive digital engagement. This perception can lead to low motivation and a lack of sustained commitment to formal learning. Nevertheless, in Chap. 4 we have substantiated that digital skills are now essential for everyday life, not only for professional advancement but also for personal and social participation. This should offer a powerful motivational entry point for adult education providers to design engaging and relevant learning experiences that moved beyond standardized, one-size-fits-all approaches. Learner-centered, flexible, and context-sensitive programs are more likely to foster sustained engagement. Traditional courses focusing solely on operational, formal, and information skills are insufficient as they do not fully cover learners' everyday realities. Integrating communication, content creation, and strategic media use into adult education makes learning more meaningful by connecting digital skills to personal interests, social relationships, and practical life applications. For instance, teaching adults how to use digital tools to create community projects, manage small businesses, or share family memories online can make learning both relevant and empowering.

Besides a decline in adult education, initiatives that focus on learning digital skills tend to focus on seniors over 65, as their exclusion from digital society is often more visible and widely discussed. For middle-aged adults who missed earlier opportunities for structured digital skills learning, informal learning remains the primary means of acquiring digital skills. While valuable, this tends to be fragmented and limited to immediate problem-solving rather than the systematic development of broader digital skills. Overall, a pressing need for structured and supportive learning opportunities for adults remains. We recommend those involved in adult and distance education to:

- *Enhance* motivation *and engagement.* Offer learning opportunities that are relevant, flexible, and rewarding, emphasizing the immediate benefits of digital skills in daily life. Include interactive, hands-on learning activities that allow adults to practice and apply skills directly.
- *Adopt learner-centered and context-sensitive approaches.* Programs that connect digital skills to adults' personal, social, and professional contexts result in meaningful learning experiences. This calls for customized learning schedules, personalized learning plans, and supportive services such as childcare and transport facilities (Edwards-Fapohunda, 2024).
- *Combine* structured instruction (e.g., workshops, online courses) with supported informal learning (e.g., mentoring, peer learning, workplace-based initiatives).
- *Leverage AI and adaptive technologies.* Use AI tools to personalize learning pathways, identify gaps, and provide tailored feedback, while maintaining human support and guidance.
- *Recognize and address the "missing middle" generation* and develop targeted initiatives.
- *Integrate* digital skills *into national lifelong learning strategies* and reduce structural barriers to participation. Think of financial incentives such as learning vouchers, tax credits, or employer co-funding schemes to reduce cost barriers (Edwards-Fapohunda, 2024). Support flexible learning formats to accommodate adults balancing work and family responsibilities.

6.6 Learning in Public Access Centers and Communities

Public access sites include a diverse range of locations, such as community access or technology centers, public libraries, municipal halls, schools, museums, hospitals, and commercial venues like supermarkets, service centers, and internet cafés. Their main functions are to provide (occasional or regular) internet access for those without connectivity at home, school, or work; offer guidance and support for users unfamiliar with online platforms and applications; and deliver training, depending on the staff's capacity and expertise. Unlike schools, public access centers typically offer non-formal, community-based learning that combines self-directed exploration with guidance from staff or peers. The effectiveness depends strongly on staff expertise, funding, and local partnerships with schools or NGOs. In most cases, the emphasis is placed on access rather than digital skills development. Educational functions are limited and usually target specific groups, such as women, marginalized communities, or low-income populations. Some governments have implemented specialized public provisions, offering on-the-spot assistance at service desks to help citizens access online government services. In some cases, these programs include full courses designed to enable home use of digital services.

In developed countries, where most households have internet access, public access centers sometimes serve as social meeting spaces or places to seek support, but primarily function as a safety net for those without reliable access or digital skills. With widespread mobile connectivity, they often serve as a last-resort option for those without reliable home internet. Most users visit infrequently, typically to resolve temporary connectivity issues or access Wi-Fi, while more regular users tend to be people with a migrant background, adults with low-income, or job seekers. In lower-income areas, rural communities, or among populations without consistent home access, public centers may still represent an important opportunity to use the internet, besides mobile internet access. In developing countries, public access often represents the first, and for many the only, opportunity for digital engagement. Limited home connectivity, combined with insufficient access points and training in workplaces or schools, makes these centers critical both as gateways to the internet and as hubs for digital skills development. They frequently also serve broader social and community functions. In contrast, users in developed countries are likely to be more goal-oriented, seeking specific services, considering these centers less welcoming than home or peer-supported access. These differences underscore the need to tailor services to local social, economic, and cultural contexts, as well as to the skills and needs of target users.

Intelligent media offer opportunities to enhance the effectiveness of public access centers. AI-driven tutorials and adaptive learning platforms can provide personalized guidance for novice users, helping them operate and navigate online services to build digital confidence. Smart devices in public centers—such as smart tablets, interactive whiteboards, and connected learning kiosks—can support experiential, hands-on learning, enabling users to practice real-life digital tasks under guided supervision. These innovations can transform public access centers from static access points into dynamic, learning-oriented environments that equip users with practical, lifelong digital skills.

We recommend those involved in the learning of digital skills in public access centers and communities to:

- *Provide guidance and support* for users unfamiliar with online platforms and applications. Ideally, support should be available at all times (rather than for example only once a week), indicating that relying solely on volunteers is insufficient.
- *Offer training programs based on staff capacity and expertise*, combining self-directed exploration with guidance from staff or peers.
- *Strengthen staff expertise, funding, and local partnerships with schools, NGOs, or community organizations* to improve program effectiveness and sustainability.
- *Focus on digital skills development*, not just internet access, particularly for marginalized or low-income groups.
- *Use intelligent media tools* (adaptive tutorials, AI-driven guidance) to provide personalized support and build confidence.
- *Transform public access centers into dynamic learning environments* rather than purely static access points, emphasizing lifelong digital skill development.

6.7 Learning among Disadvantaged Groups

In the final section of this chapter, we focus on several groups that require special support in developing digital skills. While many of these individuals face socioeconomic disadvantages, this is not always the case. For example, older adults may not be disadvantaged economically but still encounter distinct challenges. Each group faces specific barriers to digital learning. People with disabilities may experience physical or cognitive limitations that make it difficult to use digital technologies. Individuals with low levels of traditional literacy struggle to read or write, which severely restricts their ability to engage with text-based digital content. Older adults, accustomed to traditional media, must adapt to new modes of communication and often learn more slowly. Age-related issues such as declining vision, hearing, mobility, and memory can further hinder their interaction with digital tools. People with a migrant background, meanwhile, may encounter cultural and language barriers that complicate the use of digital media in their host countries.

These disadvantaged groups represent key target audiences for internet training. Experience shows that people with disabilities face the greatest challenges in developing operational and formal digital skills, a pattern also observed among many older adults. Individuals with low literacy skills struggle to read text on keyboards and screen menus, making content-related digital tasks extremely difficult. People with a migrant background often encounter similar difficulties, as digital skills frequently require knowledge of English or the host country's language, especially for more advanced or strategic skills. Because of these additional barriers, learners often need to acquire supplementary knowledge or skills before or at the beginning of digital training. People with disabilities, for instance, must learn to use assistive technologies such as screen readers, magnifiers, speech-enabled content, or Braille displays. Older adults may also benefit from such aids while becoming familiar with the operation of digital devices. Individuals with low literacy must first improve their reading and writing abilities or be introduced to multimedia-based approaches that reduce reliance on text. People with a migrant background typically need to strengthen their proficiency in the local language or English to successfully follow most computer and internet courses, as digital learning resources in migrants' native languages are often scarce or poorly adapted to their cultural contexts.

People with Disabilities

The potential benefits of having high levels of digital skills among people with disabilities are considerable. Internet use can help reduce social isolation and mitigate the stigma associated with visible disabilities by shifting the focus of interaction away from physical limitations (Dobransky & Hargittai, 2006). The internet also provides access to specialized health information and opportunities to join self-help groups for people with similar conditions. Furthermore, online communication can compensate for mobility constraints, enabling greater participation in social and professional life. However, people with disabilities face multiple barriers to developing digital skills. An important issue is the accessibility of websites, which often fail to meet the needs of this user group. Despite the existence of the W3C accessibility guidelines discussed in the prior chapter, many online platforms and websites do not comply with them, creating usability challenges. A second barrier is the shortage of digital skills courses specifically designed for people with disabilities. Furthermore, the cost and complexity of assistive technologies are a structural barrier as these are often expensive, difficult to operate, and not readily available. A fourth obstacle arises from a lack of specialized support. While many disabled individuals receive general assistance or nursing care, they rarely have access to training or guidance (with appropriate pedagogical methods for disabled learners) specific to internet use, or to the use of assistive technologies. Finally, costs of training are high, as instruction often requires one-on-one or small-group sessions (Murphy et al., 2008).

Barriers to equitable AI use for disabled individuals arise from multiple structural and technical factors. First, disabled people are frequently underrepresented or even excluded entirely from AI training datasets or are treated as statistical outliers. As a result, AI systems often fail to accurately recognize or accommodate their behaviors, interactions, and needs (Manzoor et al., 2025). This underrepresentation is compounded by industry perceptions that disability constitutes a low-priority market, which discourages investment in accessible AI design and development (Newman-Griffis et al., 2022). Second, AI systems tend to implicitly position non-disabled users as the normative default, embedding exclusion at a structural level (Dash et al., 2025). Generative AI further perpetuates these inequities by producing biased representations of disability, often reinforcing harmful stereotypes or framing disabled experiences solely through medicalized or deficit-oriented lenses. These portrayals not only misrepresent disabled lives but also undermine principles of respect and dignity, shaping public imaginaries in ways that marginalize and exclude (Tevissen, 2024).

Visually impaired learners encounter particular difficulties with operational and formal digital skills. They expend greater time and mental effort navigating websites, rely heavily on memory to understand page structures and content, and lack the perceptual cues available to sighted users. Consequently, they develop a distinct mental model of web navigation, which can make collaboration with sighted users more challenging (Murphy et al., 2008). In 2013, researchers examined the digital skills of people with visual impairments in the Netherlands, using both self-assessments and performance tests (Van der Geest et al., 2014). The study compared two groups: younger participants (aged 12–18) and older adults (aged 55+). About one-quarter of respondents used a Braille reader, while nearly half (48 percent) relied on a screen reader or magnifier. Younger participants rated themselves higher in self-assessments and performed significantly better in operational, formal, and information skills. However, older adults scored notably higher in strategic media use skills, such as making decisions and comparing outcomes against implicit criteria. Overall, the performance of disabled participants was comparable to that of the general Dutch population, with the visually impaired older adults showing particularly strong strategic skills. Given the additional challenge of mastering assistive technologies alongside general digital skills, these performance levels can be considered relatively high. This may reflect their lifelong experience in self-advocacy and independent decision-making.

We recommend those aiming to support people with disabilities to:

- *Strengthen web accessibility and inclusive design* by encouraging public and private organizations to adopt universal design principles and conduct regular accessibility audits, and by providing incentives (e.g., grants, certification, or recognition) for developers and companies that achieve exemplary accessibility standards. Moreover, participatory approaches, which involve disabled people throughout the design lifecycle, produce technologies that are both more usable and more meaningful (Almufareh et al., 2024).

- *Improve supportive AI systems* by ensuring that datasets represent diverse abilities and technologies avoid defaulting to non-disabled users. Promote accurate and respectful representations of disability, prevent harmful stereotypes, and create systems that recognize and accommodate a wide range of behaviors, interactions, and accessibility needs.
- *Expand access to affordable assistive technologies* by supporting subsidy programs or financial assistance for purchasing essential assistive devices such as screen readers, magnifiers, or Braille displays.
- *Develop specialized* digital skills *training programs* that address the specific needs of people with various disabilities, including visual, auditory, cognitive, and motor impairments. Ensure that training content integrates the use of assistive technologies and practical, real-world digital tasks. Offer flexible training formats—including blended, online, and in-person options—to accommodate different accessibility requirements.
- *Build capacity among trainers and support staff* to provide specialized professional development for digital skills instructors and support staff on accessibility tools, inclusive pedagogy, and adaptive learning strategies.
- *Leverage strengths and promote empowerment* by recognizing and building on the strategic and adaptive skills many individuals with disabilities already possess, particularly those developed through lifelong self-advocacy and problem-solving. Highlight success stories and role models within the disabled community to inspire participation and reduce stigma.

People with Low Literacy

At first glance, teaching digital skills to individuals with low literacy may appear nearly impossible, as reading and writing are fundamental prerequisites for using internet and intelligent media. However, these media are not limited to text; they are inherently multimedia platforms that incorporate sound, images, and interactive elements. By following audio and visual cues and using touchscreens, users with non-literacy and low literacy can still engage with digital media to a certain extent. For instance, many low-literate users quickly learn to recognize certain letters or visual symbols, allowing them to perform simple operational tasks such as selecting menu icons, typing short URLs, or navigating familiar websites. While these users can develop basic operational and formal skills, content-related digital skills generally remain beyond reach without literacy, as they depend heavily on reading and writing abilities.

The capacity to use digital media varies considerably according to the degree and type of low literacy. Non-literate individuals are unable to read or write at all, though some may recognize familiar letters, symbols, or words based on their visual appearance. Individuals with low literacy possess basic literacy skills but lack the proficiency required to handle routine reading and writing tasks essential for everyday life such as filling out forms, composing an email, interpreting street signs, or using automated systems like ATMs and digital ticket machines. Low literacy is far more widespread than commonly assumed. According to UNESCO (2025), approximately 754 million adults worldwide, about one in ten people, still cannot read and write with sufficient understanding to interpret a simple text. While non-literacy has declined in most developed countries, it persists among certain groups, particularly people with a migrant background, older adults, and people with intellectual disabilities. In contrast, in many developing countries, the combined prevalence of non-literacy and low literacy continues to encompass the majority of the adult population, posing a significant barrier to social and economic participation in the digital age.

Digital media present valuable opportunities for both non-literate and low-literate individuals. Unlike traditional print media, digital platforms offer a multisensory environment that integrates text, sound, visuals, and animation to support understanding. This multimodal nature enables users to interpret meaning through nonverbal cues—such as images, icons, and auditory feedback—rather than relying exclusively on written text. The increasing availability of touchscreen interfaces and icon-based navigation has further reduced dependence on written instructions, allowing users to engage in simple digital activities such as making voice or video calls, playing multimedia content, or accessing basic online services through one-click operations. However, these benefits have clear limits. As soon as digital interaction requires reading comprehension—such as navigating menus, interpreting messages, managing written information, or evaluating online content—low literacy becomes a decisive barrier. Users are unable to progress beyond basic functions to more complex forms of digital engagement. AI can play an important role in helping individuals with low literacy learn digital skills. AI applications, particularly those leveraging speech, visuals, and adaptive learning, can make digital education far more accessible, intuitive, and personalized. AI-powered voice assistants enable users to navigate devices, access the internet, and complete everyday tasks through spoken commands instead of text. These tools can offer step-by-step, interactive guidance, for instance, demonstrating how to open an app, make a video call, or search for information, allowing learners to develop basic operational and formal digital skills through hands-on experience rather than reading. Speech-to-text and text-to-speech applications can also bridge oral and written communication, helping learners gradually associate spoken and written words. Similarly, AI chatbots with voice-based interaction and local dialect recognition can act as round-the-clock digital mentors, teaching practical skills such as mobile payments, online communication, or accessing health information. By simulating real-life digital scenarios, these conversational systems promote active, experience-based learning rather than abstract instruction, offering an effective pathway for non-literate and low-literate users to participate meaningfully in the digital world.

However, while digital media and AI can open an important gateway to participation, parallel progress in literacy education remains of utmost importance. The limited engagement with information is not only a socioeconomic issue but also a cultural, cognitive, and behavioral one. Individuals with low literacy often lack the motivation or habit of active information-seeking, rarely integrating such practices into their daily lives: Their information behavior tends to be narrow in scope, incidental, locally confined, and characterized by simple, surface-level processing (Yu, 2010). Yet, teaching digital skills to people with low literacy is not impossible. To be effective, we recommend those aiming to support people with low literacy to:

- *Leverage multimedia learning*. Instruction should exploit the audio-visual features of digital media, focusing on visual and auditory interaction before introducing text-based elements.
- *Design* AI *learning tools that emphasize experiential and visual learning*. Educational technologies should rely on visual cues, icons, animations, and simulations, allowing learners with low literacy to practice real-life tasks, such as sending messages or accessing online services, without heavy text use.

- *Integrate digital and literacy education.* Digital skills training should occur alongside literacy, language, or citizenship courses so that learners perceive it as directly relevant to their lives. In general, the findings presented in Chap. 3 emphasize that digital inclusion initiatives should not overlook challenges related to reading, writing, and text comprehension, as these skills are essential for effectively using the internet and intelligent media.
- *Tailor content to low-literate learners' needs.* Courses should be adapted to participants' specific social, cultural, and practical contexts.

People with a Migrant Background

Internet and intelligent media offer substantial benefits for people with a migrant background. They can support integration into the host country, facilitate maintenance of social ties with the home country, and enable connection with co-ethnic communities. Online platforms provide practical information on navigating local services, completing immigration requirements, accessing healthcare, or enrolling in training and job programs. In some cases, digital media are even used to teach literacy to people with a migrant background who arrived in developed countries as non-literate. Despite the benefits, there are several barriers to digital skill acquisition among people with a migrant background, including low education or low literacy, language barriers due to limited proficiency in the host country's language or English, and a lack of familiarity with local cultural norms that shape websites, services, and digital interfaces.

As with all disadvantaged groups discussed in this section, digital skills training for people with a migrant background must be carefully customized. Language-sensitive instruction should build on the learner's mother tongue while gradually introducing host-country vocabulary relevant to daily life, formal education, and employment. Content should be culturally relevant and practical, addressing issues such as passing immigration exams, finding housing, accessing social services, or seeking employment. Multimedia-based learning, incorporating visuals, animations, audio, and interactive tools, is particularly important for low-literate learners, enabling comprehension without reliance on text (Redecker et al., 2010). Whenever possible, learning materials should be translated into the learner's native language to scaffold understanding and build confidence. The central goal is to facilitate language acquisition alongside digital skills, gradually enabling learners to navigate their host country's cultural and institutional systems independently.

AI offer a promising means to enhance digital skills training for people with a migrant background by addressing language and cultural barriers while providing adaptive, personalized instruction. AI-powered language support, including speech recognition, text-to-speech, and automatic translation, can help learners understand instructions, navigate websites, and practice host-country languages in context. Adaptive learning systems can assess performance, identify areas of difficulty, and adjust lesson content and delivery accordingly, allowing people with a migrant background to progress at an individualized pace and focus on immediately relevant skills. AI can also combine multimodal learning formats—audio, video, and visual cues—to support comprehension and reinforce practical tasks, such as completing online job applications, using public services, or managing immigration forms. AI-driven systems can tailor content and feedback to reflect the learner's cultural background, increasing relevance and motivation. Chatbots can provide continuous guidance in multiple languages, offering step-by-step assistance in a non-intimidating manner.

We recommend that those aiming to support people with a migrant background to:

- *Customize* digital skills *training* by considering specific needs and challenges of people with a migrant background, including low literacy and unfamiliarity with local digital culture.
- *Provide language-sensitive instruction* by building on the learner's mother tongue while gradually introducing host-country vocabulary.
- *Ensure culturally relevant and practical content* by focusing on topics that directly impact the daily lives of people with a migrant background, such as immigration processes, housing, healthcare, education, and employment.
- *Use multimedia-based learning* by incorporating visuals, animations, audio, and interactive tools to support comprehension, especially for low-literate learners. Reduce reliance on text-based materials wherever possible.
- *Leverage AI to enhance training* by implementing AI-powered language support (speech recognition, text-to-speech, and automatic translation), using adaptive learning systems to personalize instruction based on performance and progress, applying tools to reinforce

practical digital tasks (e.g., completing online forms, accessing public services), tailoring AI feedback and content to reflect the learner's cultural background to increase relevance and motivation, and using chatbots for continuous, step-by-step guidance in multiple languages.

Older Adults

Unlike the relatively limited attention given to the digital skills of people with low literacy levels, disabilities, or a migrant background, digital inclusion among older adults—commonly defined as individuals aged 65 and above—has received substantial policy attention. It is widely recognized that older adults must actively adapt from traditional to digital forms of communication. Access to the internet and intelligent media can greatly enhance their quality of life by reducing social isolation and compensating for declining mobility. Online platforms provide opportunities to maintain social connections, particularly with family members and grandchildren, and to access specialized health information and social support networks. Despite the potential benefits, older adults remain among the last groups to gain internet access and generally exhibit lower levels of digital skills compared to younger users. Digital media often involve unfamiliar interfaces, commands, and formal structures, which can make acquiring operational and formal skills challenging. This is unfortunate, as evidence suggests that once older adults develop these basic skills, they tend to excel in information and strategic media use skills, drawing on their accumulated life experience and decision-making abilities (Van Deursen et al., 2011). However, their difficulties extend beyond technical unfamiliarity. Age-related physical and cognitive changes such as reduced mobility and dexterity, visual and hearing impairments, slower information processing, and challenges with short-term memory or attention, can also pose significant barriers to meaningful digital participation.

Older adults primarily receive support in using digital media outside formal education, relying on *warm experts* for assistance, such as children, grandchildren, and close friends (Gallistl et al., 2020). While support from family and friends offers clear advantages, such as a personal understanding of the learner's needs, informal assistance cannot fully replace structured training when it comes to developing comprehensive digital skills (Gallistl et al., 2020). Recognizing this limitation, numerous initiatives have sought to enhance digital skills among older adults through adult education programs, public libraries, and community centers. In many countries, self-organized senior networks have also emerged, providing peer-led training and mutual support. Research shows that older adults are both capable and motivated learners (Wandke et al., 2012), and their motivation tends to increase when digital media are meaningfully integrated into their daily lives and provide tangible practical or social benefits. However, to achieve this, formal learning opportunities must be adapted to the specific needs and learning styles of older adults. Unfortunately, conventional courses often replicate those designed for younger learners and are frequently taught by younger instructors who may struggle to empathize with age-related learning challenges or who proceed at an overly fast pace. Peer tutoring, where an individual volunteers to provide digital support to someone of a similar age and life situation, has proven to be an effective and preferred approach for promoting digital skills in later life (Aavikko et al., 2022). Peers tend to communicate in accessible language, avoid excessive technical jargon, and offer guidance at a calm, comfortable pace (Kärnä, 2022), all of which foster a more supportive and confidence-building learning environment. Additionally, adaptive, personalized, and multimodal capabilities of AI provide opportunities to enhance both learning effectiveness and motivation among older adults. These systems can detect when a learner is struggling and automatically slow down, simplify instructions, or switch to another teaching mode (e.g., from text to video or voice). This approach respects individual differences in cognitive processing speed and attention span. Furthermore, advancements in affective computing allow AI systems to detect frustration, hesitation, or confusion through tone of voice or facial expressions, and respond empathetically. This reduces anxiety and promotes a positive learning experience, which is crucial for older adults who may feel intimidated by technology.

We recommend those aiming to support older adults to:

- Develop training programs tailored to older adults' needs, accounting for *adjusted learning pace* (older learners require more time to process new information, practice skills, and retain knowledge), *recognition of prior learning habits* (many older adults learned within the logic of traditional media; concepts like hyperlinks or menus may be unfamiliar), ***accessible instructional materials*** (instructions that are simple, clearly written, and accompanied by visuals or animations tend to be more effective than lengthy text, while some older adults might also benefit from printed materials they can consult at their own pace), ***accommodation of physical and cognitive changes*** (integrate appropriate assistive technologies to address sensory or mobility impairments), and cultural sensitivity (reflect local social norms) (Bean, 2003; Wandke et al., 2012).

- *Use peer tutoring and intergenerational learning models* where older adults teach and support one another. Note that these approaches should be complemented with professional guidance).
- *Integrate assistive and adaptive technologies* (e.g., larger fonts, voice commands, magnifiers, simplified interfaces) to address physical and cognitive barriers such as reduced mobility, vision, or hearing.
- *Ensure relevance and practical application.* Training should focus on personally meaningful tasks, such as communicating with family, accessing healthcare services, or managing finances online, to enhance motivation and sustained engagement.

6.8 Conclusions

This chapter argued that formal and adult education should play an important role in supporting the development of digital skills. Informal learning through self-study and assistance from people in the immediate environment is important and facilitated by the growing user-friendliness of internet applications and handheld devices, but not sufficient. Although natural, motivating, rapid, and convenient, many digital media cannot be intuitively learned without some prior knowledge and instruction. Furthermore, informal learning by trial and error tends to be opportunistic and inconsistent. Informal learning is most effective when combined with structured guidance, training, or courses.

For children and students, digital skills are acquired both at school and outside the classroom, primarily at home. These two contexts offer very different learning experiences. In school, skills are directed by teachers and formal curricula, focusing primarily on operational, formal, and information skills. At home, children often learn independently or with guidance from parents, with operational and formal skills acquired largely through practice. Information, communication, content creation, and strategic media use skills, however, are less likely to be effectively learned at home through trial and error, highlighting the need to integrate them into existing school curricula rather than treating them as separate lessons.

For older generations who did not encounter the internet during school or work, home support and formal computer education, such as classes and instructional materials, remain essential for acquiring digital skills. Here, learner motivation is critical. Motivation improves when courses are tailored to the needs of specific audiences. Public access centers are especially important in developing countries, where they provide both access to digital technologies and support for skill development.

After the home environment, the workplace is the most important context for learning digital skills. Employees typically learn by asking colleagues for help, with co-workers serving as the first line of support. Formal organizational solutions, such as helpdesks, often provide only emergency technical assistance, while structured ICT training is rare. Both management and employees frequently underestimate the value of training.

The chapter also highlighted groups that require specialized approaches to digital skills learning: people with disabilities, with non-literacy and low literacy, with a migrant background, and older adults. Each of these groups faces additional barriers. Some learners require supplementary tools, for example, assistive technologies for people with disabilities. Unfortunately, few trainers are familiar with the specialized tools and pedagogical methods needed to teach these groups effectively. Digital skills courses should therefore be customized, taking into account unique needs, barriers, and available tools.

References

Aavikko, L., Pihlainen, K., & Kärnä, E. (2022). Peer mentoring process for older adult's digital skills. In K. Korjonen-Kuusipuro, P. Rasi-Heikkinen, H. Vuojärvi, K. Pihlainen, & E. Kärnä (Eds.), *Older adults in the digital society—Opportunities for lifelong learning* (pp. 211–228). Gaudeamus.

Almufareh, M.F., Kausar, S., Humayun, M., & Tehsin, S. (2024). A conceptual model for inclusive technology: advancing disability inclusion through artificial intelligence. *Journal of Disability Research, 3*(1), 20230060.

Arora, P. (2019). *The next billion users: Digital life beyond the West*. Harvard University Press.

Bean, C. (2003). Meeting the challenge: Training an aging population to use computers. *The Southeastern Librarian, 51*(3), 6.

Bruner, J. S. (1961). The act of discovery. *Harvard Educational Review, 31*, 21–32.

Bruner, J.S. & Olson, D.R. (1973). Learning through experience and learning through media. In G. Gerbner, L. Gross & W. Melody (Eds), *Communications, Technology and Social Policy*. New York: Wiley.

Buckingham, D. (2012). *Beyond technology: Children's learning in the age of digital culture*. Polity.

Cedefop. (2024). *Artificial Intelligence in EU Workplaces: Another great divide?* Retrieved from https://www.cedefop.europa.eu/files/press_backgrounder_ai_surveypre_event.pdf

Cobo, C. (2013). Skills for innovation: Envisioning an education that prepares for the changing world. *The Curriculum Journal, 24*(1), 67–85.

Dash, D., Bangera, Y., Bangera, M., Vadithya, G., & Panda, S. (2025). *Who gets left behind? auditing disability inclusivity in large language models*. arXiv 2509.00963.

Dobransky, K., & Hargittai, E. (2006). The disability divide in Internet access and use. *Information, Communication & Society, 9*(3), 313–334.

Edwards-Fapohunda, D. M. O. (2024). The role of adult learning and education in community development: A case study of New York. *Iconic Research and Engineering Journals, 8*(1), 437–454.

European Commission. (2019). *2nd Survey of Schools: ICT in Education*. Retrieved from https://ec.europa.eu/digital-single-market/en/news/2nd-survey-schools-ict-education

Eynon, R. (2021). Becoming digitally literate. Reinstating an educational lens to digital skills policies for adults. *British Educational Research Journal, 47*(1), 146–162.

Freire, P., & Ramos, M. B. (1972). *Pedagogy of the oppressed*. Herder and Herder.

Gallistl, V., Rohner, R., Seifert, A., & Wanka, A. (2020). Configuring the older non-user: Between research, policy and practice of digital exclusion. *Social Inclusion, 8*(2), 233–243.

Hammer, F., Leineweber, M., Sonnega, G., & Van der Groot, L. (2025). *Onderzoek informele helpers*. Beeld & Geluid, programma Alliantie Digitaal Samenleven & Perspective.

Helsper, E. J., & Van Deursen, A. J. A. M. (2017). Do the rich get digitally richer? Quantity and quality of support for digital engagement. *Information, Communication & Society, 20*(5), 700–714.

Kalmus, V., Blinka, L., & Ólafsson, K. (2015). Does it matter what mama says: Evaluating the role of parental mediation in European adolescents' excessive Internet use. *Children & Society, 29*(2), 122–133.

Kärnä, E. (2022). Peer guidance styles and learning theories. In K. Korjonen-Kuusipuro, P. Rasi Heikkinen, H. Vuojärvi, K. Pihlainen, & E. Kärnä (Eds.), *Older adults in the digital society—Opportunities for lifelong learning* (pp. 165–188). Gaudeamus.

Kirschner, P. A., Sweller, J., & Clark, R. E. (2006). Why minimal guidance during instruction does not work: An analysis of the failure of constructivist, discovery, problem-based, experiential, and inquiry-based teaching. *Educational Psychologist, 46*, 75–86.

Livingstone, S., Haddon, L., Görzig, A., & Ólafsson, K. (2011). *EU Kids Online: Final report 2011.* London School of Economics & Political Science. Available at http://eprints.lse.ac.uk/39351/

Lucas, M., & Moreira, A. (2009). Bridging formal and informal learning – A case study on students' perceptions of the use of social networking tools. In U. Cress, V. Dimitrova, M. Specht (Eds.), *Learning in the synergy of multiple disciplines* (vol. 5794). EC-TEL 2009. Lecture Notes in Computer Science.

Manzoor, R., Hussain, W., & Anjum, M. L. (2025). Out of dataset, out of algorithm, out of mind: A critical evaluation of AI bias against disabled people. *AI & SOCIETY, 40*(5), 3941–3951.

Mayer, R. E. (2004). Should there be a three-strikes rule against pure discovery learning? *American Psychologist, 59*(1), 14.

Morandini, S., Fraboni, F., De Angelis, M., Puzzo, G., Giusino, D., & Pietrantoni, L. (2023). The impact of artificial intelligence on workers' skills: Upskilling and reskilling in organisations. *Informing Science, 26*, 39–68.

Mühlemann, S. (2024). *AI adoption and workplace training*. IZA Discussion Papers, No. 17367, Institute of Labor Economics.

Murphy, E., Kuber, R., McAllister, G., & Strain, P. (2008). An empirical investigation into the difficulties experienced by visually impaired internet users. *Universal Access to the Information Society, 7*, 79–91.

Nadrljanski, Ð., Nadrljanski, M., & Pavlinović, M. (2022). Digitalization of education. In M. Ivanović, A. Klašnja-Milićević, & L. C. Jain (Eds.), *Handbook on intelligent techniques in the educational process: Vol 1 recent advances and case studies* (pp. 17–39). Springer.

Newman-Griffis, D., Rauchberg, J. S., Alharbi, R., Hickman, L., & Hochheiser, H. (2022). *Definition drives design: Disability models and mechanisms of bias in AI technologies*. arXiv 2206.08287.

OECD. (2018). *PISA 2018 Results (Volume V): Effective policies, successful schools*. OECD Publishing. https://doi.org/10.1787/ca768d40-en

OECD. (2025). *Trends in adult learning: New data from the 2023 survey of adult skills, getting skills right*. OECD Publishing. https://doi.org/10.1787/ec0624a6-en

Office of Educational Technology. (2017). *Reimagining the role of technology in Education: National Education Technology Plan Update*. Retrieved from https://files.eric.ed.gov/fulltext/ED577592.pdf

Redecker, C., Haché, A., & Centeno, C. (2010). *Using information and communication technologies to promote education and employment opportunities for immigrants and ethnic minorities*. JRC(European Commission)/IPTS.

Rott, K. J., & Schmidt-Hertha, B. (2024). Transforming adult learning in the digital age: Exploring environmental, content, and technological changes. *International Journal of Lifelong Education, 43*(4), 319–323.

Schank, R. C., & Cleary, C. (1995). *Engines for education*. Lawrence Erlbaum Associates.

Sousa, M. J., & Wilks, D. (2018). Sustainable skills for the world of work in the digital age. *Systems Research and Behavioral Science, 35*(4), 399–405.

Tevissen, Y. (2024). *Disability representations: Finding biases in automatic image generation*. arXiv 2406.14993.

Unesco. (2025). *What you need to know about literacy*. Retrieved from https://www.unesco.org/en/literacy/need-know

Van der Geest, T., Van der Meij, H., & Van Puffelen, C. (2014). Self-assessed and actual Internet skills of people with visual impairments. *Universal Access in the Information Society, 13*(2), 161–174.

Van Deursen, A. J. A. M., & van Dijk, J. A. G. M. (2014). Loss of labor time due to malfunctioning ICTs and ICT skill insufficiencies. *International Journal of Manpower, 35*(5), 703–719.

Van Deursen, A. J. A. M., Van Dijk, J. A. G. M., & Peters, O. (2011). Rethinking Internet skills: The contribution of gender, age, education, Internet experience, and hours online to medium-and content-related Internet skills. *Poetics, 39*(2), 125–144.

Van Dijk, J. A. G. M. (2020). *The digital divide*. Polity Press.

Wandke, H., Sengpiel, M., & Sönksen, M. (2012). Myths about older people's use of information and communication technology. *Gerontology, 58*(6), 564–570.

Webster, M. (2015). *Reimagining learning: Defining strategies for engagement*. Retrieved from https://www.gensleron.com/cities/2015/7/6/reimagining-learning-defining-strategies-for-engagement.html

Yu, L. (2010). How poor informationally are the information poor? Evidence from an empirical study of daily and regular information practices of individuals. *Journal of Documentation, 66*(6), 906–933.

Zhang, D., & Livingstone, S. (2019). *Inequalities in how parents support their children's development with digital technologies*. LSE Department of Media and Communications.

CHAPTER 7

Conclusions and Policy Perspectives

7.1 Conclusions

Digital Skills as the Key to Internet and Intelligent Media

This book has demonstrated that digital skills are a crucial factor in the appropriation of digital media, ranging from traditional internet-based platforms to advanced forms of intelligent media. Without these skills, digital media cannot be used beneficially, regardless of their motivation or material access. Motivation may drive the appropriation process, and material access may provide the necessary means, but digital skills ultimately determine whether digital media can be meaningfully employed. The emphasis on digital skills aligns with the concept of the second-level digital divide. While the first-level divide mainly concerns material access to digital media, the second-level divide highlights disparities in skills and patterns of use. The consequences of these skill gaps for social and informational inequality may be deeper and more enduring than the relatively straightforward and temporary issues associated with material access. As digital media become more complex, multifunctional, and intelligent, differences between those who can use them beneficially and those who cannot grow wider. Adaptive platforms, algorithmic recommendation systems, voice-controlled assistants, and AI-driven applications demand skills such as critical interpretation of algorithmic outputs, understanding system boundaries, and strategically selecting or rejecting

A. van Deursen and J. van Dijk, *Digital Skills*, Digital Education and Learning, https://doi.org/10.1057/978-1-349-96162-7_7

automated suggestions. Without such skills, users may become increasingly dependent on intelligent media in ways that limit autonomy rather than enhance it.

At one end of the spectrum lies a digitally skilled elite, capable of using both internet and intelligent media in varied and purposeful ways, especially in support of work, education, political participation, and career advancement. These individuals are not only comfortable performing complex tasks but also able to leverage internet and intelligent media to their advantage, gaining greater efficiency, insight, and opportunities. At the other end of the spectrum are individuals with minimal skills, whose digital media use tends to be infrequent, narrow, or confined largely to entertainment-oriented activities, patterns often reinforced by the design of many media and platforms that privilege ease-of-use while hiding complexity. Those with insufficient strategic media choice, operational, and formal skills are particularly vulnerable, as they struggle to benefit from more sophisticated content-related skills and may rely heavily on automated features without understanding how they function. Between these two extremes, the majority of the population is likely to develop moderate levels of skill and to engage with internet and intelligent media for both functional and leisure purposes. However, this middle group is also increasingly exposed to gradual forms of relative disadvantage as the digital environment shifts from static platforms to adaptive, data-driven systems that reward higher levels of strategic media use skills. The evolving media landscape reinforces Van Dijk's (2005, 2020) expectation of a tripartite information and network society. The combination of conventional digital inequality and new disparities caused by intelligent media may produce a society segmented into an empowered elite capable of using complex systems effectively and critically, a large middle group with moderate skill levels, and a marginalized group excluded from meaningful participation due to persistent skill deficits. In this sense, intelligent media do not eliminate digital inequalities; it intensifies them by raising the skill threshold required for full participation.

The Concept of Digital Skills

Throughout this book, we have preferred the term digital skills over expressions that include the word *literacy or competency*. Historically, *literacy* is rooted in reading, writing, and related cognitive processes that characterized earlier phases of media development. While these remain relevant, they no longer capture the complexity of contemporary media landscapes. Interacting with internet and intelligent media involves far more than the interpretation of texts or audiovisual content. Users must interact with interfaces, communicate with other users, negotiate transactions with goods and services, and evaluate, respond to, and sometimes co-produce outputs generated dynamically through algorithms and AI. For this broader and more active set of practices, the term *skills* offers a more suitable and precise conceptualization. Furthermore, *competency* can imply an underlying potential rather than an observable, enacted skill. Digital skills, as defined in this book, are grounded in actual user behavior in digital contexts. In the case of intelligent media such as recommendation systems, generative AI, algorithmically curated social feeds, or wearables and smart devices, effective use hinges on the skills to interact meaningfully with media and platforms that do not merely present information but transform, personalize, and sometimes autonomously generate it. This expanded understanding of digital skills therefore requires a multidisciplinary perspective. The concept used in this book draws on insights from media and communication studies, computer and information sciences, educational sciences, and a blend of sociology and psychology. Collectively, these fields illuminate the diverse skills needed to use not only internet but also intelligent media.

This is not to suggest that digital skills fundamentally diverge from those required for traditional media. As discussed in Chap. 1, there are several similarities and areas of overlap. Digital media still depend on reading and writing, as well as on the skills to interpret and produce audiovisual content. Yet the multifunctional, interactive, and adaptive nature of digital media demands additional skills. These include navigating complex interfaces, evaluating dynamically generated information, formulating effective search objectives and queries, understanding algorithmic cues, and making decisions in media landscapes where content is continuously reshaped by user inputs and AI-driven processes. In this book, these skill types are referred to as *content-related skills*, and they apply most directly to internet and intelligent media. Comparable skills existed in traditional media, but in digital contexts they have become broader, more dynamic, and more demanding. Moreover, digital media presuppose skills that traditional media never required to the same extent.

Chapters 1 and 2 laid out a conceptual framework for digital skills related to internet and intelligent media, which was then assessed empirically using both survey-based self-assessments and laboratory-based performance tests. Seven types of digital skills were distinguished: strategic media choice, operational, formal, information, communication, content creation, and strategic media use skills. This framework has three defining characteristics.

1. *A distinction between medium-related and content-related skills.* Medium-related skills (strategic media choice, operational, and formal skills) differ markedly in digital media and advanced further in intelligent media environments where interactions are often adaptive or algorithmically driven. Content-related digital skills (information, communication, content creation, and strategic media use) share similarities with those required for traditional media, but in digital contexts they rely on a prior command of strategic media choice, operational, and formal skills, and gain more emphasis due to increased complexity of digital media. The framework makes careful analytical distinctions among skill sets to enable rigorous and reliable investigation.
2. *A sequential and conditional structure.* The seven types of skills are organized sequentially, reflecting the assumption that complex, content-related skills can only be acquired once medium-related skills are sufficiently mastered. This structure is also salient in intelligent media landscapes, where tasks such as prompting generative systems or assessing system outputs presume a stable command of strategic media choice, operational, and formal skills. The sequential skills structure reflects not only a logical dependency between simpler and more complex skills but also the layered nature of digital media landscapes themselves, where every advanced interaction depends on the successful mastery of multiple underlying skills.
3. *The inclusion of both technical and substantive skills.* Operational and formal skills are primarily technical, whereas information, communication, content creation, and strategic media use skills are substantive, involving knowledge, creativity, and goal-oriented decision-making. This differs from everyday understandings of digital skills, which often restrict them to technical operations.

The framework is limited to the skills individuals need to use internet and intelligent media satisfactorily. It does not encompass advanced skills such as professional programming and editing, or specialized applications intended for a minority of expert users. This focus also means that the framework avoids adopting a predetermined normative stance, something that is common in many definitions of media literacy. Such definitions often assume that users *should* be critical evaluators of media, recognizing the interests of content producers and understanding how media may influence them. The framework presented in this book aims to remain as objective as possible. Through observations of various forms of internet and intelligent media use, the skills necessary for users to fully benefit from digital media were identified. For example, in the domain of information skills, users must be able to recognize the sources provided by search engines or generative AI systems and compare the intentions or reliability of those sources. Once these skills are in place, users can interact meaningfully with intelligent search agents or recommendation systems. However, they do not need to evaluate content producers' goals according to predetermined societal or ideological criteria to use these systems satisfactorily.

Throughout this book, particular attention has been given to skills for internet and intelligent media for two main reasons. First, the internet remains the most versatile digital landscape, offering the full spectrum of skill demands, from basic operational tasks to complex interactions with adaptive and generative systems. Second, nearly all other digital media are converging with or are embedded in internet and intelligent media. Smartphones, smart televisions, voice assistants, e-readers, and even everyday household devices rely on algorithmic processing, personalization, and connectivity. For this reason, extending or adapting the seven-skill framework to other media should be relatively straightforward. The tables in Chap. 1 provide a conceptual foundation for such expansions, and the rise of intelligent media only increases the relevance and urgency of understanding digital skills in this broader, interconnected landscape.

Empirical Evidence

After proposing a framework of digital skills, it is essential to demonstrate its value and test it empirically. Conceptual models of digital literacy and digital skills are often developed without sufficient empirical support. This book presents the results of nationwide Dutch surveys reporting self-assessed levels of all seven skills, alongside task-based performance tests.

Expanding the framework to include intelligent media makes empirical validation even more important. Despite the growing relevance of skills such as interpreting system-generated outputs, crafting effective prompts for generative AI, and understanding algorithmic recommendations, the body of empirical research on them remains limited. Chapter 3 discusses the primary empirical approaches that are generally used to assess digital skills. Most used are surveys measuring the use of digital media which are taken to provide indirect evidence of skill levels, surveys asking respondents to self-assess their skills, and performance tests in laboratory or controlled environments in which participants complete specific tasks designed to reveal actual skill levels. The latter is the most valid method. Indirect measures only record whether an application is used, not whether it is mastered. Self-assessments frequently lead to overestimation of actual skills.

An important conclusion from the available evidence is that medium-related skills are generally more advanced than content-related skills. Most individuals have at least a basic command of the operational skills required to use internet media. Information skills continue to pose significant challenges, especially when users must compare perspectives or identify the reliability of search results or system outputs. Challenges become even greater in intelligent media contexts, where users must judge the quality, validity, or bias of AI-generated information. Communication and content creation skills also remain underdeveloped, partly because they encompass advanced skills such as curating online identities, managing complex social media interactions, or producing multimodal content. Strategic media use skills are the least developed overall. Many users struggle to translate their digital actions into meaningful outcomes.

A second important conclusion is that insufficient medium-related skills inhibit the acquisition of content-related skills, yet possessing adequate medium-related skills does not guarantee mastery of these substantive skills. This helps explain why middle-aged and older adults often outperform so-called "digital natives" in information and strategic media use skills, *provided* they have attained the required operational and formal skills. Their advantage stems from domain knowledge, traditional literacy, critical reasoning, and life experience, all of which matter greatly when evaluating sources or interpreting algorithmic suggestions. These findings also reinforce a broader insight: experience with digital media does not automatically lead to higher skill levels, except in basic operational and formal skills. Repeated exposure does not replace targeted learning, also not in (autonomous) intelligent media landscapes.

Further evidence speaks to socio-demographic patterns in digital skill inequality. Age, educational level, and traditional literacy emerge as the strongest predictors of skill disparities. Digital skills generally decline with age, except for information and strategic media use skills among those who have mastered the necessary operational and formal skills. Educational attainment and traditional literacy are even more powerful factors, consistently predicting all skill types across all age groups. Highly educated individuals perform better, reflecting greater reading ability, broader background knowledge, and greater familiarity with abstract problem-solving, qualities that are increasingly crucial in intelligent media environments.

Gender differences in digital skills are typically small or nonexistent in affluent societies with high levels of gender equality. Women tend to show lower skill levels mainly in developing societies characterized by limited socioeconomic opportunities. Ethnic disparities occasionally appear—as in the United States, where Hispanic, Native American, and African American populations often score lower than Asian or Anglo-American groups—but these patterns reflect broader socioeconomic inequalities and cultural patterns rather than intrinsic differences.

The Problem of Exclusion

The patterns of digital skill inequalities suggest a reflection of broader societal inequalities, yet this explanation is only partial. While similar forms of inequality exist for traditional media, internet and intelligent media introduce additional, often more complex, barriers. These barriers can be particularly detrimental for older generations whose accumulated knowledge and practical experience cannot be fully leveraged without sufficient operational and formal skills. They also disadvantage individuals with physical or cognitive disabilities, as well as those who have a genuine interest in digital culture, education, or information but lack confidence or skills. In the context of intelligent media, the challenge is even greater: navigating adaptive systems, interpreting algorithmic outputs, or benefiting from autonomous systems requires not only basic operational skills but also advanced information, communication, content creation, and strategic media use skills.

The primary impact of digital skill inequality is differential participation, or even exclusion, from multiple spheres of society. In a smart society, digital skills have become essential for full engagement, and skilled use of internet and intelligent media confers tangible advantages across economic, educational, political, social, cultural, spatial, and institutional domains. Economically, individuals with advanced digital skills gain better employment opportunities, higher incomes, greater career mobility, and access to cost-saving digital services. In education, they benefit from easier access to online courses, learning platforms, and a wide range of educational resources. Politically, participation increasingly relies on internet and intelligent media, including automated news curation, recommendation systems, and data-driven civic engagement tools, which facilitate access to information, voting resources, and public debate. Socially, digital skills enable maintaining personal networks, engaging in civic activities, and participating in online communities, while culturally, it allows for engagement with events, entertainment platforms, and the creation or consumption of user-generated content. Digital skills also enhance spatial participation, improving mobility, flexibility, and efficiency in daily life through tools such as navigation apps and AI-assisted scheduling or logistics systems. Finally, in the institutional sphere, individuals with sufficient digital skills gain improved access to public services, healthcare, and social benefits.

Although many of these advantages were once accessible through traditional media, relying solely on these channels is becoming increasingly difficult. In highly connected societies, traditional media are disappearing or require disproportionate effort to use, contributing to forms of absolute exclusion. At the same time, relative exclusion persists: individuals with high levels of internet and intelligent media skills gain disproportionately greater benefits, outperforming others in employment, social status, political influence, access to services, and even social and romantic networks through online platforms. This growing relative inequality reinforces existing structural disparities across all societal spheres. As illustrated in Chap. 4, unequal participation leads to uneven access to resources, opportunities, and societal positions. This inequality is amplified in complex intelligent media landscapes where automated systems, algorithms, and AI-driven platforms reward skillful engagement while marginalizing those lacking the required skills. The result is a self-reinforcing cycle that tends to exacerbate inequality over time, creating an increasingly stratified smart society in which digital skills determine not only participation but also social and economic advantage.

Solutions

To break the cycle of digital skill inequality, a range of strategic interventions is required. Some of these interventions specifically target inequality arising from differences in digital skills, while others address the broader socioeconomic and cultural inequalities that shape access to and engagement with internet and intelligent media. This book focuses primarily on interventions aimed at mitigating digital inequality by improving digital skills, while continually emphasizing the importance of social, economic, and cultural contexts. Individuals without jobs involving computer and internet use, without access to educational institutions, without school-age children at home, without financial resources to purchase devices or pay for internet connections, without command of the majority language, or without stable housing are at a significant disadvantage when it comes to acquiring digital skills. Many of these conditions are widespread in developing countries, highlighting that interventions addressing digital skills alone may be insufficient; for many, improving employment or income opportunities may be a more effective first step than providing devices or training.

Chapters 5 and 6 explore specific solutions for reducing digital skill inequalities. These solutions fall into two broad categories: preventive measures through improvements in interface design and content and targeted educational interventions. Enhancing digital interfaces can reduce the demands on users' medium-related skills, particularly operational and formal skills. Designers often prioritize aesthetic appeal over accessibility or usability, but adopting User- and Human-Centered Design approaches can shift this focus, compelling designers to test their assumptions about how diverse users will interact with their creations. Consistency across media and platforms is another important consideration, as users with lower skill levels must otherwise relearn interfaces repeatedly. Content design and delivery can also support skill development. For example, intelligent search systems can guide users by limiting the overwhelming number of large-scale platforms, supporting query formulation, improving text readability, providing concise and focused content, and applying quality markers that indicate verified, high-quality information. From the perspective of communication skills, content improvements may involve helping users manage online contacts, moderating discussion boards, encouraging responsible profile creation, and supporting collaboration. Content creation skills can be enhanced through platforms that simplify technical requirements while simultaneously raising awareness of what users are producing. Strategic media use skills can be supported through decision-making assistance systems that help users maintain focus, take appropriate actions, and make informed choices across a variety of daily life situations.

Educational interventions remain a cornerstone of digital skill development. While many individuals naturally attempt to learn through trial and error or by seeking help from their social environment, these methods, though important, are often insufficient. Natural learning processes may support basic medium-related skills, but they rarely foster content-related skills, which require background knowledge, creativity, practical experience, and structured guidance. As internet and intelligent media become more intuitive, natural learning remains relevant, yet increasingly complex tasks in work, education, and leisure contexts demand systematic educational support. Formal education must integrate digital skills throughout the curriculum at all levels. In some cases, this may involve dedicated courses, but in most instances, content-related digital skills can be embedded into existing subjects such as languages, history, science, mathematics, and media education. For adults over fifty who did not acquire digital skills at school or in the workplace, targeted adult education programs are essential. Public access sites, libraries, and community centers can offer short courses, guided activities, or one-on-one support to help learners acquire digital skills. In developing countries, such public venues are often the primary setting for digital skill acquisition across age groups. Certain groups require specially tailored approaches, including older adults, individuals with low literacy, people with disabilities, homeless populations, and migrants with limited proficiency in the local language or English. Digital skills education for these groups must be adapted to their specific needs, motivations, and cultural contexts. This principle of adapting instruction to the learner is central to all forms of effective digital skills education. The following sections discuss educational solutions within the context of current policy approaches aimed at addressing digital skill disparities.

7.2 General Policy Perspectives

The discussion of contemporary policies addressing inadequate digital skills begins with a set of general principles designed to guide policymakers in selecting among available strategies and instruments. Following this, the societal actors responsible for addressing the issue are identified. These actors extend beyond governments and educational institutions to include tech companies and developers, training institutes, publishers of digital learning tools, labor organizations, public access sites, libraries, user support groups, and users themselves, all of whom bear specific roles and responsibilities. Finally, the discussion turns to the concrete strategies and instruments currently available to each of these actors, illustrating how coordinated efforts can effectively enhance digital skills across society.

The discussion of contemporary policies for addressing inadequate digital skills begins with several general principles that all responsible actors must consider. The first and most important is a social-contextual perspective, which this book argues is far more effective for understanding and addressing digital skill deficiencies than a purely technical perspective. Learning digital skills is not a temporary task of mastering a few tricks on a device or completing steps in a single program. When digital media first emerged in the 1980s and 1990s, a popular view was that acquiring basic keyboard skills and learning office programs like word processors and spreadsheets would suffice to include individuals in the digital world. These tasks were seen as temporary and primarily technical, and once mastered, users were considered digitally literate. In contrast, this book emphasizes that the social context of internet and intelligent media use is decisive, shaping the entire learning process from initial motivation to the realization of tangible benefits. Individuals who are unmotivated to use particular media will not acquire skills, and those who fail to experience benefits will discontinue use. Digital media must fit into everyday routines; otherwise, use remains sporadic and limited to necessity. When operational difficulties arise, users typically turn to proximate peers with similar social backgrounds rather than distant technical helpdesks. Learning venues such as adult education centers, public access sites, or libraries must be attractive and culturally relevant, and digital courses must align with learners' needs. Skills taught in one context, such as a classroom, must be practiced in work, study, or leisure environments to be retained. Across this book, social and contextual factors are repeatedly highlighted as critical determinants of digital skill acquisition.

A technical perspective has historically dominated policy, often emphasizing hardware provision as a solution. For a long time, governments and educational institutions worldwide prioritized equipping schools with computers and internet connections, with software adaptation and teacher retraining implemented much later (Selwyn, 2012). Similarly, public access sites and libraries focused on maximizing the number of terminals and devices, while staff training received lower priority. While equipment, software, connectivity, and subscriptions are necessary prerequisites for learning digital skills, they are not sufficient. In developed countries with high-access rates, government and corporate programs providing computers at discounted prices or tax reductions have had limited impact on either access or skill development (Van Dijk, 2005). In contrast, widespread adoption of affordable, "always-on" broadband that enables learning by doing in rich multimedia environments has had a far greater effect. In developing countries, collective and low-cost public access remains a viable approach for the foreseeable future. Large-scale initiatives in developing countries, such as the One Laptop per Child and the Indian Hole in the Wall projects (see Sect. 7.4, technology provision), exemplify the limitations of a purely technical approach. While these projects gained global recognition for their ambition, they illustrate that providing hardware alone neglects the social, cultural, and educational contexts critical for effective skill acquisition.

Technical and hardware-focused approaches have also reinforced an overemphasis on medium-related skills at the expense of content-related skills. Programs that teach only technical procedures offer temporary benefits. They may help individuals gain initial access to digital media, but these skills quickly become outdated as media evolve, and practical, context-driven applications demand broader knowledge, creativity, and problem-solving skills. Furthermore, policy and research often assume that difficulties in digital tasks stem primarily from the digital design of applications or services. In reality, the substantive knowledge required to navigate complex tasks, such as filing online tax forms or using digital banking platforms, can be a greater barrier than technical skill. Individuals may struggle not with navigating menus or completing forms, but with understanding regulatory requirements, financial concepts, or administrative language. Effective solutions therefore require combining digital skills support with clear, accessible explanations of the underlying subject matter.

Another key principle is the adoption of a target group strategy in digital skills education. Standardized, one-size-fits-all courses focused on office programs, email, or general internet use rarely meet the diverse needs of learners. Tailored approaches for specific groups, such as older adults, people with disabilities or low literacy, or migrants, are essential. Similarly, workplace-focused training that aligns with employees' tasks can be more effective than generic courses. This strategy emphasizes adapting both design and educational solutions to individual needs and local cultures. Internet and intelligent media can be made more accessible and relevant by customizing interfaces, offering only the necessary functions, or providing content in the learner's language. Courses and training should engage learners with culturally appropriate and personally relevant content. Such customization addresses the primary driver of digital skill acquisition: motivation. When learners perceive relevance and attain tangible benefits, engagement and learning outcomes are likely to improve.

7.3 Policy Actors

Addressing the problem of inadequate digital skills requires coordinated action by a wide range of societal actors. It cannot be resolved by schools, libraries, or public access centers alone. Responsibility for developing and implementing effective digital skills policy extends to governments, tech companies, training institutes, software and content publishers, labor organizations, educational institutions, public access centers, and user support groups. Among these actors, governments are uniquely positioned to coordinate efforts. For this reason, the discussion begins with the role of governments as key policy actors.

Governments

Both national and local governments recognize a responsibility to address the widespread lack of digital skills among citizens. Their motivation stems from multiple policy domains—political, economic, innovation, educational, social, and cultural—and the strategies they adopt are influenced by broader national models of information and network societies (Venturelli, 2002; Bradford, 2023). For instance, the United States follows a market-driven, liberal model in which digital skills are largely supported by corporations and the workforce, with governments providing general education and R&D incentives for innovation. In contrast, European countries, guided by human rights principles, consider digital access and the skills required to exercise it as a public interest or citizen right, primarily supported through government and public educational institutions (Helsper & Van Deursen, 2015). East-Asian and Chinese state-driven models emphasize coordinated state intervention to build national digital infrastructure and ensure that corporate workforces acquire necessary digital skills. In many developing countries, governments initially prioritize technical infrastructure, followed by products, services, and eventually education and digital skills for the population (Van Dijk, 2020). Across all contexts, however, *economic considerations remain the dominant driver*: adequate digital skills expand business opportunities, improve employment prospects, and foster innovation and productivity. Innovation policies further reinforce the importance of digital skills, with governments investing heavily in research and development to ensure that populations are prepared for emerging tech sectors. Educational policies require ongoing updates of school curricula, teaching facilities, and teacher training to reflect internet and intelligent media applications. Social and cultural policies aim to equip citizens with the skills to live effectively in smart societies.

Governments have a wide range of instruments to promote digital skill development. See Box 7.1.

Box 7.1 Government Instruments to Support Digital Skills

- Provision of infrastructure.
- Development and standardization of digital skills frameworks.
- Organizing technical assessments for emerging technologies.
- Promoting awareness of digital skills needs across society.
- Coordination of stakeholders and facilitation of partnerships.
- Implementation and updating of educational policies.
- Design and delivery of targeted digital skills interventions and training.
- Stimulating citizens to use electronic government services.
- Provision of public access points.

The first and most fundamental is providing *infrastructure*, particularly in schools. Without access to digital media, students and citizens cannot develop digital skills. For example, broadband deployment in the United States is prioritized because it enables access to a broader range of applications that encourage skill development. Globally, the provision of sufficient computer terminals and reliable internet connections in schools remains an essential first step.

Recognizing that hardware provision alone is insufficient, governments have invested in *digital skills framework development*. This involves defining the necessary skills, as has been done in this book, standardizing and certifying them, and integrating them into curricula, including areas such as *AI literacy* in secondary education (Casal-Otero et al., 2023).

Governments also organize *technical assessments* for new digital media, evaluating both opportunities and risks, and engage in *awareness-raising initiatives* among the population and the leadership of local institutions, emphasizing that adequate digital skills are essential and cannot be achieved simply by providing infrastructure. After 2000, many governments recognized this need and established research and policy groups to investigate the issue and to inform businesses, schools, and other public institutions that it required dedicated attention. In some cases, these efforts were accompanied by concrete regulations, such as the *EU AI Act*.

Another key instrument is *stakeholder coordination*. Governments convene actors across sectors—employers, employees, educational institutions, adult education organizations, public libraries, and municipalities—to develop coherent national or local digital skills strategies. The scope of these initiatives varies: large-scale, broad programs are typically government-led, while smaller, targeted partnerships may emerge from private or public-private collaboration.

Educational policy constitutes a central tool. Governments oversee public education and are responsible for its continual adaptation to technological change. Digital media in classrooms have driven ongoing curriculum renewal, teacher training, educational software development, and innovations in pedagogy. Ministries of Education often provide funding, guidance, and evaluation frameworks to support these changes.

Governments can also implement *direct interventions and training programs* to improve digital skills. An evaluation of seven European initiatives found significant increases in the use of information and communication technologies, though gains in the outcomes of use were more modest (Martinez et al., 2024). Notably, participants with higher socioeconomic resources and preexisting basic digital skills benefited the most, reflecting both the Matthew effect and the Resources and Appropriation theory: individuals with more resources and prior experience derive greater advantage. Psychological factors, such as confidence, also play a role. It is important that training programs become more closely aligned with participants' needs and experiences and are better embedded within broader initiatives (Martinez et al., 2024), a finding consistent with the social-contextual perspective emphasized throughout this book.

Governments have a vested interest in *encouraging citizens to engage with digital government services*, including online information portals and transactional platforms. Many governments leverage this opportunity to simultaneously promote digital skills. Some countries offer specialized courses that teach citizens how to navigate digital service desks, while in other cases civil servants provide hands-on guidance at in-person service points, helping users complete tasks and gain practical experience with online services.

A final key government instrument is the *provision of public access points* in libraries, community centers, and other public facilities. These sites become particularly effective for digital skills development when staff possess sufficient expertise and time to assist users or when structured computer and internet courses are offered. By combining access with guidance and training, public access initiatives can support both medium- and content-related skills, including the skills needed to use intelligent AI-enhanced services.

Tech(nology) Industry

The tech industry has played a central role in both creating and potentially resolving the digital skills problem. On one hand, the widespread introduction of complex and technically demanding hardware and software has contributed to difficulties for users, particularly those with lower levels of digital skills. On the other hand, the industry has the capacity to alleviate much of this problem by designing more intuitive, user-friendly devices and applications. In Chap. 5, several strategies were proposed for developers and designers to accommodate users with lower levels of both medium- and content-related digital skills, emphasizing the importance of usability, guidance, and thoughtful interface design.

The shift toward highly intuitive, easy-to-operate devices such as smartphones, tablets, and all kinds of smart devices has successfully reduced challenges related to medium-related skills. However, these devices have done little to address the persistent difficulties in acquiring content-related skills, which require more complex cognitive engagement, creativity, evaluation, and decision-making. In fact, the growing reliance on mobile and smart devices may inadvertently exacerbate the so-called "usage gap." Mobile applications often constrain user agency, limiting opportunities for performing content-related tasks or generating creative input compared to desktops and laptops with full functionality. As a result, individuals who primarily rely on mobile devices may find themselves at a disadvantage relative to users of more versatile computing platforms, potentially widening disparities in digital engagement and skills application (Napoli & Obar, 2014; Van Deursen & Van Dijk, 2019).

Intelligent media, including AI-driven recommendation systems, generative platforms, adaptive learning tools, and algorithmic content curation, introduces new dimensions of digital skills. Users must learn to craft effective prompts, interpret system-generated outputs, evaluate algorithmic recommendations critically, and integrate automated feedback into decision-making. Without sufficient guidance and support, intelligent media risk widening skill disparities. The tech industry can play a pivotal role by intentionally designing products that not only reduce operational complexity but also actively scaffold content-related skill development. Several approaches can be pursued. First, applications can provide embedded learning support such as step-by-step tutorials, contextual tips, or AI-driven coaching, guiding users in performing complex tasks while fostering critical thinking and creative problem-solving. Second, platforms can offer experimental modes that allow users to explore functions freely and gain hands-on experience without real-world consequences. Third, transparency should be prioritized in intelligent media, helping users understand how algorithms make recommendations and giving them tools to adjust and interpret outputs.

Finally, telecom providers, as a distinct segment of the tech industry, have an important role to play. While their local stores have traditionally focused on selling subscriptions and hardware for mobile and internet services, they are uniquely positioned to support digital skills development. By shifting their focus beyond transactional sales, telecom stores can become community hubs that empower users. Approaches might be offering one-on-one in-store guidance or transforming the store into a personalized learning environment. They might for example offer bundles that combine hardware, subscriptions, and digital skills training, making learning an integral part of the customer experience.

Internet Training Institutes

General computer and internet training institutes that offer certifications play a central role in shaping and standardizing digital skills. These institutes can define the skills required, provide structured curricula, and issue certifications that signal mastery of the most important skills. Specific providers that cater to professional groups such as healthcare workers, bank employees, or educators perform a similar role for more specialized digital skills. In these professional contexts, digital skill training is closely linked to the knowledge, decision-making, and practical tasks relevant to the profession, making content-related skills a larger component than in general courses, which typically focus on office programs or basic internet use.

Despite their significance, both general and professional training institutes tend to define digital skills largely according to prevailing public perceptions, which often prioritize technical skills. The broader and more nuanced set of content-related digital skills discussed in this book remains insufficiently standardized and certified in most training programs. General training institutes, which provide thousands of courses annually worldwide, are unlikely to take on this task, as they usually view professional skill development as the responsibility of specialized institutes. In combination, general and professional training providers form complementary pillars in the ecosystem of digital skills development, but substantial work remains to align curricula, assessment, and certification with the full spectrum of skills required in a smart (and information-rich) society.

Publishers of Learning Tools

High-quality educational software and learning materials for digital skills remain relatively rare, which gives publishers of digital learning tools a crucial role in fostering skill development. Such tools include self-assessment platforms, instructional computer books, and online resources that provide guided exercises and assignments across the full spectrum of digital skills outlined in this book. Publishers face two major challenges. First, rapid technological change means that hardware, software, and digital media and platforms are constantly evolving, quickly rendering instructional materials obsolete. This requires publishers to continually update content and provide timely revisions, often at significant cost. Second, the market for digital skills learning tools is relatively limited. Many learners believe they can acquire digital skills more effectively on-the-job, through trial and error, or with personal guidance from peers, mentors, or instructors. This perception reduces the demand for stand-alone educational products. Similarly, the market for teacher-oriented materials is often small, as many educators rely instead on the help functions and embedded tutorials included with each new version of popular software. Despite these challenges, publishers have an important role to play in supporting digital skills. Well-designed instructional tools can complement formal training, provide accessible resources for self-directed learning, and offer structured pathways for learners who do not have immediate access to professional training or guided instruction. Publishers can also innovate by creating interactive and adaptive additional resources that integrate simulations or gamification, helping learners practice skills. Additionally, by collaborating with schools, professional institutes, and online learning platforms, publishers can help ensure that content remains current, pedagogically sound, and aligned with both general and profession-specific digital skills.

Labor Organizations

Company management often leaves employees largely on their own when it comes to solving problems related to digital skills and tends to underestimate the productivity lost due to employees' insufficient digital skills (Van Deursen & Van Dijk, 2014). Less than one-quarter of employees learn the most from formal training programs or helpdesks, the traditional solutions offered by management. Instead, they rely on informal methods, such as learning by doing or seeking help from colleagues and people outside the workplace. Raising *awareness among management* about the scale and impact of digital skills gaps is therefore a critical first step. Once aware, organizations can implement a range of effective measures. One approach is to *formalize informal assistance* currently provided by colleagues. Employees with advanced digital skills and some teaching or mentoring ability could be appointed as designated digital skill mentors to assist colleagues. Networks of these mentors could collaborate with internal helpdesks to provide more structured support, creating a peer-supported ecosystem that reinforces learning across departments.

Another priority is re-evaluating *the role of helpdesks*. Traditionally, helpdesks are seen as reactive, technical support services, resolving hardware and software issues as they arise. However, helpdesks could play a more proactive role in digital skills development by offering guidance, explanations, and small training sessions to prevent recurring failures. For this expanded role, helpdesk staff would require training in didactic methods.

Organizations also need to *expand the focus of digital skills training* beyond traditional office software to include internet and intelligent media. Skills for internet applications and AI-driven platforms are frequently neglected in corporate training programs. Conducting an inventory of workplace-relevant tools such as collaboration platforms, AI-assisted data analysis tools, or industry-specific digital applications can help management identify skill gaps and prioritize training initiatives.

Systematic assessment of employees' digital skills is another key step. Self-assessments or performance-based evaluations can identify gaps across age groups, with particular attention to older adults and low-educated employees who may face the greatest challenges. Young employees should also be evaluated, as hiring digital natives does not guarantee sufficient workplace-ready skills. Results from the assessments can inform the design of targeted courses, on-the-job training, and collaborations with external educational institutions. Evidence suggests that training interventions are more effective than many employees expect, highlighting the value of structured learning opportunities (Van Deursen & van Dijk, 2014).

Special emphasis should be placed on intelligent media, popular under the notion of *AI literacy*. Emphasis should not primarily be about learning to program advanced language models but about developing basic programming skills and recognizing that every element of a line of code can influence outcomes. As Seaver (2019, p. 418) notes, "To know an algorithm is to know its decision-making criteria." AI literacy involves the ability to understand, use, and critically evaluate AI applications (Tsz Kit Ng et al., 2021). These skills are increasingly necessary both in modern industrial and organizational work and in the use of seemingly simple, everyday AI applications. In labor organizations, workers and employees need more advanced intelligent media skills, potentially including aspects of programming, to remain competitive in relation to AI systems. More and more, the job will involve *collaborating* with AI in order to avoid becoming redundant. Organizations that integrate these skills into formal training, complemented by peer and helpdesk support, are better positioned to maximize employee productivity and engagement with intelligent media. Similarly, training in *efficient communication* needs more attention. Training in email and digital communication skills can reduce significant time waste and improve workplace workflow.

Schools and Universities

Schools occupy a unique position as the first institutions systematically supported by governments and other funders, such as charitable organizations, to enhance digital skills. Historically, the primary focus has been on providing hardware and software, with plans for digital skills development often relegated to secondary priority. These plans typically list teacher training as the top priority; however, such training often comes last or does not occur at all.

In primary education, the emphasis is often on operational and formal skills, building on skills developed at home or in pre-school. Computers are often used to reinforce traditional literacy and numeracy, but opportunities to develop content-related skills remain limited. In secondary education, the hope is to expand students' digital skills to include content-related skills, particularly information skills. However, many teachers do not provide adequate instruction in effectively using search engines, generative AI platforms, or integrating online sources into assignments. Students' communication, content creation, and strategic media choice and use skills are often assumed rather than explicitly taught, even in higher education.

The central didactic principle should be to draw on the *mutual enrichment between the ways of learning that children and students develop in their home environments and the methods used at school*. Currently, these styles are often worlds apart. When pupils and students are allowed to use their own preferred methods of engaging with digital media, their motivation increases. They also become more receptive to teachers' suggestions for improving their subject-specific skills.

In the former chapter, it was suggested to *embed digital skills into existing curricula*. This is more effective than creating isolated subjects. Information and strategic media use skills can be integrated into language, history, geography, biology, physics, and mathematics courses, while communication and content creation are suited to media education programs. Realizing this integration requires curriculum development, clear learning objectives, and adequate teacher retraining. Educators must be given time and resources to design materials that foster digital skills within the context of subject-specific learning.

The prior chapter also suggested several new avenues for learning enabled by intelligent media. Schools can incorporate AI-assisted platforms for personalized learning, simulations, and project-based tasks to develop digital skills. For example, students can practice evaluating AI-generated information, constructing prompts for generative systems, and using algorithmic recommendations responsibly, preparing them for both academic and professional environments.

Public Libraries

Public libraries, in both developed and developing countries, have a widely recognized role in providing access to digital resources, offering assistance, and delivering computer and internet training. However, the scope, scale, and approach to these activities vary considerably depending on how libraries perceive their role. Some libraries place a high priority on digital access, support, and education, while others maintain a more traditional focus on print collections and archival resources. In some countries or regions, public libraries adopt a reactive stance, offering assistance primarily upon request rather than actively engaging visitors or promoting structured learning opportunities. In contrast, in other places, libraries take a proactive approach, fostering digital engagement through workshops, outreach programs, and community initiatives.

The diversity of visitors' needs complicates the task of public libraries. Some visitors possess advanced digital skills and come to the library mainly for free wireless access. Others have limited or no access at home and very low skill levels; they primarily seek opportunities to use computers and the internet. Still others require assistance with specific tasks that call for information, communication, content creation, or strategic media use skills. Especially information skills are an area in which libraries have expertise. Public libraries and their staff vary in how they respond to potential requests for help. Some staff members wait at service desks for visitors to approach, while others circulate through the space, observing and offering assistance proactively. Opportunities to participate in internet courses depend on the library's program, available expertise, and staffing levels. However, many public libraries lack the necessary funding to provide such intensive and resource-demanding services.

Public and Community Access Centers

The roles and opportunities of public and community access centers are similar to those of public libraries, focusing on providing access, guidance, and training in digital media. These centers offer computer and internet access to individuals without home or workplace connectivity, provide on-the-spot assistance for specific questions, and deliver longer-term digital skills courses. However, access centers typically have a broader social function than public libraries. Their role is often tied to the primary public services they support, such as health services in hospitals, administrative services in government buildings, or adult education in public schools. Community centers in particular serve social and cultural functions for local neighborhoods, facilitating community organization and engagement. Digital media and online communities can act as catalysts for these initiatives, encouraging the formation of digital networks and online community participation.

The importance of public and community access centers differs sharply between low- and high-internet access countries or between developing and developed nations. In low-access or developing countries, these centers are important for providing access to populations with limited resources and skills. They often serve as key social spaces, particularly for young people, where learning, social interaction, and digital engagement intersect. Even commercial internet cafés may fulfill similar functions, offering both access and informal support for digital learning. In high-access countries and developed nations, the roles of public and community access centers are much more specialized. Because most people have internet access at home, these centers primarily provide wireless and fixed access for the small portion of the population who do not. They no longer serve as general gathering places for the entire community, but rather as hubs for specific groups involved in activities such as health support, community building, immigration courses, or political engagement. Internet training is similarly targeted, focusing on groups such as older adults, people with an immigrant background, people with disabilities, or patient communities.

In all contexts, effective access centers must be embedded in the local culture and adapted to the specific needs of their visitors. Unlike public libraries or adult education institutions, which often focus on individual learning, access centers frequently offer collective activities. These group-based programs, ranging from community action projects to collaborative digital workshops, may have goals that extend beyond individual digital skills development, combining social, cultural, and technological objectives. When designed thoughtfully, these centers can both empower local communities and foster meaningful engagement with internet and intelligent media.

User Support Services and Citizen Initiatives

The responsibility for improving digital skills extends beyond public institutions, educational organizations, and private companies. Individual users, consumers, and citizens also play a crucial role in developing their skills. First, individuals must make a realistic assessment of their own digital skills, identifying both strengths and areas that require improvement. Second, they need to actively seek solutions, whether through social support networks, educational opportunities, or self-directed learning. The internet itself provides numerous applications and platforms for these purposes. Both online and offline courses and training programs are increasingly accessible, even in resource-constrained environments. Motivated learners can take advantage of internet cafés, libraries, or community centers to gain hands-on experience, seek guidance from peers, or consult friends and acquaintances with more digital experience.

Beyond individual efforts, collective initiatives play an important role in fostering digital skills. Across countries, organizations such as older adult-focused online networks provide tailored courses, guidance, and support specifically designed to meet their needs. Similar initiatives exist for people with disabilities, immigrants, and people with low literacy, combining specialized instruction with practical support to reduce barriers to digital engagement. Many of these initiatives operate on a commercial basis, while others rely on public funding or volunteer contributions. Intelligent media present both new opportunities and challenges for these initiatives. Collective programs can leverage them to provide personalized guidance, automated feedback, and interactive exercises, helping learners acquire digital skills more efficiently. For instance, AI-powered learning platforms can adapt to a user's existing skill level, suggest targeted exercises, or simulate real-world scenarios for practice, thus extending the reach and effectiveness of traditional community programs.

Both individual and collective efforts should receive stronger social, public, and government support. Even modest additional resources such as funding for training facilitators, access to intelligent learning tools, or promotion of local digital networks could dramatically increase the effectiveness of these initiatives.

7.4 A Synopsis of Strategies and Instruments

In the final part of this book, a concise synopsis of the main practical strategies and instruments for addressing the digital skills challenge is offered. This overview is intentionally condensed, as the goal is not to present a fully developed action plan but rather to highlight key approaches and tools. The strategies and instruments are organized thematically in Fig. 7.1.

Awareness and Organization

Large sections of society are still insufficiently aware of the seriousness and far-reaching consequences of digital skills inequality, a problem that has been a central motivation for this book. When governments, corporations, educational authorities, and institutions of adult education recognize the scope and impact of this issue, they might organize *awareness programs*. Such programs should not only highlight the existence and importance of the problem but also offer practical, actionable solutions tailored to the needs of the populations concerned.

Addressing digital skills inequality often requires the *coordinated effort of multiple actors*. Institutions with the largest reach, such as national and local governments or major educational bodies, are particularly well placed to convene relevant stakeholders. These collaborations frequently take the form of *public-private partnerships*, combining public interest objectives with material or immaterial incentives, such as skills development and workforce improvement. Common stakeholder combinations include government departments, private-sector companies, schools, and professional training organizations. The coordination of these actors ensures that interventions are both comprehensive and contextually appropriate, addressing the technical, social, and educational dimensions of digital skills.

Government departments such as Ministries of Education, Economy, or Innovation play a central role in *monitoring the* population's digital skills. Continuous monitoring supports policy development, guides intervention planning, and enables the evaluation of progress over time. For example, the authors of this book participate in bi-annual trend surveys

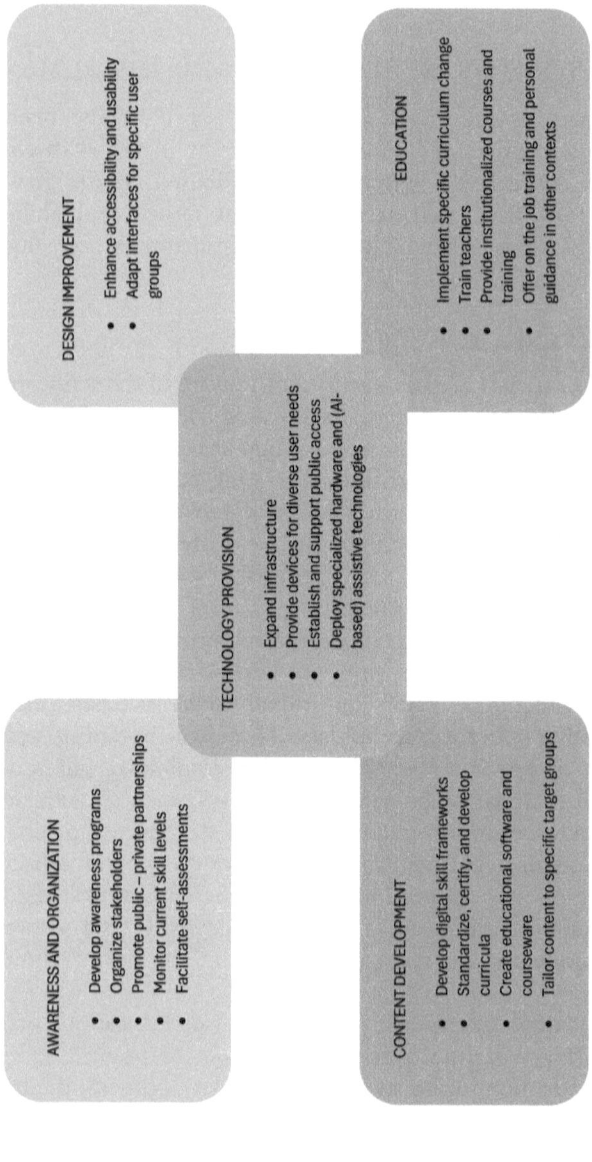

Fig. 7.1 Clusters of strategies and instruments for digital skills improvement

of internet and intelligent media skills and use among the Dutch population. These surveys rely on proxy questions that estimate current levels across the seven skills identified, allowing for both broad trend analysis and targeted interventions. Monitoring can also take place through online *self-assessments*. These enable individuals to evaluate their own digital skills against a standardized framework. Ideally, these self-assessments should be interactive, providing personalized guidance and suggestions for addressing specific skill gaps. When combined with institutional awareness campaigns and stakeholder coordination, such tools can significantly enhance both individual and collective understanding of digital skills needs, fostering more effective learning and skill acquisition across society.

Design Improvement

In Chap. 5, strategies for enhancing the *accessibility and usability of both interfaces and content* were explored to mitigate digital skills challenges. Improving design is not solely a matter of aesthetics; it directly influences whether users can beneficially use internet and intelligent media and platforms. We proposed specific ways to optimize interfaces and online content to accommodate a broad spectrum of users, not just those with disabilities or special needs.

Many individuals encounter difficulties in using internet media because the designs of websites, applications, and software tools are overly complex or unintuitive. This is a serious concern, as much information, public services, and commercial transactions are delivered online with the implicit assumption that all citizens can access and use them effectively. Poorly designed interfaces can amplify existing digital inequalities, excluding individuals who are otherwise motivated but struggle with operational and formal skills. These challenges extend to mobile devices such as smartphones and tablets. Mobile applications have been lauded for their convenience and portability, but many remain constrained by limited functionality or design choices that restrict user agency. Similarly, intelligent media and platforms demand additional content-related skills which can further amplify difficulties for users who are insufficiently skilled. Complex navigation, pre-programmed workflows, and poorly explained features across these platforms can exacerbate challenges.

Developers and designers have the opportunity and responsibility to create intuitive, user-friendly, and inclusive interfaces that empower a diverse user base to access, understand, and interact with internet and intelligent media effectively. This includes explicitly ***adapting interfaces and content for groups with specific accessibility needs***, such as older adults, users with low literacy, and people with disabilities. By ensuring that interfaces are both technically and socially inclusive, designers can support all users to engage meaningfully.

Technology Provision

Adequate ***infrastructure*** is a necessary precondition for developing digital skills, particularly in developing nations where internet access is limited. This also applies to intelligent media systems. However, an overemphasis on technology provision alone without paying attention to implementation, guidance, and user support can be overly simplistic and produce disappointing results in terms of actual skills and meaningful usage. Equipping schools with hardware, software, internet connectivity, and intelligent media is often the first step considered by governments and educational institutions when planning educational innovation, while complementary measures such as teacher training, curriculum integration, and ongoing support are frequently treated as secondary considerations. Examples of this technical orientation include several technology-provision projects in the Global South that specifically target children. In the *Hole in the Wall* project in India, for instance, computer kiosks were installed in public spaces to give children access to a limited set of computer and internet applications, though with minimal guidance or skill support. Similarly, in the well-known *One Laptop per Child* (OLPC) initiative, implemented in various developing countries since 2005, selected children were provided with inexpensive (around $200 or less) and durable laptops. Despite their good intentions, these examples of technology provision overlook the social, cultural, educational, and material contexts in which they operate. Warschauer and Ames (2010), as well as Selwyn (2012), offer strong critiques of OLPC's "technocentric vision," describing it as "technologically Utopian development schemes that have unsuccessfully attempted to solve complex social problems with overly simplistic solutions" (Warschauer & Ames, 2010, p. 33). Warschauer and Ames provide a detailed analysis of these projects, highlighting several issues: the limited affordability of large-scale laptop programs (which tend to be feasible only for middle- and higher-income developing countries); unrealistic expectations about educational impact in the absence of substantial guidance and teacher support; design flaws in the specialized operating system; frequent hardware failures; and the disappointing reality that the benefits primarily accrue to high-performing students. They conclude that "instead of an approach of simply handing computers to children and walking away, there needs to be large-scale integrated education improvement efforts" (p. 34). They argue further that "the poorest countries targeted by OLPC cannot afford laptop computers for all their children and would be better off building schools, training teachers, developing curricula, providing books and subsidizing attendance" (p. 34). By contrast, public access centers and specialized hardware tools for people with disabilities or for older adults tend to yield more immediate and practical benefits. Although they do not provide comprehensive solutions, they offer crucial support to individuals who are already motivated, evident in their willingness to seek out these services, and they are typically accompanied by assistance from staff with at least some level of professional expertise.

Content Development

An important task in addressing digital inequality is to determine which digital skills are needed and to develop a *conceptual framework* that captures them. This book offers one such framework. This framework identifies seven types of skills that all users need in order to use internet and intelligent media beneficially. However, in the context of specific jobs, educational levels, or public and private services, more specialized frameworks might be required. Every profession demands its own skill set, and university students, for example, need more advanced digital skills than those in secondary education. Once a framework has been established, it must be made operational by means of *standardization, certification, and curriculum development*. This task falls primarily to professional organizations, sectoral bodies, training institutions, and certification agencies. It typically involves designing modules that target specific skills, creating assessment tools, and establishing certification pathways that culminate in diplomas, badges, or other credentials. Current training modules overwhelmingly focus on medium-related skills, such as operating devices, navigating interfaces, or using common office applications. In contrast, content-related skills remain underdeveloped or entirely absent from most curricula. These are precisely the skills that determine whether people can engage critically with online information, evaluate AI outputs, participate meaningfully in digital communication, and use internet and intelligent media to achieve personal and professional goals. In this regard, substantial development work is still needed to address the full spectrum of digital skills.

The next step, and arguably the most crucial, is the *development of high-quality educational software, courseware, and learning materials* that are suitable for specific contexts and target groups. The relevance and effectiveness of digital skills training are determined largely by the quality of these materials. To be effective, digital skills content must be adapted to *the social, cultural, linguistic, and practical realities of the learners*. This includes aligning learning pathways with users' lived experiences; incorporating adaptive or intelligent tutoring systems where appropriate; and ensuring that content is accessible for people with specific needs.

Education

Once frameworks, standards, and certification systems for digital skills have been developed, educational institutions must *embed them into their curricula* and *prepare teachers* to guide students effectively. This typically requires substantial teacher training, not only in the technical use of tools but also in understanding which types of digital skills need emphasis within a given curriculum. As argued earlier, especially for content-related skills, integration into existing school subjects is more effective than teaching these skills in isolated computer classes. When digital skills are tied to subjects such as language, science, social studies, or vocational training, teachers are more motivated, learning becomes authentic, and students are better able to connect digital skills to real academic tasks. Importantly, this approach helps teachers recognize that their disciplinary expertise is central to cultivating digital skills that extend beyond the basic skills students may already possess.

Beyond formal schooling, workplaces represent the second major context in which digital skills are learned. Here, organizations must choose between *on-the-job training and structured classes* offered by schools, vocational centers, or adult education providers. In most cases, on-the-job training is more effective and efficient, as it directly aligns digital skill development with the practical tasks employees must perform. However, external or remote courses can be valuable when workers require uninterrupted time for concentrated learning or when new digital media require basic skills to be developed before they can be applied in the workplace.

The distinction between on-the-job learning and external training highlights a broader insight: digital skill learning is not a narrow, technical activity but a deeply social and contextual process. It is shaped by workplace norms, social relationships, cultural expectations, and everyday practices. For this reason, education alone cannot fully address digital skill gaps. Preventive strategies—especially improving the usability, accessibility, and inclusiveness of interface design—are equally essential. Finally, broader social and economic policy plays a decisive role. Investments in quality schooling, teacher training, job creation, and inclusive public services indirectly foster digital skills by improving the environments in which people live, learn, and work. In the long term, such structural policies may be more effective in narrowing digital inequalities than digital skills programs alone. Strengthening education and social opportunity therefore remains central to enabling all individuals to participate meaningfully in a smart society.

7.5 Closing Remark

Digital skills are essential for making meaningful use of the internet and intelligent media and, therefore, for participating fully in a smart society. This book has shown that digital inequality will not resolve itself and that mere access to digital media is only the first step. Real progress demands thoughtful policy, inclusive design, well-developed content, robust educational infrastructure, and continuous attention to the social context in which people learn and live. Our central message is clear: digital skills are cultivated by people, not by technology alone. By embedding internet and intelligent media meaningfully in education, work, and daily life; by improving interface designs; by aligning training with real user needs; and by accounting for differences in opportunity, motivation, and capability, we can ensure digital skills benefit everyone. When policymakers, designers, educators, organizations, and users collaborate, digital skills can become a force that unites rather than divides. The challenge is complex, but the reward is a society where most people can participate. With targeted, sustainable efforts, this promise can be achieved.

References

Bradford, A. (2023). *Digital empires: The global battle to regulate technology*. Oxford University Press.

Casal-Otero, L., Catala, A., Fernández-Morante, C., Taboada, M., Cebreiro, B., & Barro, S. (2023). AI literacy in K-12: A systematic literature review. *International Journal of STEM Education, 10*(1), 29.

Helsper, E.J. & van Deursen, A.J.A.M. (2015). Digital skills in Europe: Research and policy. In K. Andreasson (Ed.), *Digital divides: The new challenges and opportunities of e-inclusion* (pp. 125–148). CRC Press.

Martinez, D., Helsper, E., d'Haenens, L., Vissenberg, J., Donoso, V., Edisherashvili N., Puusepp, M., Kasemets, M., Martinez, G., Larranaga, N., Garmendia, M., Tomczyk, Ł., Kielar, I., Tiihonen, S., Sormanen, N., Wilska, T.-A., Irani, F., Makniemi, E., Hietajarvi, L., & Salmela-Aro, K. (2024). *Report on Twelve Evaluation Studies of Media Literacy and Digital Skills Interventions*. KU Leuven, REMEDIS.

Napoli, P. M., & Obar, J. A. (2014). The emerging mobile Internet underclass: A critique of mobile Internet access. *The Information Society, 30*(5), 323–334.

Ng, T. K., Leung, J. K. L., Chu, K. W. S., & Qiao, M. S. (2021). AI literacy: Definition, teaching, evaluation and ethical issues. *Proceedings of the Association for Information Science and Technology, 58*(1), 504–509.

Seaver, N. (2019). Knowing algorithms. In J. Vertesi & D. Ribes (Eds.), *DigitalSTS: A field guide for science & technology studies* (pp. 412–422). Princeton University Press.

Selwyn, N. (2012). *Education in a digital world: Global perspectives on technology and education*. Routledge.

Van Deursen, A. J. A. M., & van Dijk, J. A. G. M. (2014). Loss of labor time due to malfunctioning ICTs and ICT skill insufficiencies. *International Journal of Manpower, 35*(5), 703–719.

Van Deursen, A. J. A. M., & Van Dijk, J. A. G. M. (2019). The first-level digital divide shifts from inequalities in physical access to inequalities in material access. *New Media & Society, 21*(2), 354–375.

Van Dijk, J. A. G. M. (2005). *The deepening divide: Inequality in the information society*. Sage.

Van Dijk, J. A. G. M. (2020). *The network society*. Sage.

Venturelli, S. (2002). Inventing e-regulation in the US, EU and East Asia: Conflicting social visions of the Information Society. *Telematics and Informatics, 19*(2), 69–90.

Warschauer, M., & Ames, M. (2010). Can one laptop per child save the worlds' poor? *Journal of International Affairs, 64*(1), 33–51.

References

Aavikko, L., Pihlainen, K., & Kärnä, E. (2022). Peer mentoring process for older adult's digital skills. In K. Korjonen-Kuusipuro, P. Rasi-Heikkinen, H. Vuojärvi, K. Pihlainen, & E. Kärnä (Eds.), *Older adults in the digital society—Opportunities for lifelong learning* (pp. 211–228). Gaudeamus.

Antonio, A., & Tuffley, D. (2014). The gender digital divide in developing countries. *Future Internet, 6*(4), 673–687.

Anttiroiko, A. V., Lintilä, L., & Savolainen, R. (2001). Information society competencies of managers: Conceptual considerations. In P. Eero, R. Savolainen, & P. Tynjälä (Eds.), *In search for a human-centred information society* (pp. 27–56). Tampere University Press.

Arora, P. (2019). *The next billion users: Digital life beyond the West*. Harvard University Press.

Bawden, D. (2001). Information and digital literacies: A review of concepts. *Journal of Documentation, 57*(2), 218–259.

Bean, C. (2003). Meeting the challenge: Training an aging population to use computers. *The Southeastern Librarian, 51*(3), 6.

Beniger, J. R. (1986). *The control revolution: Technological and economic origins of the information society*. Harvard University Press.

Berners-Lee, T. (2000). *Weaving the web: The original design and ultimate destiny of the world wide web*. Harper Business.

Best, P., Manktelow, R., & Taylor, B. (2014). Online communication, social media and adolescent wellbeing: A systematic narrative review. *Children and Youth Services Review, 41*, 27–36.

Boerkamp, L. G., Van Deursen, A. J. A. M., Van Laar, E., Van der Zeeuw, A., & Van der Graaf, S. (2024). Exploring barriers to and outcomes of internet

A. van Deursen and J. van Dijk, *Digital Skills*, Digital Education and Learning, https://doi.org/10.1057/978-1-349-96162-7

appropriation among households living in poverty: A systematic literature review. *SAGE Open, 14*(1).

Bommasani, R., Hudson, D. A., Adeli, E., Altman, R., Arora, S., von Arx, S., ..., & Liang, P. (2021). *On the opportunities and risks of foundation models.* arXiv preprintarXiv 2108.07258.

Bradford, A. (2023). *Digital empires: The global battle to regulate technology.* Oxford University Press.

Brand-Gruwel, S., Wopereis, I., & Vermetten, Y. (2005). Information problem solving by experts and novices: Analysis of a complex cognitive skill. *Computers in Human Behavior, 21*(3), 487–508.

Briggs, C. F. (2000). Literacy, reading, and writing in the medieval West. *Journal of Medieval History, 26*(4), 397–420.

Briggs, A., & Burke, P. (2009). *A social history of the media: From Gutenberg to the Internet.* Polity.

Bruner, J. S. (1961). The act of discovery. *Harvard Educational Review, 31*, 21–32.

Bruner, J. S. (1974). *Toward a theory of instruction.* Harvard University Press.

Buckingham, D. (2012). *Beyond technology: Children's learning in the age of digital culture.* Polity.

Carroll, J. M., & Carrithers, C. (1984). Training wheels in a user interface. *Communications of the ACM, 27*(8), 800–806.

Carvin, A. (2000). More than just access: Fitting literacy and content into the digital divide equation. *Educause Review, 35*(6), 38–47.

Casal-Otero, L., Catala, A., Fernández-Morante, C., Taboada, M., Cebreiro, B., & Barro, S. (2023). AI literacy in K-12: A systematic literature review. *International Journal of STEM Education, 10*(1), 29.

Cedefop. (2024). *Artificial Intelligence in EU Workplaces: Another great divide?* Retrieved from https://www.cedefop.europa.eu/files/press_backgrounder_ai_surveypre_event.pdf

Cobo, C. (2013). Skills for innovation: Envisioning an education that prepares for the changing world. *The Curriculum Journal, 24*(1), 67–85.

Coiro, J., & Dobler, E. (2007). Exploring the online reading comprehension strategies used by sixth-grade skilled readers to search for and locate information on the Internet. *Reading Research Quarterly, 42*(2), 214–257.

Collins, R. (2000). Comparative and historical patterns of education. In M. T. Hallinan (Ed.), *Handbook of the sociology of education* (pp. 213–239). Springer.

Courtois, C., & Verdegem, P. (2016). With a little help from my friends: An analysis of the role of social support in digital inequalities. *New Media & Society, 18*(8), 1508–1527.

Daft, R. L., & Lengel, R. H. (1984). *Information richness: A new approach to managerial behavior and organizational design.* JAI Press.

Danielson, D. R. (2003). Transitional volatility in web navigation. *It & Society, 1*(3), 131–158.

Dash, D., Bangera, Y., Bangera, M., Vadithya, G., & Panda, S. (2025). *Who gets left behind? auditing disability inclusivity in large language models*. arXiv 2509.00963.

De Boer, P. S., Van Deursen, A. J. A. M., & Van Rompay, T. J. (2020). Internet-of-things skills among the general population: Task-based performance test using activity trackers. *JMIR Human Factors, 7*(4), e22532.

De Boer, P. S., Van Deursen, A. J. A. M., & Van Rompay, T. J. (2023). Health on the move—Can we keep up? Activity tracker performance test to measure data and strategic skills. *International Journal of Human–Computer Interaction, 39*(17), 3377–3387.

De Boer, P. S., Van Deursen, A. J. A. M., & Van Rompay, T. J. (2024). The lights are on, but no one's home: A performance test to measure digital skills to use IoT home automation. *New Media & Society, 26*(9), 5259–5290.

De Castell, S., & Luke, A. (1988). Defining "literacy" in North American Schools. In E. R. Kingten, B. M. Kroll, & M. Rose (Eds.), *Perspectives on literacy* (pp. 159–174). Southern Illinois University Press.

De Greef, M., Segers, M., Nijhuis, J., Lam, J. F., van Groenestijn, M., Van Hoek, F., et al. (2015). The development and validation of testing materials for literacy, numeracy and digital skills in a Dutch context. *International Review of Education, 61*(5), 655–671.

Dennis, A. R., Fuller, R. M., & Valacich, J. S. (2008). Media, tasks, and communication processes: A theory of media synchronicity. *MIS Quarterly, 32*(3), 575–600.

DiMaggio, P., & Bonikowski, B. (2008). Make money surfing the web? The impact of Internet use on the earnings of US workers. *American Sociological Review, 73*(2), 227–250.

Dobransky, K., & Hargittai, E. (2006). The disability divide in Internet access and use. *Information, Communication & Society, 9*(3), 313–334.

Dwivedi, R., Dave, D., Naik, H., Singhal, S., Omer, R., Patel, P., et al. (2023). Explainable AI (XAI): Core ideas, techniques, and solutions. *ACM Computing Surveys, 55*(9), 1–33.

Edwards-Fapohunda, D. M. O. (2024). The role of adult learning and education in community development: A case study of New York. *Iconic Research and Engineering Journals, 8*(1), 437–454.

European Commission. (2019). *2nd Survey of Schools: ICT in Education*. Retrieved from https://ec.europa.eu/digital-single-market/en/news/2nd-survey-schools-ict-education

Eynon, R. (2021). Becoming digitally literate: Reinstating an educational lens to digital skills policies for adults. *British Educational Research Journal, 47*(1), 146–162.

Fau, S., & Moreau, Y. (2018). *Managing tomorrow's digital skills-what conclusions can we draw from international comparative indicators?* Published by the United Nations Educational, Scientific and Cultural Organization, UNESCO 2018.

Filonik, D., Medland, R., Foth, M., & Rittenbruch, M. (2013). A customisable dashboard display for environmental performance visualisations. In S. Berkovsky & J. Freyne (Eds.), *Persuasive technology: 8th International conference* (pp. 51–62). Springer.

Freire, P., & Ramos, M. B. (1972). *Pedagogy of the oppressed.* Herder and Herder.

Gallistl, V., Rohner, R., Seifert, A., & Wanka, A. (2020). Configuring the older non-user: Between research, policy and practice of digital exclusion. *Social Inclusion, 8*(2), 233–243.

Gerbaudo, P. (in press). TikTok and the algorithmic transformation of social media publics: From social networks to social interest clusters. *New Media & Society.*

Gill, K. S. (1991). Summary of human-centred systems research in Europe, Part 1. *Systemist, the Journal of the UK Systems Society, 13*(1), 7–27.

Goldfarb, B. (2002). *Visual pedagogy: Media cultures in and beyond the classroom.* Duke University Press.

Gottfried, J. (2024). *Americans' Social Media Use: YouTube and Facebook are by far the most used online platforms among U.S. adults; TikTok's user base has grown since 2021.* Pew Research Center.

Hall, R. (2009). Towards a fusion of formal and informal learning environments: The impact of the read/write web. *Electronic Journal of e-Learning, 7*, 29–40.

Hammer, F., Leineweber, M., Sonnega, G., & Van der Groot, L. (2025). *Onderzoek informele helpers.* Beeld & Geluid, programma Alliantie Digitaal Samenleven & Perspective.

Hasebrink, U., & Hepp, A. (2017). How to research cross-media practices? Investigating media repertoires and media ensembles. *Convergence, 23*(4), 362–377.

Hasebrink, U., & Popp, J. (2006). Media repertoires as a result of selective media use. A conceptual approach to the analysis of patterns of exposure. *Communications, 31*(3), 369–387.

Helsper, E. J. (2012). A corresponding fields model for the links between social and digital exclusion. *Communication Theory, 22*(4), 403–426.

Helsper, E. J., Schneider, L. S., Van Deursen, A. J. A. M., & Van Laar, E. (2020). *The youth Digital Skills Indicator: Report on the conceptualisation and development of the ySKILLS digital skills measure.* ySKILLS.

Helsper, E. J., & Van Deursen, A. J. A. M. (2015). Digital skills in Europe: Research and policy. In K. Andreasson (Ed.), *Digital divides: The new challenges and opportunities of e-inclusion* (pp. 125–148). CRC Press.

Helsper, E. J., & Van Deursen, A. J. A. M. (2017). Do the rich get digitally richer? Quantity and quality of support for digital engagement. *Information, Communication & Society, 20*(5), 700–714.

Hoem, J., & Schwebs, T. (2005). *Personal publishing and media literacy: Designing a virtual learning arena based on weblogs and wikis*. Paper presented at the IFIP World Conference on Computers in Education (WCCE), Cape Town, South Africa.

Horst, H. A., Herr-Stephenson, B., & Robinson, L. (2010). Media ecologies. In M. Ito et al. (Eds.), *Hanging out, messing around, and geeking out: Kids living and learning with new media* (pp. 29–78). MIT Press.

Hughes, L., Davies, F., Li, K., Gunaratnege, S. M., Malik, T., & Dwivedi, Y. K. (2026). Beyond the hype: Organizational adoption of Generative AI through the lens of the TOE framework—A mixed-methods perspective. *International Journal of Information Management, 86*, 102982.

Jeager, P. T., Bertot, J. C., Thomson, K., Katz, S. M., & Decoster, E. J. (2012). The intersection of public policy and public access; digital divides, digital literacy, digital inclusion, and public libraries. *Public Library Quarterly, 31*, 1–20.

Jenkins, H. (2009). *Confronting the challenges of participatory culture: Media education for the 21st century*. MIT press.

Jovanovic, M., & Campbell, M. (2022). Generative artificial intelligence: Trends and prospects. *Computer, 55*(10), 107–112.

Kalmus, V., Blinka, L., & Ólafsson, K. (2015). Does it matter what mama says: Evaluating the role of parental mediation in European adolescents' excessive Internet use. *Children & Society, 29*(2), 122–133.

Kärnä, E. (2022). Peer guidance styles and learning theories. In K. Korjonen-Kuusipuro, P. Rasi Heikkinen, H. Vuojärvi, K. Pihlainen, & E. Kärnä (Eds.), *Older adults in the digital society—Opportunities for lifelong learning* (pp. 165–188). Gaudeamus.

Karvalics, L. Z. (2014). Emerging new information literacies: A conceptual outlook. In S. Kurbanoğlu, S. Špiranec, E. Grassian, D. Mizrachi, & R. Catts (Eds.), *European conference on information literacy* (pp. 37–46). Springer.

Katz, E., Blumler, J. G., & Gurevitch, M. (1973). Uses and gratifications research. *The Public Opinion Quarterly, 37*(4), 509–523.

Kirschner, P. A., Sweller, J., & Clark, R. E. (2006). Why minimal guidance during instruction does not work: An analysis of the failure of constructivist, discovery, problem-based, experiential, and inquiry-based teaching. *Educational Psychologist, 46*, 75–86.

Kwan, M. P. (2001). Cyberspatial cognition and individual access to information: the behavioral foundation of cybergeography. *Environment and Planning B: Planning and Design, 28*(1), 21–37.

Lee, M. J. (2005). Expanding hypertext: Does it address disorientation? Depends on individuals' adventurousness. *Journal of Computer-Mediated Communication, 10*(3), JCMC1036.

Lehaney, B., Clarke, S., Kimberlee, V., & Spencer-Matthews, S. (1999). The human side of information development: A case of an intervention at a British visitor attraction. *Journal of End User Computing, 11*(4), 33–39.

Livingstone, S., Haddon, L., Görzig, A., & Ólafsson, K. (2011). *EU Kids Online: Final report 2011.* London School of Economics & Political Science. Available at http://eprints.lse.ac.uk/39351/

Lucas, M., & Moreira, A. (2009). Bridging formal and informal learning – A case study on students' perceptions of the use of social networking tools. In U. Cress, V. Dimitrova, M. Specht (Eds.), *Learning in the synergy of multiple disciplines* (vol. 5794). EC-TEL 2009. Lecture Notes in Computer Science.

Madianou, M. (2014). Polymedia communication and mediatized migration: An ethnographic approach. In K. Lundby (Ed.), *Mediatization of communication* (pp. 323–346). De Gruyter Mouton.

Madianou, M., & Miller, D. (2013). *Migration and new media: Transnational families and polymedia.* Routledge.

Manzoor, R., Hussain, W., & Anjum, M. L. (2025). Out of dataset, out of algorithm, out of mind: A critical evaluation of AI bias against disabled people. *AI & SOCIETY, 40*(5), 3941–3951.

Marchionini, G. (1995). *Information seeking in electronic environments* (Vol. 9). Cambridge University Press.

Martinez, D., Helsper, D., Casado, M. A., Martinez, G., Larrañaga, N., Garmendia, M., Olveira, R., Salmela-Aro, K., Spurava, G., Hietajärvi, L., Maksniemi, E., Sormanen, N., Tiihonen, S., Wilska, T.-A., Vissenberg, J., Puusepp, M., Edisherashvili, N., Tomczyk, L., Opozda-Suder, S., Sepielak, D., Pedaste, M., & d'Haenens, L. (2023). *Co-developing media literacy and digital skills interventions: Report on preliminary results.* REMEDIS.

Mayer, R. E. (2004). Should there be a three-strikes rule against pure discovery learning? *American Psychologist, 59*(1), 14.

Miller, K. (2006). *Organizational communication: Approaches and processes.* Thomson Wadsworth.

Mizrach, S. (1998). *From orality to teleliteracy.* Retrieved from http://www2.fiu.edu/~mizrachs/orality.htm

Mossberger, K., Tolbert, C. J., & Stansbury, M. (2003). *Virtual inequality: Beyond the digital divide.* Georgetown University Press.

Mühlemann, S. (2024). *AI adoption and workplace training.* IZA Discussion Papers, No. 17367, Institute of Labor Economics.

Murphy, E., Kuber, R., McAllister, G., & Strain, P. (2008). An empirical investigation into the difficulties experienced by visually impaired internet users. *Universal Access to the Information Society, 7*, 79–91.

Nadrljanski, Đ., Nadrljanski, M., & Pavlinović, M. (2022). Digitalization of education. In M. Ivanović, A. Klašnja-Milićević, & L. C. Jain (Eds.), *Handbook on intelligent techniques in the educational process: Vol 1 recent advances and case studies* (pp. 17–39). Springer.

Napoli, P. M., & Obar, J. A. (2014). The emerging mobile Internet underclass: A critique of mobile Internet access. *The Information Society, 30*(5), 323–334.

Newman-Griffis, D., Rauchberg, J. S., Alharbi, R., Hickman, L., & Hochheiser, H. (2022). *Definition drives design: Disability models and mechanisms of bias in AI technologies*. arXiv 2206.08287.

Ng, T. K., Leung, J. K. L., Chu, K. W. S., & Qiao, M. S. (2021). AI literacy: Definition, teaching, evaluation and ethical issues. *Proceedings of the Association for Information Science and Technology, 58*(1), 504–509.

OECD. (2018). *PISA 2018 Results (Volume V): Effective policies, successful schools*. OECD Publishing. https://doi.org/10.1787/ca768d40-en

OECD. (2025). *Trends in adult learning: New data from the 2023 survey of adult skills, getting skills right*. OECD Publishing. https://doi.org/10.1787/ec0624a6-en

Office of Educational Technology. (2017). *Reimagining the role of technology in Education: National Education Technology Plan Update*. Retrieved from https://files.eric.ed.gov/fulltext/ED577592.pdf

Ong, W. J. (1984). Orality, literacy, and medieval textualization. *New Literary History, 16*(1), 1–12.

Palczyńska, M., & Rynko, M. (2021). ICT skills measurement in social surveys: Can we trust self-reports? *Quality & Quantity, 55*(3), 917–943.

Rahmat, A. M., Mohd, I. H., Omar, M. K., Kamalludeen, R., Zahari, W. M. Z. W., Azmy, N., & Adnan, A. (2022). Integrating socio-digital skills in the Industry 4.0 era for graduates' employability: An employers' perspective. *Journal of Positive School Psychology, 6*(3), 8493–8507.

Redecker, C., Haché, A., & Centeno, C. (2010). *Using information and communication technologies to promote education and employment opportunities for immigrants and ethnic minorities*. JRC(European Commission)/IPTS.

Reeves, B., & Nass, C. (1996). *The media equation: How people treat computers, television, and new media like real people*. Cambridge University Press.

Rott, K. J., & Schmidt-Hertha, B. (2024). Transforming adult learning in the digital age: Exploring environmental, content, and technological changes. *International Journal of Lifelong Education, 43*(4), 319–323.

Rury, J., & Rury, J. L. (2005). *Education and social change: Themes in the history of American schooling*. Routledge.

Schank, R. C., & Cleary, C. (1995). *Engines for education*. Lawrence Erlbaum Associates.

Scheerder, A., Van Deursen, A. J. A. M., & Van Dijk, J. A. G. M. (2017). Determinants of Internet skills, uses and outcomes. A systematic review of the second-and third-level digital divide. *Telematics and Informatics, 34*(8), 1607–1624.

Seaver, N. (2019). Knowing algorithms. In J. Vertesi & D. Ribes (Eds.), *DigitalSTS: A field guide for science & technology studies* (pp. 412–422). Princeton University Press.

Seneviratne, O., & Monroy-Hernandez, A. (2010). Remix culture on the web: A survey of content reuse on different user-generated content websites. In W. Nejdl, F. Abel, K. Tochtermann, & H. Sack (Eds.), *Proceedings of the WebSci10: Extending the frontiers of society on-line* (pp. 26–27).

Søby, M. (2003). *Digital competence: From ICT skills to digital "bildung"*. University of Oslo.

Sousa, M. J., & Wilks, D. (2018). Sustainable skills for the world of work in the digital age. *Systems Research and Behavioral Science, 35*(4), 399–405.

Springer, A., & Whittaker, S. (2019, March). Progressive disclosure: Empirically motivated approaches to designing effective transparency. In *Proceedings of the 24th international conference on intelligent user interfaces* (pp. 107–120).

Statistics Netherlands. (2023). *Digital proficiency continues to rise*. https://www.cbs.nl/en-gb/news/2023/45/digital-proficiency-continues-to-rise

Statistics Netherlands. (2024). *Internettoegang en internetactiviteiten; persoonskenmerken*. Retrieved from https://www.cbs.nl/nl-nl/cijfers/detail/84888NED

Stone, L. (1969). Literacy and education in England 1640–1900. *Past & Present, 42*, 69–139.

Tate, M., & Alexander, J. (1996). Teaching critical evaluation skills for World Wide Web resources. *Computers in Libraries, 16*(10), 49–55.

Tevissen, Y. (2024). *Disability representations: Finding biases in automatic image generation*. arXiv 2406.14993.

Tichenor, P. J., Donohue, G. A., & Olien, C. N. (1970). Mass media flow and differential growth of knowledge. *Public Opinion Quarterly, 34*, 159–170.

Tilly, C. (1998). *Durable inequality*. University of California Press.

Treem, J. W., & Leonardi, P. M. (2013). Social media use in organizations: Exploring the affordances of visibility, editability, persistence, and association. *Annals of the International Communication Association, 36*(1), 143–189.

Unesco. (2025). *What you need to know about literacy*. Retrieved from https://www.unesco.org/en/literacy/need-know

Van der Geest, T., Van der Meij, H., & Van Puffelen, C. (2014). Self-assessed and actual Internet skills of people with visual impairments. *Universal Access in the Information Society, 13*(2), 161–174.

Van der Zeeuw, A., Van Deursen, A. J. A. M., & Jansen, G. (2024). The orchestrated digital inequalities of the IoT: How vendor lock-in hinders and playfulness creates IoT benefits in every life. *New Media & Society, 26*(10), 5658–5676.

Van Deursen, A. J. A. M. (2012). Internet skill-related problems in accessing online health information. *International Journal of Medical Informatics, 81*(1), 61–72.

Van Deursen, A. J. A. M., Courtois, C., & Van Dijk, J. A. G. M. (2014). Internet skills, sources of support, and benefiting from Internet use. *International Journal of Human-Computer Interaction, 30*(4), 278–290.

Van Deursen, A. J. A. M., De Boer, P. S., & Van Rompay, T. J. (2025). Smart devices require skilled users: Home automation performance tests among the Dutch population. *International Journal of Human–Computer Interaction, 41*(2), 1688–1699.

Van Deursen, A. J. A. M., Görzig, A., Van Delzen, M., Perik, H., & Stegeman, A. G. (2014). Primary school children's internet skills: A report on performance tests of operational, formal, information, and strategic internet skills. *International Journal of Communication, 8*, 1343–13656.

Van Deursen, A. J. A. M., & Helsper, E. J. (2015). The third-level digital divide: Who benefits most from being online? In L. Robinson, S. R. Cotten, J. Schulz, A. Williams, & T. M. Hale (Eds.), *Communication and information technologies annual: Digital distinctions & inequalities* (pp. 29–52). Emerald Group Publishing.

Van Deursen, A. J. A. M., & Helsper, E. J. (2018). Collateral benefits of Internet use: Explaining the diverse outcomes of engaging with the Internet. *New Media & Society, 20*(7), 2333–2351.

Van Deursen, A. J. A. M., & Helsper, E. J. (2020). *Digitale vaardigheden: Een onderzoeks- en beleidsagenda*. Centrum voor Digitale Inclusie, Universiteit Twente.

Van Deursen, A. J. A. M., & Helsper, E. J. (2021). *Mediawijsheid: Conceptualisering en belang in een gemedieerde samenleving. Lacunes in bestaand onderzoek en beleid*. Universiteit Twente.

Van Deursen, A. J. A. M., Helsper, E. J., & Eynon, R. (2016). Development and validation of the Internet Skills Scale (ISS). *Information, Communication & Society, 19*(6), 804–823.

Van Deursen, A. J. A. M., & Mossberger, K. (2018). Any thing for anyone? A new digital divide in Internet-of-Things skills. *Policy & Internet, 10*(2), 122–140.

Van Deursen, A. J. A. M., & Van Diepen, S. (2013). Information and strategic Internet skills of secondary students: A performance test. *Computers & Education, 63*, 218–226.

Van Deursen, A. J. A. M., & Van Dijk, J. A. G. M. (2009). Using the Internet: Skill related problems in users' online behavior. *Interacting with Computers, 21*(5–6), 393–402.

Van Deursen, A. J. A. M., & Van Dijk, J. A. G. M. (2011a). Internet skills and the digital divide. *New Media & Society, 13*(6), 893–911.

Van Deursen, A. J. A. M., & van Dijk, J. A. G. M. (2011b). Internet skills performance tests: Are people ready for eHealth? *Journal of Medical Internet Research, 13*(2), e1581.

Van Deursen, A. J. A. M., & van Dijk, J. A. G. M. (2014a). Loss of labor time due to malfunctioning ICTs and ICT skill insufficiencies. *International Journal of Manpower, 35*(5), 703–719.

Van Deursen, A. J. A. M., & Van Dijk, J. A. G. M. (2014b). The digital divide shifts to differences in usage. *New Media & Society, 16*(3), 507–526.

Van Deursen, A. J. A. M., & Van Dijk, J. A. G. M. (2016). Modeling traditional literacy, Internet skills and Internet usage: An empirical study. *Interacting with Computers, 28*(1), 13–26.

Van Deursen, A. J. A. M., & Van Dijk, J. A. G. M. (2019). The first-level digital divide shifts from inequalities in physical access to inequalities in material access. *New Media & Society, 21*(2), 354–375.

Van Deursen, A. J. A. M., Van Dijk, J. A. G. M., & Peters, O. (2011). Rethinking Internet skills: The contribution of gender, age, education, Internet experience, and hours online to medium-and content-related Internet skills. *Poetics, 39*(2), 125–144.

Van Deursen, A. J. A. M., Van Laar, E., Helsper, E. J., & Schneider, L. S. (2023). *The youth Digital Skills Performance Test Results: Report on the results of real-life information navigation and processing, communication and interaction, and content creation and production skills tasks*. ySKILLS.

Van Dijk, J. A. G. M. (2005). *The deepening divide: Inequality in the information society*. Sage.

Van Dijk, J. A. G. M. (2020a). *The digital divide*. Polity Press.

Van Dijk, J. A. G. M. (2020b). *The network society*. Sage.

Van Dijk, J., & Hacker, K. (2003). The digital divide as a complex and dynamic phenomenon. *The Information Society, 19*(4), 315–326.

Van Dijk, J. A. G. M., & Van Deursen, A. J. A. M. (2014). *Digital skills: Unlocking the information society*. Palgrave Macmillan.

Van Laar, E., Van Deursen, A. J. A. M., Helsper, E. J., & Schneider, L. S. (2025). Developing performance tests to measure digital skills: Lessons learned from a cross-national perspective. *Media and Communication, 13*, 8988.

Venturelli, S. (2002). Inventing e-regulation in the US, EU and East Asia: Conflicting social visions of the Information Society. *Telematics and Informatics, 19*(2), 69–90.

Wandke, H., Sengpiel, M., & Sönksen, M. (2012). Myths about older people's use of information and communication technology. *Gerontology, 58*(6), 564–570.

Warschauer, M. (2004). *Technology and social inclusion: Rethinking the digital divide*. MIT Press.

Warschauer, M., & Ames, M. (2010). Can one laptop per child save the worlds' poor? *Journal of International Affairs, 64*(1), 33–51.
Webster, M. (2015). *Reimagining learning: Defining strategies for engagement*. Retrieved from https://www.gensleron.com/cities/2015/7/6/reimagining-learning-defining-strategies-for-engagement.html
Webster, J., & Ahuja, J. S. (2006). Enhancing the design of web navigation systems: The influence of user disorientation on engagement and performance. *MIS Quarterly, 30*(3), 661–678.
Wei, K. K., Teo, H. H., Chan, H. C., & Tan, B. C. (2011). Conceptualizing and testing a social cognitive model of the digital divide. *Information Systems Research, 22*(1), 170–187.
Yu, L. (2010). How poor informationally are the information poor? Evidence from an empirical study of daily and regular information practices of individuals. *Journal of Documentation, 66*(6), 906–933.
Zhang, D., & Livingstone, S. (2019). *Inequalities in how parents support their children's development with digital technologies*. LSE Department of Media and Communications.

Index

A
Accessibility, 148
Adaptive guidance, 156
Adaptive interfaces, 150
Adult education, 137, 182, 202, 203, 216, 232
AI, 3–5, 7, 10, 13, 15, 20, 21, 24–26, 31, 35, 36, 44, 47, 51, 54–56, 61, 67–69, 80, 89, 91, 96, 97, 99, 101, 103, 112, 125–127, 130, 132–134, 136, 139, 140, 148, 157–160, 162, 165, 167, 171–173, 175, 178, 184, 187, 188, 190–194, 196–198, 201, 204, 206, 211, 214, 223, 225, 228, 230, 237–239, 242–244, 251
AI literacy, 189, 237, 242
Algorithmic ranking, 55
Algorithms, 10, 12, 16, 20, 35, 53, 55, 56, 67, 128, 190, 198, 225, 230, 239
Analog media, 8, 16, 28, 29, 34
Appropriation of Technology, 1
Digital skills, 4, 117, 119
Material access, 3, 11, 117, 119
Motivation, 2, 6, 11, 117, 119
Outcomes, 6
Usage, 5, 119
Audio, visual, and audiovisual media, 18, 27
Authenticity, 61, 62, 67, 196, 197
Autonomous, 5, 7, 31, 43, 119, 157, 229
Autonomy, 112, 138, 157, 158, 177, 178, 224

B
Browser, 22–26, 30, 81

C
Collective intelligence, 62
Communication skills, 13, 25, 27–30, 32, 37, 56, 57, 62, 95, 108, 112, 166, 194

A. van Deursen and J. van Dijk, *Digital Skills*, Digital Education and Learning, https://doi.org/10.1057/978-1-349-96162-7

Community, 13, 60, 127, 142, 170, 182, 185, 203, 205, 206, 239, 244–246
Community center(s), 182
Computer anxiety, 2
Computers, 22–26, 28, 30, 45, 202, 234, 243, 244, 251
Consistency, 154, 157, 158, 165
Contacts, 57, 58, 93, 128, 155, 156, 166, 200, 232
Content creation skills, 13, 25, 27–29, 31, 33, 37, 64–66, 99, 106, 109, 112, 196–198
Content-related skills, 11, 21, 135, 224–226, 228, 232, 234, 238–240, 243, 249, 251, 252
Control revolution, 18
Copyright, 25, 31, 65, 66, 112, 196, 197
Critical thinking, 15, 32, 33, 36, 79, 138, 177, 186, 188, 190, 198, 239
Curricula, 117, 124, 182, 189, 191, 192, 195, 196, 199, 202, 217, 236, 237, 240, 243, 251, 252

D
Data literacy, 124
Decision-making, 6, 12, 14, 20, 26, 33, 36, 43, 56, 58, 62, 67, 68, 79, 101, 112, 126, 163, 165, 174, 177, 190, 197, 199, 209, 215, 226, 232, 239, 240, 242
Decision Support System, 175, 179
Decoding, 21, 27–29, 38, 93, 167, 195
Design, 153, 212, 231, 236, 249
Designers, 147
Digital divide, 1, 3, 8, 120, 223
Digital identities, 61, 194
Digital inclusion, 2, 8, 77, 112, 213, 215
Digital inequality, 1, 6, 8, 10, 103, 117, 126, 133, 135, 224, 231, 249, 251, 253
Digital literacy, 4, 37, 187, 227
Disabilities, 135, 140, 148, 150, 182, 207–211, 215, 218, 229, 232, 235, 245, 246, 249–251
Disorientation, 51, 52

E
Education, 16–19, 45, 64, 112, 125, 126, 142, 151, 170, 181, 182, 188, 190, 191, 194, 196, 200, 202, 203, 212–215, 217, 218, 224, 230, 235, 237, 243, 244, 247, 251–253
Employers, 122, 199–201, 237
Encoding, 21, 27, 29, 38, 59, 93, 167, 195
Ethical, 31, 44, 66, 67, 99, 152, 153, 177, 188, 191, 195–197, 199
Evaluation, 6, 53, 56, 68, 92, 165, 237, 239, 247
Explainability, 171
Explainable AI, 157, 165, 171

F
Fairness, 25, 65, 66, 99, 153, 196, 197
File formats, 48
Formal skills, 12, 21, 23, 27, 29, 30, 32, 37, 49, 85
Formats, 8

G
Generative AI, 14, 33, 123, 130, 136, 138, 174, 208, 225, 227, 228
Guidance, 157, 189, 197, 204, 206, 208, 215, 217, 232, 237, 239, 241, 245, 249

H
History of media skills, 16
Human-AI collaboration, 7, 33, 113
Hypermedia, 23, 30, 37, 49–52, 85, 87

I
Industrial revolution, 18
Informal learning, 204, 217, 241
Information skills, 13, 24, 27, 29, 37, 53, 92, 107, 193, 228
Information society, 18, 19
Installation, 22, 29, 46, 49
Instruction, 16, 45, 92, 124, 125, 183, 185, 187, 192–194, 196–198, 200, 204, 208, 212–214, 217, 232, 241, 243, 246
Intelligent media, 15, 34, 36, 157, 194, 200, 201, 206, 215, 223, 225–229, 239, 242, 249, 250
Interaction, 28, 135, 149, 167, 207, 208, 212, 226, 245
Interface, 5, 25, 112, 119, 131, 135, 148, 150, 151, 154, 177, 183, 213, 215, 217, 225, 231, 235, 249, 251
Internet of Things. *See* IoT
IoT, 4, 36, 70, 78, 84, 112, 157, 158, 163, 178, 192–194, 198, 199, 201
Iterative design, 152

K
Knowledge, 12, 17

L
Learning, 10, 12, 17, 156, 181, 188, 191, 193, 195, 198–204, 206, 207, 213, 214, 216–218, 229, 230, 232, 233, 235, 239, 240, 242–245, 249, 252
  Adaptive learning, 210, 212
  AI mediated learning, 194, 198, 204, 206, 212, 214, 239, 244, 246
  Blended learning, 184, 200
  Informal learning, 181, 182, 186, 190, 204, 217
  Intergenerational learning, 217
  Learning by doing, 183, 184, 241
  Lifelong learning, 182, 202, 204
  Multimodal Learning, 212
  On-the-job learning, 253
  Self-directed learning, 186, 189, 202, 241, 246
Level of communication skills, 93
Level of content creation skills, 97
Level of formal skills, 85
Level of information skills, 88
Level of operational skills, 81
Level of strategic media choice skills, 79
Level of strategic media use skills, 100
Libraries, 182, 205, 216, 232–235, 237, 238, 244–246
Literacy, 4, 16, 18, 118, 135, 207, 210, 211, 213, 224, 228, 242
Low literacy, 182, 207, 210, 212, 213, 218, 232, 235, 246, 250

M
Machine learning, 20
Material access, 6, 223
Measurement, 76
Media, 21
  Audio, visual, and audiovisual media, 20
  Computers, 20
  Connected Intelligent media, 31
  Internet media, 29

Print media, 20
Media landscape(s), 10, 187, 224–226, 229, 230
Media literacy, 4, 91, 134, 194, 227
Media repertoires, 10, 12, 42, 187
Media Richness Theory, 42
Media Synchronicity Theory, 42
Medium-related skills, 11, 21, 22, 226
Migrant, 205, 207, 211, 213–215, 218
Mobile banking, 124, 150

N
Natural Language Processing, 162
Navigation, 50, 87, 149, 154, 155, 166, 183, 199, 209, 230, 249
Negotiation, 62, 63, 96, 123, 195
Netiquette, 60, 93, 112, 167, 178, 195
Networks, 63, 68, 118, 127, 137, 177, 185, 215, 216, 230, 245–247

O
Older adults, 3, 13, 82, 85, 86, 88, 109, 136, 139, 148, 151, 155, 182, 186, 187, 207, 209, 211, 215–218, 228, 232, 235, 242, 245, 250, 251
Online profiles, 61
Operational skills, 12, 21, 22, 27, 29, 37, 45, 46, 48, 111

P
Parental guidance, 185
Parents, 136
Participation, 122
Cultural participation, 128
Economic participation, 122
Educational participation, 124
Institutional participation, 131
Political participation, 126
Social participation, 127
Spatial participation, 130
Performance tests, 76, 78, 79, 209, 226, 227
Personalization, 150
Photography, 18
Plain Language Action and Information Network, 164
Policy, 2, 75, 101, 112, 141, 143, 147, 215, 232–235, 237, 247, 253
Policy actors, 235
Governments, 235, 237, 238
Labor organizations, 241
Public and Community Access Centers, 245
Public Libraries, 244
Publishers, 240
Schools, 243
Tech(nology) Industry, 238
Training institutes, 240
Polymedia, 42
Print media, 21–26
Privacy, 32, 43, 82, 96, 111, 112, 153, 177, 195
Problem definition, 28, 29, 53, 54, 92, 160
Progressive disclosure, 150, 155
Public access, 205, 218, 232
Publishers, 233, 235, 240

R
Resources, 2, 6, 66, 118, 119, 121, 182, 199, 203, 230, 231, 238, 240, 245, 246
Resources and Appropriation Theory, 2, 117, 118, 140, 143

S
Schools, 182, 189, 190, 192, 243, 244
Search query, 47, 54, 89, 161, 193
Self-assessments, 75, 209, 225, 249
Smart devices, 5, 10, 21, 32, 33, 53, 56, 83, 92, 101, 111, 119, 138, 153, 156, 163, 175, 199, 225, 238
Smartphones, 28, 64, 133, 153, 185, 238, 249
Smart society, 7, 38, 42, 53, 67, 121, 122, 130, 137, 141, 144, 182, 189, 195, 230, 231, 253
Social networking, 13–15, 31, 34, 35, 59, 122, 128, 153, 166, 182
Stakeholders, 139, 236, 247
Strategic media choice skills, 12, 22, 27, 37, 42, 43, 190
Strategic media use skills, 14, 20, 26–29, 31, 33, 34, 36, 38, 67, 68, 102, 108, 110, 112, 159, 171, 174, 175, 192, 197–199, 209, 215, 218, 224, 226, 228, 229, 232, 244
Strategies for addressing digital skills, 247
Support, 7, 113, 142, 161, 169, 188, 191, 192, 199, 201, 204, 206, 207, 210, 211, 213–216, 224, 227, 231–233, 235–239, 241, 242, 244–246, 250
  AI support, 163, 164, 187, 214
  Guided and contextual support, 149
  Informal support, 185, 215, 218
  Multimodal support, 150
  Parental support, 182
  Support from coworkers, 186, 218
  Technical support, 4

T
Tablets, 28, 121, 133, 142, 153, 192, 206, 238, 249
Teacher, 124, 185, 189, 190, 192, 195–197, 234, 236, 237, 243, 250, 252
Tech industry, 143, 238, 239
Technology Provision, 250
Traditional media, 133
Training institutes, 233, 235, 240
Transparency, 67, 111, 157, 165, 171, 196, 239
Trial and error, 35, 62, 63, 183, 188, 193, 195, 217, 218, 232

U
User-centered design, 151
Uses and Gratifications Theory, 42

W
W3C, 148
WCAG, 148
Wearables, 13, 36, 70, 78, 225
Workplace, 35, 64, 111, 123, 142, 167, 182, 185, 188, 199–201, 218, 232, 235, 241, 245, 253
World Wide Web, 19, 56, 202

www.ingramcontent.com/pod-product-compliance
Lightning Source LLC
Chambersburg PA
CBHW050209250826
50385CB00018B/201
* 9 7 8 1 3 4 9 9 6 1 6 1 0 *